Interac[illegible] Narrat[illegible] Tran[illegible]dia Storytelling

Interactive Narratives and Transmedia Storytelling provides media students and industry professionals with strategies for creating innovative new media projects across a variety of platforms. Synthesizing ideas from a range of theorists and practitioners across visual, audio, and interactive media, Kelly McErlean offers a practical reference guide and toolkit to best practices, techniques, key historical and theoretical concepts, and terminology that media storytellers and creatives need to create compelling interactive and transmedia narratives. McErlean takes a broad lens, exploring traditional narrative, virtual reality and augmented reality, audience interpretation, sound design, montage, the business of transmedia storytelling, and much more.

Written for both experienced media practitioners and those looking for a reference to help bolster their creative toolkit or learn how to better craft multi-platform stories, *Interactive Narratives and Transmedia Storytelling* serves as a guide to navigating this evolving world. An accompanying online resource site, www.Storyfort.ie, will feature regularly updated articles and links to related content.

Kelly McErlean has developed graduate and postgraduate programs in film and new media for local and international delivery and successfully delivered eLearning and onsite contracts for international broadcast organisations on behalf of the European Broadcasting Union. Kelly lectures on new media, film and entrepreneurship in the Department of Creative Arts, Media, and Music at Dundalk Institute of Technology, Ireland. He has won several awards including a Golden Spider Award and a Digital Media Award for his film, new media, and photographic works. Kelly holds a PhD in visual culture from the National College of Art and Design, Dublin.

Interactive Narratives and Transmedia Storytelling

Creating Immersive Stories Across New Media Platforms

Kelly McErlean

Routledge
Taylor & Francis Group
NEW YORK AND LONDON

First published 2018
by Routledge
711 Third Avenue, New York, NY 10017

and by Routledge
2 Park Square, Milton Park, Abingdon, Oxon OX14 4RN

Routledge is an imprint of the Taylor & Francis Group, an informa business

Library of Congress Cataloging in Publication Data
A catalog record for this book has been requested

ISBN: 978-1-138-63881-5 (hbk)
ISBN: 978-1-138-63882-2 (pbk)
ISBN: 978-1-315-63757-0 (ebk)

Typeset in Warnock
by HWA Text and Data Management, London

Visit the eResources: www.storyfort.ie

For Esther

Contents

1

Introduction

> Forms move and are born, and we are forever making new discoveries.
>
> Kasimir Malevich – *Suprematist Manifesto* (1916)

This book explores contemporary and traditional storytelling concepts and ideas. It encourages theoretical research and experimentation in the development of interactive narratives and transmedia stories. It considers the work of a wide range of practitioners across a multitude of creative fields. These include writing, music, film, photography, theatre, art and new media. It identifies and examines key texts and includes interviews with industry practitioners and academic researchers. Throughout history artistic inspiration has often come from the most unlikely sources. An openness to new ideas always brings about original, exciting and challenging storytelling opportunities.

WHO IS THIS BOOK FOR?

The book is aimed at storytelling creatives who are looking to develop and deliver interactive narratives and transmedia titles using new technologies and distribution platforms. It is a synthesis of storytelling strategies and related theoretical concerns with regard to interactive content creation. It considers many of the current questions regarding interactive storytelling and is intended to guide and inform the reader's knowledge and to promote ideas generation. A key concern of the text relates to story navigation: how will storytellers resolve the difficulties in creating interactive points within a plot to encourage a natural, rather than forced, story interaction? Who and where is the intended audience for interactive content and what issues are anticipated or currently experienced in targeting and then delivering to particular demographics? Does an interactive content audience need to have access to specific (perhaps the latest) technologies, do they need to have interactive story experience, a history of social media engagement, platform awareness or particular software application experience? What are the most appropriate skillsets and previous experience of an interactive story developer? Which elements of the traditional storytelling experience can be exploited within these new narrative paradigms? Sound design and music are considered within a broad storytelling context to look at their potential to fully realise narrative worlds and to promote audience immersion and engagement. The future of interactive storytelling is explored, and artistic and commercial projects, completed and in development, are considered. Throughout the book I have avoided taking a technocentric approach. The emphasis is on the creation of engaging stories which (through trial and error) take advantage of the most innovative yet appropriate modes of delivery to effectively communicate story ideas across multiple platforms. The book includes the most useful content that I have identified over many years teaching this subject in universities and colleges across Europe. You will note that there are many references to the works of traditional artists. I have made observations on their workflows when I considered them to be relevant to the development of interactive and transmedia stories. I have drawn on existing best practices from traditional media, to identify and give insight into creative works that are both experimental and engaging and to synthesise complex theories to make them accessible to a wide audience.

DEFINING INTERACTIVE NARRATIVES AND TRANSMEDIA STORIES

An interactive narrative offers a pre-specified level of story agency or choice to the audience, allowing them to exert an influence on the plot. The interactive experience is 'highly context-dependent' and involves some form of interface such as text input (entered at the command line), a hand-held controller or a gesture-sensing device (Laurel, 1991 p. 21). Each interaction results in various levels of impact on the story depending on the narrative design. Producer Hideo Kojima states that the challenge for interactive narrative developers is to offer increased agency without sacrificing the story emotion developed through 'cut sequences' (edited scenes rather than interactive gameplay) (Ashcraft, 2008). Brighton-based artists group Blast Theory released a very interesting interactive narrative titled *Karen* (2015). Using a phone-based app to facilitate a series of 'video calls', the user takes the role of a client and interacts with a life-coach called Karen over several days. The multiple choice responses given to Karen's often leading questions are used to construct a psychometric profile of each user which can be purchased at the end of the story. The story progresses along a satisfying narrative arc and includes a good level of story conflict, drama and humour. User engagement is designed around well-constructed questions (delivered by Karen) and equally valid answer options for the user. The result is an interactive narrative that feels like you are a performer within a finely tuned theatrical experience.

Transmedia stories are delivered across multiple distribution platforms, in various formats that can include feature films, short films, episodic television, streaming content, social media, games, print media, music and audio clips. Transmedia stories are defined as 'many franchises developed around a core story and characters' (Blumenthal & Xu, 2012 p. 190). Transmedia story elements exist within a single story world despite their perceived distance from each other. Blast Theory's #FindTheGirl transmedia campaign to promote *Thirteen* (2016) delivered story content within the five-episode online drama itself, but also on social media platforms and across various websites (Puschmann, 2016).

THE AUTHOR

At 18 years old I took full advantage of the UK's education grant system and left Ballymoney, Northern Ireland to study computer programming at Birmingham Polytechnic, UK. I graduated in 1989 and soon began my career as a computer programmer working for Marconi Command and Control Systems at a UK Ministry of Defence site in Leicester. I designed and coded software in Ada (the defence sector's traditional language of choice) to perform phonetic searches on London Fire Brigade's database of geographical locations. The system allowed emergency telephone call operators to enter street names as they heard them phonetically without the need to check spelling. However, I found working at the 'command line' lacked the creativity I sought so I returned to education to study photography at Bournville Art College under the inspirational guidance of my tutor John Hodgett. With a small child in tow, my then girlfriend Esther and I returned to Dublin in the mid-1990s where I was able to combine my software engineering, film and photography skills. I was hired by the influential sculptor and academic Aileen McKeogh to work in Arthouse, a trailblazing multimedia arts organisation in a newly refurbished, purpose-built premises in Temple Bar. As Head of Training and Production I project-managed European-funded projects and designed and delivered new media education contracts on behalf of the Irish government. In 2000 I raised €250,000 private funding to set up a new media training college in Dublin city centre. I travelled extensively throughout Eastern Europe and North Africa helping international broadcast organisations to establish digital strategies and to develop new media training programmes for their personnel. In each country I would work on a photo-essay to pass the extended time between meetings. I almost got arrested in Pakistan on the road to Rawalpindi for photographing an enormous toll booth in the middle of nowhere. In Egypt, my now wife Esther and I interviewed prospective course participants and she was happy to receive numerous confidence-building proposals of marriage. On a visit to Media Production City, near Giza, a simple linguistic error left uncorrected led to me being mistakenly identified as the Director General of Radio Telefis Eireann (RTE). In too deep, we spent the day being whisked around the impressive film studio complex introduced to movie stars and forcing a fully attended water park to wait for our arrival beifre starting a show.

During my travels I always noted the international language of storytelling and the potential of new technologies to create new narrative paradigms. I continued to research the subject and was extremely fortunate to be supervised by Dr. Kevin Atherton and Dr. Paul O'Brien when successfully completing a PhD in visual culture at the National College of Art & Design, Dublin. By 2012 our award-winning college was fully accredited and delivering graduate and postgraduate programmes in film, theatre, games design, photography and animation, welcoming students from 22 countries. We produced the animated logo for the Eurovision Song Contest, which aired before and after commercial breaks and was watched by over 120 million people each year. Our students won national and international awards and were highly sought after by audiovisual production companies. In 2014 the Irish immigration service's heavy-handed approach to international students forced the closure of dozens of private education facilities in Ireland, including ours. In the years since, I have worked in the public education sector and I am now researching and lecturing in the highly innovative Creative Arts, Media and Music Department, Dundalk Institute of Technology.

I have always been interested in experimental narrative projects and generally prefer arthouse films to traditional commercial fare. I take inspiration from my children's engagement and interaction with games and social-media platforms and I continue to develop my own projects – interactive stories, films and photo books. My most recent film work *Singularitas* was conceived as a multilingual short, with languages intermixed throughout and no subtitles. The intention was to create a concept piece, an audiovisual spectacle which would be currently incomprehensible, yet in a few years, be viewed via commonplace language translating devices. The translation would 'free-up' the text and remove the linguistic barriers of language, dialect, intonation and prosody, making it accessible to anyone, in any country, speaking any language. In short, the film was really for the future.

NEW MODES OF STORYTELLING

In this book I also consider how evolving technologies will impact storytelling media and modes of delivery. Narrative interpretation depends on our understanding of the technologies used to create and deliver stories (Wood, 2007 p. 42). Audiences are increasingly knowledgeable about production tools, workflows and distribution platforms. If the spectacle focuses our attention on technology itself, then it creates in the audience a desire to learn more about the process of production. Individual digital elements compete for audience attention while driving the narrative and helping to create an immersive environment (Wood, 2007 p. 45). The effect may work with real elements or act as a counterpoint, expanding and developing their meaning. There may be an over-emphasis on visual spectacle through attempts to recreate that which no longer exists or does not yet exist. In this sense new media technologies are no different than the special effects of early cinema. If the audience knows how an effect is produced then the impact is reduced and immersion in the story may be lost. The fluidity of perception leads to the creation of narrative perspective. The world is constantly changing and the author's narrative is altered during its creation, and again when it is observed by the reader:

> the shift of an object or area out of the center of vision even to the inner edge of the periphery transforms it ... perceptual constancy is a phantom, and the world thus seen is no longer identical to itself.
>
> (Crary, 2001 p. 298)

The observer's engagement with the technological invention manipulates the optical display. This is an alternative to the theatrical tradition of perception (Crary, 2001 p. 191). I will use as an example an interactive film I made called *The Little Extras* (see Appendix 1) which was created to extend the relationship between author and observer. In this film, viewer interaction alters their perspective of the story and creates a flexible or plastic narrative experience.

In interactive film the process of interaction may be considered a representational vehicle for the development and presentation of the characters. Navigation through the narrative leads to changes in our interpretation of the representation. The belief system that makes the representation possible is an acceptance of what is real both within the context of the story and the viewer's world (Mitchell, 1995 p. 356). The representation of characters within the interactive narrative text is distanced from the reality of the actors who are playing the roles and the mode of interaction itself. We can consider representation as a process or mode of interaction as well as relating to a 'particular kind of object' (Mitchell, 1995 p. 420). The immersive nature of the story allows the distance to be traversed and a multiplicity of character perspectives to cohabitate the metanarrative. The mode of interaction is blended to the narrative to function as a natural method of 'reading' the story, 'all representations are conventional in the sense that they depend upon symbol systems that might, in principle, be replaced by some other system' (Mitchell, 1995 p. 351). The mode of interaction in *The Little Extras* is rooted in simple hyperlinking. If the viewer has been properly encouraged and stimulated to 'read' the text and look for interactive opportunities, they will seize upon a symbol system that allows them to navigate more freely. *The Little Extras* creates a temporal reality within the interactive text. The temporal period is known to the audience in that it deals with historically familiar concepts including the emotions of jealousy and anger (Mitchell, 1995 p. 353).

Filmic representations of reality can be considered uncinematic (Carroll, 2008 p. 203). Narrative disclosure is unrealistic in that it does not replicate the reality we experience in everyday life where most issues remain unresolved and facts stay hidden. Theorists who favour the Italian Neorealist recording of experiences emphasise the value of photography in creating cinematic works where the camera simply photographs the reality in front of it. An alternative theoretical position is to emphasise the creation of narrative structure through editing. Pacing and juxtaposition of narrative elements create the relationships between shots and scenes for the audience and drive the narrative according to the author's vision. Mitchell notes the difference in time between the writing of the story and its reading, 'narrative seems to be a mode of knowing and showing which constructs a region of the unknown, a shadow text or image that accompanies our reading, moves in time with it' (Mitchell, 1995 p. 190). The author of the non-linear story creates an organic text that lives and grows through interactivity. As the story develops, the relevance of its own past and future is in state of flux. Dialogue in the text offers the characters a voice as an alternative to the absolutism of diegesis. This mimesis can be flexibly interpreted by the audience as they develop a greater understanding of the characters and their situations (Mitchell, 1995 p. 191). Most film-makers create work that their target audience will understand and cognise (Carroll, 2008 p. 212). This includes incorporating known features specific to their genre such as high-key lighting in film noir thrillers and the lone gunman in westerns. A film that is 'truly, ontologically incomparable with any other would be ... an incomprehensible artifact. Faith in the consummately singular motion picture derives from a romantic-modernist fantasy of the genius' (Carroll, 2008 p. 216).

Jerome Bruner explored the transference of knowledge and the assimilation of narrative. He points out that knowledge always represents someone's perspective, so that the 'normativeness of narrative, in a word, is not historically or culturally terminal. Its form changes with the preoccupations of the age and the circumstances surrounding its production' (Bruner, 1991 p. 16). Bruner is stating that a perspective on a story is therefore influenced by one's consideration of the author's intent. It depends on what we know about both the author as a person and the subject under discussion. He refutes the concept of knowledge as a fixed entity. It is instead highly flexible and changing, mediated and remediated by successive readers, who have been influenced in turn by their background, friends, books, cultural experience and conventions. The reality created by a narrative is an interpretation of the facts presented to us.

Different cultures will adopt and exploit digital interactive media developments in different ways (Jenkins & Thorburn, 2003 p. 5). Political, cultural and economic forces will shape the interactions between the people and emerging technologies. The book includes an analysis of the communication and processing technologies that will be used to develop and distribute new media formats including interactive films. The relationship between author and observer is explored. Digital media allow the reader to alter original texts through interactivity including the use of inserts and links (Landow, 2006 p.126). The role of the author is changing. The reader is empowered to actively construct meaning by adding layers of interpretation. However, readers have always 'read' texts from particular perspectives and in doing so altered their interpretation of meaning to suit themselves. In this way, the act of adding content to the published text is simply another step in the information reception process. This process leads to an interpretation and position taken by the reader in relation to the content.

A SUMMARY OF THE CHAPTERS

Chapter 2, 'Traditional Narrative Texts', explores the works of various creative artists including photographers, playwrights, authors, film-makers and academic theorists. It considers the extent to which non-linear narrative developers can exploit traditional storytelling structures, techniques and literary devices to produce a unique story experience. The chapter introduces relevant terminology and reflects on the prospective augmentation of linear narratives by the addition of interactive interfaces. The chapter also examines classic film-making techniques including the incorporation of narrative conflict, promoting audience immersion and the use of sound. Subtitles in film are also considered with regard to the potential incorporation of hypertext within interactive film products.

Chapter 3, 'Subjective Interpretation', examines how an audience interprets meaning within narrative texts. The relative position of the author and reader is assessed. Burgess and Dovey are considered with regard to the linguistic construction of texts and the interactive storyteller's relinquishment of authorial control. Bellantoni's research into our emotional response to colour sequences is explored alongside Kandinsky's theory on the psychology of colour and Mortenson's description of our instinctual responses to geometric patterns.

Chapter 4, 'Sound Design', examines the explicit nature of music via the theoretical texts of Adorno and Eisler. The chapter also looks at Goodall's research into the history of music development and Storr's work on the emotional meaning of music. It considers the exploitation of musical devices and techniques including counterpoint, syncopation, allusionism, psychological time and instrumentation. It explores the use of music in cinematic works and examines the implementation of music in feature-film soundtracks.

Chapter 5, 'Visual Montage', takes a detailed look at spatially presented audiovisual works and assesses the meaning and interpretation of both spatial montage and the juxtaposition of story elements. The chapter also considers the work of Hockney, Marker and Burroughs and examines how spatial presentation techniques used in traditional film and print media can be employed in an interactive narrative context.

Chapter 6, 'Codifying Story Elements', considers the classification of interactive narrative elements using a predetermined database schema. Codification of content requires the identification of story components which can be stored in a database. Codified data can be accessed non-sequentially to present the audience with a non-linear narrative. The chapter also looks at the codification techniques proposed by Propp and Bal. It introduces narratology terminology and considers Barthes 'message without a code'. It further examines the metatagging of digital content, data visualisation, trend-identifying algorithms, data analytics and hypernarrative. The chapter also explores the historical archive and reflects on the work of Brecht, de Quincey and Perec.

Chapter 7, 'Interactive Narratives', looks at ergodic texts, interactive titles, interfaces, narrative immersion, story structures, latency, distribution platforms and related technologies. It considers both historical and contemporary interactive narrative works with particular emphasis on the theatrical tradition. Interaction methodologies and their impact on users is assessed, including gesture-controlled interfaces and the study of proprioception. Virtual reality (VR), virtual identities and augmented reality (AR) are also explored. VR creates a fully rendered computer graphics environment for the viewer whereas AR overlays computer generated text and graphics over our real world vision.

Chapter 8, 'The Business of Transmedia Storytelling', looks at the commercial implementation of interactive narratives and transmedia stories across international markets. It considers the work of several ground-breaking experimental storytelling companies such as Blast Theory (UK) and the content-creation department of Marriott International (US). The chapter explores a range of new storytelling platforms including social media, and examines some highly innovative and commercially successful attempts to monetise interactive content. It looks at the international news agencies' development of data analytics tools to measure audience engagement, the development of augmented reality products and geo-located narratives.

In Appendix 1, 'Making *The Little Extras*', I discuss the development of this interactive film. The film concept is compared and contrasted to the works of Brueghel, Manovich and Tarkovsky. Conceptually the film created a paradigm shift that fundamentally differs from traditional linear narrative. In Appendix 2 I have given a brief explanation of digital data compression. The exploration of new storytelling platforms, developing experimental narratives using digital workflows, is much improved by a good understanding of compression.

COMMERCIAL IMPERATIVE

During my research I spoke to media-industry professionals and academic theorists here in Ireland and abroad. While the former naturally seek to exploit the commercial potential of new storytelling platforms, the latter's theoretical approach and openness to experimentation without a commercial imperative has resulted in the development of innovative products that could eventually be successfully monetised. Therefore, my approach has been to consider the potential success of all commercial opportunities within this highly experimental and inventive storytelling environment. The stories considered in this book have been delivered in a wide variety of formats from self-contained entertainment products to a media segment within a content creation department's audience-building marketing strategy. Depending on your approach, you may believe the commercial imperative of content creation to be irrelevant. Generating income from interactive content is a challenge. However, it is worth noting that when one considers the income generation potential of the passive consumption of traditional media (selling commercial advertising space to clients based on projected audience figures and demographics), it seems likely that the commercial potential of individually identifiable interactive engagements with story elements is significantly greater.

THE COMMAND TO READ

To expand upon this practice of exploring traditional media I encourage the reader to continue to study a wide range of texts and to certainly move outside their comfort zone. Reading is not always easy, nor even pleasurable in some cases, as many worthwhile texts require significant effort to get through. As a film and photography lecturer I have always promoted the importance of critically analysing narrative texts. Keep reading until it becomes more than a thought, it becomes an opinion. With the rise of online broadcasting I have found it necessary to encourage 'reading not watching'. Reading a text requires a greater level of engagement with the author's text to fully consider their intention and line of argument. Reading creates a much more profound understanding of a concept. Watching an online documentary may be useful in some circumstances, but it tends to result in a simple regurgitation of facts – it lacks criticality. When reviewing student work, it is always obvious to me who has conducted their research by 'reading' and who has simply 'watched'.

When considering relevant published materials as part of your research, go to a library with a good stock of visual reference books and simply browse through the texts one by one. Eventually, a narrative technique or visual style will appeal to you, it will make itself known and provide the starting point for future research and practice. Experimentation with techniques, styles and approaches often uncovers something original. The film-maker Alan Parker attributes his success in film-making to the large number of television commercials he made during his early career in advertising. It was here he says that he was able to make mistakes, experiment with new ideas and eventually hone his craft. It also allowed him to develop a unique storytelling style, a personal aesthetic. The repetition of the short storytelling process, conceiving ideas, shooting then completing the product allowed him to continually analyse his work and thus grow as an artist. In fact, in my experience as a teacher, it is the student who completes a large number of smaller projects, rather than getting part way through several larger and more ambitious ones, who is the most capable, confident and ready to work in a competitive industry.

LATERAL THINKING

A high level of critical analysis in turn results in a good degree of lateral thinking, considering an idea from various angles, thinking around the concept. In storytelling this allows the writer to produce unique, thought-provoking narratives. As the story creator engages with the development process while keeping an open mind, they will achieve a greater level of ownership of their work. This ownership, the act of critiquing your work and its intention as the narrative develops, encourages one to 'say something' with each story. This always results in a much more compelling narrative, one which has an opinion, is eloquently expressed and which promotes debate. The increased engagement with the intention of the author also increases the potential for commercial success. It is important to have an opinion on something that you wish to engage with both creatively and intellectually. The artistic artefact that you produce will create an intellectual discourse between you and your audience. In this regard, the most successful works 'speak out'. Your opinion, the point of view you have adopted in relation to the subject being discussed, should come from an informed position, evidencing research, knowledge and synthesis.

PITCHING YOUR IDEA

It is beneficial to pitch your idea to an audience. The pitch forces you to consider who and where the market is for the product you intend to create. An intellectual academic may experiment with concepts and storytelling paradigms having little interest in their commercial potential, yet most students are engaged in a programme of academic study in order to launch a successful career. Therefore, I consider it important to both identify the audience for a story idea that is being pitched and decide how the story will be delivered to them. This constraint, forcing the creative individual or team to tailor a product for a particular audience, is an opportunity to employ the techniques of lateral thinking to develop a fresh perspective and personal style.

DEVELOPING AN IDEAS BOOK/VISUAL DIARY

An ideas book or visual diary is an invaluable resource in ideas generation. It should include all manner of visuals, texts, references, both obscure and well-known. Whatever takes your fancy. The important thing is to get it down on paper, scanned, copied or drawn. The best ideas books I have seen tended to be messy affairs, with bits of paper and assorted materials bulging out at the sides. In this personal volume, the individual is storing up a series of narrative elements, for future reference. The visual diary is an important tool for communicating ideas to both clients and other creatives. Note why you are including content; it is a common occurrence for visually exciting work to be included in an ideas book, only for the creative to forget what the (significant) point of its inclusion was.

* * *

This book has been written in order to be accessible, engaging, incisive and informative to the creative storyteller. The research that went into it was highly selective and concentrated on the simplification and clarification of complex, often abstract ideas. It highlights the vocabulary and knowledge most relevant to the development of new narrative structures. It identifies story products and creators, industry practitioners and academic researchers, and includes pertinent literary references to guide and inspire. It's all in there, it just needs to be 'unpacked'.

2

Traditional Narrative Texts

This chapter looks at a range of traditional linear texts and considers various successful attempts to break away from narrative conventions. It explores the storytelling works of photographers, film-makers, playwrights; classical narrative structures, the differences between linear and non-linear narratives and the film-editing theories and techniques most relevant to interactive storytelling. A thorough knowledge of traditional story composition, story devices and narrative techniques allows for much greater experimentation with new delivery platforms. If storytellers are going to exploit new technologies effectively they will need to engage in a significant degree of trial and error to create new user experiences. Audiences must be encouraged to participate in the development of new narrative structures and interactive interfaces. Their engagement will be of fundamental importance to the organic development of new storytelling ideas. A storyteller with a significant grasp of traditional storytelling concepts and techniques will connect emotionally with their audience regardless of the delivery mechanism.

'TALKING PICTURES': FINDING NARRATIVE IN PHOTOGRAPHY

The photographer Daniel Meadows started taking pictures as a student in Manchester in the 1970s. He was primarily interested in documenting people's lives. Early influences included the oral historian Studs Terkel and the photographer Bill Brandt who 'used the camera as a passport to slip between the social classes' (Meadows, interview 2016). Photography was a cheaper medium than video and Meadows preferred the significant level of engagement that stills photography offered. He would meet the subject, take their picture, process the film, then arrange to meet the subject again to give them the photograph and discuss the outcome. Meadows did not always have a tape recorder with him and it kept breaking down. He says he was recording audio just 'to get good caption information'. At that time, the cost of editing was prohibitive, so he did not immediately combine the audio and visuals together. Years later, when he started working with digital editing technologies, he revisited this work and created his series of 40 *Talking Pictures,* short two-minute pieces, individual photographs with first-person voices. He describes these as a 'window onto my archive'. Meadows' documentary work considers the world from the bottom up, from the point of view of the common man. He wanted to work in a collaborative way, to produce work that was more 'convivial, agreeable, democratic'. The result is a highly individual, unique work of social anthropology. He has captured a time and place, accents and behaviours that are long gone. The selected still image in each of the 'Talking Pictures' communicates its own narrative and is augmented by the edited audio. Meadows has created a sense of 'presence'.

GEOMETRY IN PHOTO COMPOSITION

A contemporary of Meadows was the photographer Tony Ray-Jones. In New York, Ray-Jones studied under the influential European artist Alexey Brodovitch at the Design Laboratory. Brodovitch encouraged artists to interact 'with aspects of modern life' and his teaching 'involved the posing of "moral and philosophical problems" in the pursuit of success, encouraging open debate and the search for a personal aesthetic' (Russell, 2004 p. 11). Ray-Jones work was highly influenced by American street photography of the 1960s, particularly Garry Winogrand and his friend Joel Meyerowitz. The social-commentary format of his images found his photographic subjects 'arranged like actors on a set with each character appearing to exist independently and collectively within the frame' (Russell, 2004 p. 16). Ray-Jones wrote several diaries that included a number of 'to-do lists' for himself. These were intended to guide future photographic projects and editorial assignments. The list of entries included phrases like 'get in closer', 'don't take boring pictures' and 'not all eye level'. He sought to explore the medium of photography and develop an individual style that communicated his particular vision of people and places. His images are geometrically balanced compositions. Each one constructs a complex narrative within a single frame. They exist both spatially and temporally, a dynamic representation of his unique perspective.

STORY SEQUENCES IN STILLS

The artist Duane Michals creates sequential-format photographic works to build an unfolding narrative across several images, exploring human emotions and reflecting on his philosophical musings.

> [These] sequences stand in a similar relation to movies as poems do to novels: they act on the imagination not through the accumulated evidence of description and explanation, but through a compression of single images rich in metaphorical allusion.
>
> (Livingstone, 1997 p. 8)

Michals also adds handwritten text to the surface of his images, suggesting the photograph alone is unable to communicate the complex ideas of the artist. The addition of language and symbols to the photograph creates a high-concept interpretative work, layered with meaning.

Photobooks function as narrative devices and reveal the photographer's 'patterns of thought' (Gibson, 1999 p. 705). The photo exhibition space allows for greater control on the part of the viewer to consider the work from various angles, distances, time and social context. A book constrains an audience in that it is normally held in one's own hands at a fixed distance and its tactile nature influences the experience of reading it. However, the book retains a certain flexibility in that it can be viewed at any time, without the need for further curation, encouraging critical engagement with the author's intention: 'books turn into thought and then become memory' (Gibson, 1999 p. 707).

Nicholas Nixon has photographed his wife and her three sisters every year since 1975 using a large format camera. His book *The Brown Sisters: Thirty-Three Years* (2007) features one representative image of the sisters for each year up to 2007 (Nixon, 2007). While they are positioned in the same order in every shot, the familial dynamic within each frame is different. We feel we can identify subtle changes in the sisters' relations to each other and observe the impact of life experience, evidenced by their slowly aging faces.

PEDRO MEYER'S *THE ILLUSION OF REAL SPACE*

Pedro Meyer was an early adopter of digital-imaging technologies. He used them to reconstruct 'the illusion of real space; no one will notice his alteration, performed with scalpel precision' (Meyer, 1996 p. 13). His creative workflow included traditional image capture on negative film, followed by digital scanning and manipulation 'to restore the picture to my memory of what actually happened' (Meyer, 1996 p. 108). For Meyer, the image captured by the negative alone was not an accurate record of the reality he had experienced; it did not reflect his memory of being there. He felt he had to digitally retouch it to improve its authority. Meyer also exploited the potential of his visual archive by regularly revisiting it, searching for new narratives, story structures and meanings to be created through the digital manipulation and juxtaposition of historical images.

NAVIGATING NON-LINEAR TEXTS

While film texts are traditionally linear in structure, film-makers have experimented successfully with non-linear presentations of the fabula.[1] This is a complex method of storytelling and requires both solid direction and an engaged viewer. *The Summit* , directed by Nick Ryan, is a film about the 2009 K2 mountain climbing tragedy. Ryan setup key story elements in advance, allowing the narrative to develop these points later in the film. Presenting the story in a linear order would have been tedious, lacked narrative immersion and would have given away important plot details too early. So Ryan restructured the fabula to make it more engaging; he said 'the whole point of editing is to navigate the story' (Ryan, interview 2016).

VERISIMILITUDE

Susan Hayward notes that the dominant ideology of classical cinema was one of verisimilitude, the implementation of a contrived plot development. Stories began with a disruption to the norm, followed by the blunt implementation of cause and effect to progress the narrative. The film ends with narrative closure and the sense that the world is right again. Here, the objective of social stability, as defined in the concept of Oedipal trajectory, involves the resolution of a crisis. However, this crisis offers opportunities for user interaction where the reader selects distinct navigational pathways, thereby creating an independent and autonomous route through the story (Hayward, 2006 p. 82).

BRECHTIAN REALISM

The Brechtian aesthetic brought science and practical action together, rejoining physical and mental activities. Brecht created 'educational' works for the enjoyment of audiences, for their immediate gratification. This realist approach promoted an active investigation of the text:

> The 'realistic' work of art is one in which 'realistic' and experimental attitudes are tried out, not only between its characters and their fictive realities, but also between the audience and the work itself ... the threefold dimensions of such a practice of 'realism' clearly explode the purely representational categories of the traditional mimetic work.
>
> (Adorno et al, 1986 p. 205)

Here, the text is considered revolutionary; it can stimulate debate and change opinion. Content generated for mass-media distribution will achieve greater success by avoiding the elite modernist approach. This means creating an accessible product that is not a novelty. The modernist invention needs to be constantly renewed just to be modern, leaving too little time for critical evaluation and reflection. The product will not become streamlined and made more efficient if it undergoes rapid fundamental changes that leave the audience baffled. The author of the interactive work needs to consider the audience's needs and expectations.

Brecht's translation of Marlowe's *Edward II* created 'free but irregular rhythms' which allowed the lines to 'stumble' (Willett, 1988 p. 95). Brecht later used the technique in his own plays to reject the flowing style of the iambic pentameter and to reflect the coarse, harsh characters and scenarios he sought to create. Brecht designed the text to be spoken in a theatrical context; characters had short, sharp lines, saying just what he wanted them to say and no more. This approach was intended to remove anything elegant from the sentence structures, which Brecht believed would obscure the true meaning of the text. The use of syncopation in verse, as in jazz music, serves to fragment the general rhythm of speech. The underlying attitude of each verse is conveyed with individual truth, rather than allowing an actor to apply a single emotion to long passages of text (Willett, 1988 p. 101). Brecht later employed further techniques to prevent the audience becoming immersed in the play including directing actors to leave the stage and join the audience at various points during the play. During rehearsals, actors would say their lines using indirect speech, as though they were an eyewitness to their own character's actions. This also informed the actor as to how the audience would view them. Preventing the audience from becoming immersed was meant to retain their critical frame of mind, to promote an intellectual engagement and consideration of the content of the play. Maintaining a critical frame of mind is important to interactive story texts. The dynamic process of interaction means the audience must be thinking at all times, to not become a passive, non-participating viewer. Brecht 'posited that catharsis is not complete until the audience members take what they have assimilated from the representation and put it to work in their lives' (Laurel, 1991 p. 31).

ARISTOTLE'S *POETICS*

Aristotle had a healthy respect for human emotions and the effect of storytelling on them. He believed that emotions were a rational human response that should be interpreted and not dismissed as being too animalistic and non-spiritual. He considered emotions to be more than irrational impulses, and indicated that there is a time and a place for correct and satisfying emotional responses appropriate to the circumstances. Malcolm Heath summarises Aristotle's first argument for the primacy of the plot in narrative:

> Tragedy aims to excite fear and pity; these emotions are responses to success and failure; success and failure depend on action; hence action is the most essential thing in tragedy; therefore plot is the most important element.
>
> (Heath, 1996 p. xxi)

Characters develop independently of the plot; in fact characters that exist within a predefined plot develop their own arc, their own voice. They speak within their natural dimensions, so that text and plot are fully separate entities. The characters do not limit the plot. Writers of stories based on real events should not be constrained by actualities. If they were, the emphasis on the facts would be to the detriment of the plot. The events only need to be connected, within the context of the story. Aristotle defined the rules of creating plot-driven narratives. The best plot involved moving a virtuous person from a position of good fortune to bad. The second-best plot has a double line of development with good characters achieving good fortune in the end, while bad characters end in misfortune (Heath, 1996 p. xxxiv).

HOGARTH'S *A RAKE'S PROGRESS*

William Hogarth's series of paintings *A Rake's Progress* (1731–33) shows the decline and fall of Tom Rakewell, a wealthy merchant's son who inherits a fortune and loses it all through gambling and high living. This series adhered to Aristotle's 'best plot' structure in that the character's fortunes decline as the story progresses. In the end all is lost and only his faithful friend Sarah Young (whom he earlier rejected despite his promise to marry her) loyally remains with him when he ends up in Bedlam asylum.

Aristotle argued against the use of one-dimensional characters that are overtly good or overtly bad, without complexity or facets. He believed that characters should be moral, or at least they should not be morally bad without good reason. They should be believable within the perspective of the narrative (Heath, 1996 p. xxi). Within the plot, they should seek to be virtuous, or as virtuous as the plot will allow them to be. Within the reality created by the plot, characters must behave according to the constraints of that reality, while also enhancing the plot. Events can happen to characters within the plot as long as they are necessary to move the plot forward, to convey the story the author wishes to tell.

BAUDELAIRE'S *L'ART MNEMONIQUE*

Sylviane Agacinski continues the analysis of Aristotle: 'there is no time without movement or change, and it is in perceiving movement that we perceive time' (Agacinski, 2003 p. 34). The tempo of change can be alternated to maintain interest in the text. Time does not have a 'single measure'. This is important in creating an immersive environment in film to encourage audience 'interaction' with the text. The audiences of interactive narratives are working with the author to create the story. 'Baudelaire attributes the formation of the interior image to a procedure by which the memory breaks with applied observation and achieves a perceptual synthesis ... imagining the real at the very moment of perceiving it' (Agacinski, 2003 p. 74). Baudelaire defined *l'art mnemonique* which 'suggests that memory and imagination takes place in the execution of the work itself and not before' (Agacinski, 2003 p. 74). The emphasis is on the processes of creation and interaction, rather than the definition of a completed work.

FILM EDITING: WALTER MURCH

Walter Murch described editing as 'cutting – the sudden disruption of reality' (Murch, 2001 p. 16). Although the human eye 'cuts' (blinks) when we look from one person to another or from one object to another, the edit can take the viewer 'out' of the story. A clumsy edit is generally considered clumsy because it is unnecessary and does not place the viewer where they want to be within the dramatic context. A smooth cut will seamlessly move the viewer from one shot to the next so that they think they have simply 'blinked' as they changed views. Various techniques are used to make the cuts smoother. These include cutting on movement (while a character moves to sit on a chair, the sudden change in shot perspective and potential continuity errors are hidden by the abruptness of the physical movement), cutting the audio before the visuals (the transition between shots appears 'smoother'), and cross-fade edits, where one shot actually merges with another.

'THE RULE OF SIX'

During his extensive career as a film and sound editor Murch created 'the rule of six'. This was a list of six criteria used to identify and to optimise each edit within a scene and the sequential placement of each individual cut. He also developed a method of use for this set of rules, 'satisfying the criteria of items higher on the list tends to obscure problems with items lower on the list, but not vice-versa' (Murch, 2001 p. 18). He classified their ratio of importance in percentages. At 51 per cent, 'emotion' was rated as the most important consideration by far. If the edit is true to the emotion of the moment then it is correct. This was followed by 'story' at 23 per cent – does the edit advance the story? 'Rhythm' is rated at 10 per cent – does the edit occur at the moment that is rhythmically interesting and 'right'? 'Eye-trace' at 7 per cent – is the edit concerned with the location and movement of the audience's focus of interest within the frame? Interestingly, the classic continuity considerations of 'two-dimensional plane of screen' and 'three-dimensional space of action' are rated low in terms of their relevance to the edit at just 5 per cent and 4 per cent (Murch, 2001, p. 18). According to Murch, the ideal cut will satisfy all criteria at once. But the decision to make a cut should be based on the priority of each rule in this weighting system. Therefore, finding the right emotion is most important and the relationship between characters (within the three-dimensional space) is least important. Finding the right emotion takes priority over story, story takes priority over rhythm etc.

By using this rating system to assess each edit, Murch moves the viewer through the story on various levels including emotion, narrative, rhythm and composition, allowing them to think critically about each edit and its impact on the story. The film audience will always assume that an edit is there for a reason and this system allows Murch to ensure that every edit serves the narrative and is fully justified.

While editing a film, Murch selects a 'representative frame' from every shot sequence, then blows it up into a photograph. He displays these photographs on a wall, in story order. Where a shot is visually complex he uses more than one photograph. Murch compares these images to Cartier-Bresson's 'decisive moment': the theory that within every period of time there exists a 'representative frame' that communicates its very essence (Murch, 2001 p. 41). These photo boards allow him to view the story 'all at once', to consider alternative edits and potential scene structures. They are also useful as a reminder of the shot options available to him.

When organising test screenings, Murch recommends speaking to the audience several days after seeing the film. The film has had time to sink in. This avoids what he calls 'referred pain'. With referred pain, the audience may indicate a scene they do not like and there is pressure on the editor to rework it. However the audience may be only be unhappy because the scene has not been properly set up, perhaps due to an issue with an earlier scene. Murch likens this process to a doctor who suspects that a patient's pain is the result of an as yet unidentified ailment. It is the ailment that needs to be fixed if the pain is going to go away.

Test audiences are often questioned about a film right after they have viewed it. This puts pressure on them to come up with immediate impressions, despite the fact that people often need several hours/days to decide on their long-term response to a film. The time immediately following a film is often spent 'replaying' parts of the story in one's head. This replaying and conversations with other viewers gives us time to enjoy once more the significant scenes, or to realise that the story does not stand up to critical evaluation and we soon forget it. While production companies want to know straightaway what people thought of their product, they are ignoring the fact that the audience's most important impressions are probably established some days after. In reality, audiences may recommend seeing a film only after this time of reflection is over. But they will continue to recommend a film for some time after.

Murch poses the question, why do we accept edits in film? They are visually unlike anything we experience in real life. He believes that we accept the cut because it resembles the way images are juxtaposed in our dreams. Murch also notes the similarity of the cut to a blink of an eye. When we move our heads to look at one object after another, we blink to avoid the 'rush of detail' as our head/eyes pass the intervening visuals. The cut also allows us to edit out unnecessary detail in a scene. We can move temporally, focusing on the moments that are most significant. Slow motion allows the viewer to go beyond 'real-time' and watch a 'hyper-real' version of a shot. This is used in action sequences, and often intercut with speeded up clips for emphasis.

Murch quotes John Huston:

> [T]o me, the perfect film is as though it were unwinding behind your eyes, and your eyes were projecting it themselves, so that you were seeing what you wished to see. Film is like thought. It's the closest to thought process of any art.
>
> (Murch, 2001 p. 60)

The opening sequence of Fellini's *8½* (1963) moves seamlessly through edits so that they are hardly noticed. Instead, the viewer is caught up in the visual feast that Fellini presents and is immersed in the film's reality.

In the 1990s Murch was a great exponent of digital-editing technologies and their inherent advantages over traditional linear systems. He believed their advantage lay in the greater options they offered editors as opposed to their speed. They allowed the editor to stay flexible with the edit, putting off commitment for as long as possible. Digital-editing systems allowed the editor to view multiple versions of an edited piece in quick succession. This meant that more ideas could be experimented with, more concepts developed and negotiated. He noted that the flexibility of new technologies necessitates different disciplines than traditional equipment. Films can now be edited right up until a few days before release. The flexibility is such that the editor must work towards a specific narrative goal rather than continually making changes in the hope that something good will turn up. This flexibility also means that editors can throw 'everything' in there without worrying about stock damage or increasing costs. With traditional film editing, even testing a transition had significant processing and optical equipment costs associated with it. The editor had to pre-visualise the work and make informed decisions as to the potential success or failure of a cut.

Traditional processes also involved lengthy waits for the lab to process the edits forcing editors to think much more laterally about the whole film.

Sometimes too many stylistic elements are included in a single piece, just because it is possible to do so, not because it helps the film. This is why Murch's 'rule of six' is so important. It regulates the edits being made and ensures that they are in keeping with the overall 'style' of the film.

Murch observes that people tend to blink their eyes when they are saying non-vocalised consonants – 's', 'f', 'th' but not 'd' (uh). Murch uses this blink of the eye to identify the frame to 'cut' shots. He edits when the actor blinks. 'The same thing that makes a person blink ... is also making the audience 'blink' – the audience is more receptive to a shift of attention at that moment' (Ondaatje, 2004 p. 142). This is also true when we move our head to look from one object to another. As the head turns the eye will 'pan' to the next object. The pan will cause slight disorientation and dizziness so we 'blink' to miss it. As the head starts to turn, the eyes close and only reopen when the head has almost completed the movement. In this way, we are always performing natural edits in our heads. We are editing out the unimportant information that we do not want to receive, the information that sits between the two objects of interest. It is interesting to note this point as it explains why early cinema audiences accepted the traditional 'edit' so readily.

With regard to the timeline of films Murch says that it is acceptable to have an actor dressed in the same clothes over a long plot time because the audience subconsciously thinks, 'I've only been here for two hours'. This is an interesting observation on how a film is 'read' by audiences. In real time the character would have changed clothes etc. but in the compressed time of the narrative this is not an issue. It is also interesting to note that most films show main characters eating and drinking. Without this type of refreshment it seems that the audience are reminded of their own reality and the fact that they are hungry or thirsty.

In the film *The Conversation* (1974) the main character 'Harry' is a recording expert played by Gene Hackman. The film was directed by Francis Coppola and edited by Murch. Murch notes that Harry would have been a peripheral character in a traditional film and part of the film's objective was to view a story from the viewpoint of a peripheral character. Characters that are incidental and exist in the periphery of the narrative do not have any significant influence on plot development.

THE THIRD EFFECT

Murch reiterates Eisenstein's theory of montage and considers how our right and left eyes view a scene from two slightly different perspectives. These alternate fields of vision are very similar yet different. When the brain tries to see both at once, a 'third concept' is introduced which is 'an arena in which both perspectives can exist' (Ondaatje, 2004 p. 209). Thus, the brain is able to extrapolate depth information from the two 2D images created by the retinas. Murch is talking about the juxtaposition of visual elements that result in a meaning that is neither one nor the other, it is something completely new. As a photographer I have often explored the potential of this 'third effect' of seemingly separate visuals that come together to create a new meaning that is independent of the parts that created it. Each image is a diptych of two unconnected photographs. The interpretation of the two images together as one, is fundamentally distinct from the interpretation derived from the individual images. Eisenstein's theory of montage is explored in more detail in the *Visual Montage* chapter.

EISENSTEIN'S DIAGRAMMATIC SCORE

Florian Brody (quoted in Lunenfield, 2000 p. 140) considers the diagrammatic 'score' which Eisenstein developed for *Alexander Nevsky* (1938). Each frame was constructed as an entity within a choreographed temporal flow, 'the spatial and temporal composition of both the image and the development of the story, together with the sound, are evident' (quoted in Lunenfeld, 2000 p. 140). Eisenstein proposed an ambitious exploitation of the audiovisual medium, by controlling all aspects of the content, including music, visuals, audio and geometry. His work left little room for open-ended interpretation, and cinema projectors already fixed the frame rate of audio and visuals and the ordering of scenes.

PRECIPITANT SOUNDS

Murch has worked as sound recordist on many films and has built up an extensive array of 'meaningful' sounds. He describes these as 'precipitant sounds, something we associate with a specific environment but that is itself distinct, then the other sounds come along automatically' ... 'I spent a lot of time trying to discover those key sounds that bring universes along with them' (Murch quoted in Ondaatje, 2004 p. 244). 'I spent a lot of time trying to discover those key sounds that bring universes along with them' (Ondaatje,

2004 p. 244). By employing the text of the sound or the universe that comes with it, Murch can inject many more layers of meaning into a scene. Murch has recorded and used sounds in films that 'enhance' the world the film-maker is trying to create. He gives various examples including the use of an almost imperceptible sound of a wrench being dropped in the distance to locate the audience spatially within the geographical limits of the film's location. This piece of audio, subconsciously informed the audience that the scene was being played out near a dockyard location, seen earlier in the film, but which had no establishing shot in this scene.

Sound has colouration that may not match the visual colour. Murch suggests that film-makers should both visualise and auralise (listen to the space in which the sound is contained) to create a contiguous piece (Murch quoted in Ondaatje, 2004 p. 247). Mismatched colour and sound will appear disjointed and may even fragment the narrative.

Edits are created 'purely with thought and emotion, with rhythm and musicality' (Ondaatje, 2004 p. 269). In practice Murch edits on what he calls 'flinch' points. In this regard he aims to hit the same frame that he intends to cut on every time he watches a shot. He says there is something 'organically true' about the moment that indicates to him that this is the frame to cut on. 'Made in America', the concluding episode of *The Sopranos* (2007), is a striking example of a perfectly crafted edit. The final scene in the diner is deliberately disjointed. Tony Soprano has been at war with his enemies all season and could likely be killed at any moment. The rhythm of the scene is 'off' and the scene includes a disorientating 'jump cut'. An incoherent visual sequence creates an uneasy atmosphere. Something's not right, but what? While all appears well on the surface we believe Tony is sensing something, although probably too late. The edits take us inside and outside the diner, which continues to confuse and disconnect. The last shot is in keeping with some earlier contemplations on the death experience within the show. Tony symbolically looks up in expectation of his daughter Meadow walking through the diner door, a signifying bell rings (denoting the guardian angel Clarence Odbody in *It's a Wonderful Life* [1946]) and his story collapses into a dark, black silence. Like Chantal Ackerman's French short film *J'ai faim, j'ai froid* (1984) the scene may simply be a recollection of an event. This was Ackerman's filmic representation of her adult self's memory, the memory of her arrival in Paris as a runaway teenager. Perhaps the final scene in *The Sopranos* is Meadow's account of that fateful night in the diner, retold many years later. Now, filled with profound, philosophical perceptions, the scene takes on a new resonance.

Murch is inspired by the work achieved by Guido d'Arezzo in music notation and he has examined the concept of creating a similar system of notation for the staging of a scene in film. But he believes that film-makers have not reached this stage and compares them to the medieval cathedral builders whose craft was 'hands-on yet mystically intuitive'. They could create these incredible pieces of work that last for centuries, yet there was no system of notation to explain the rules for the buildings they created. According to Murch, an equivalent cinematic notation is possible but has yet to be developed.

Murch edited *Cold Mountain* (2003) using Apple's Final Cut Pro. He gave a frank account to Charles Koppelman of this pioneering work editing a large-scale feature film using low budget technologies originally designed for amateur use. It was his first time using Final Cut Pro and he experienced many workflow issues while editing on location in Romania. He moved the technical set-up to London to complete the final edit with the director Anthony Minghella. The move itself caused many problems in terms of striking a set-up in one country and trying to rebuild it again in another. Due to the experimental nature of the project (no feature film had ever been edited using Final Cut Pro), Murch did not get any official support from Apple. They were concerned that if the project failed their technology would be blamed. Despite the obvious advantage of having their consumer-model editing software being used for a major feature film, they were unwilling to offer official help. The cost of the equipment was significantly cheaper than Murch's usual editing system, Avid. This meant that he was able to buy four Final Cut Pro systems for the same money and allowed him to hire technicians to work on elements of the edit under his supervision. Significantly, Murch's team solved many problems by changing the 'workflow'. Editing a film is a series of repetitive tasks including logging, editing, tweaking edits etc. They were able to remove elements of the workflow to increase the overall speed of the edit. For Murch, finessing the workflow (incorporating several technologies) was more important than the technologies themselves.

The non-linear edit suite allowed Murch and Minghella to produce a complex narrative incorporating spatial and temporal shifts: 'as the story progresses ... it makes internal leaps forward in time. Minghella likes this structural motif. He tells non-linear stories and expects an audience to work a little harder to follow them' (Koppelman, 2004 p. 211). Early scenes in the movie intercut two characters. Their time frame (pace) is different until they come to the same 'time frame'. Then 'the two main characters are intercut by location' (Murch quoted in Koppelman, 2004 p. 213).

EMBODIED SOUNDS

When the first edit of a film is complete Murch says that 30 per cent can be removed (as fat) without affecting the story. After that, the film will be changed and the story needs rethinking. He describes speech as 'encoded sound' where 'the listener must decode it using linguistic tools to associate meaning' (Murch quoted in Koppelman, 2004 p. 288). Music is 'embodied sound' which 'requires no code for understanding.' It can be experienced directly without analysis. In between speech and music are sound effects which are half language, half music. Murch wrote in a 1998 article *Dense Clarity, Clear Density*:

> A well-balanced painting will have an interesting and proportioned spread of colours from complementary parts of the spectrum, so the soundtrack of a film will appear balanced and interesting if it is made up of a well-proportioned spread of elements from our spectrum of 'sound-colours.'
>
> (Murch, 2005)

Murch states that the audience can keep track of two sounds but not three. Three sounds are treated as a single sound. 'A soundtrack shouldn't contain more than three major elements and a minor third – not unlike a musical chord' (Murch, 2005). This is Murch's 'law of two-and-a-half':

> Clarity, which comes through a feeling for the individual elements (the notes), and Density, which comes through a feeling for the whole (the chord). I found this balance point to occur most often when there were not quite three layers of something – my 'Law of Two-and-a-Half.'
>
> (Murch, 2005)

The physical properties of sound make such layering possible, what Murch calls 'harmonic superimposure.' Like musical tones, sounds can be added together while each element retains its identity. The notes C, E and G create something new, a C-major chord, but you can also hear each of the original notes. Too many notes together leads to 'white noise' that does not mean anything – this can be heard when too many background sounds are used in a film. Digital technology will make it possible to create endless variations of film edits that are customised to suit geographic, demographic, emotional responses etc. of audiences. 'Here cinema becomes more like live-theatre where actors respond to the feedback they're getting from the audience' (Koppelman, 2004 p. 331).

NARRATIVE PROGRESSION

Traditional film narrative structures exploit the audience's prior knowledge of specific genres gained through previous film-going experiences. Early film theorists created stories that audiences easily understood and which allowed them to engage in a shared participatory experience. In his book *On Film-Making*, Alexander Mackendrick offers advice on creating a compelling narrative based on his experience as a film director and successful educationalist. He describes storytelling as 'the knack of swiftly seizing the imagination of the audience and never letting it go' (Mackendrick, 2004 p. 77). The audience will remain hooked if the story promises a degree of gratification in the end. Narrative tension may be loosened now and again, but it must be 'snapped tight' to quickly regain audience attention if their focus begins to wane. Mackendrick permits a degree of flexibility in the telling of a story, digressions are allowed. But the goal is to capture the audience within a fictive reality and keep them there.

Narrative progression is the forward movement of the story, taking the audience on a journey where they can never quite catch up to the narrator. A good film-maker will alternate the pace of the film to maintain a steady interest in an unsteady and unpredictable narrative. Tension may be latent, but it is always present. Taking the attention off the main narrative (using sub-narratives and asides) enhances the impact of the plot when the audience is brought back to it again. Mackendrick highlights the essential nature of tension in film. It may not be at plot level or between characters onscreen, but it is a 'tension of the imagination' which leads to curiosity, suspense and apprehension (Mackendrick, 2004 p. 11).

Without dramatic tension there is no reason for the audience to stay immersed in the story, they have no function in relation to understanding or following plot development. Mackendrick states that the passive character in film threatens dramatic values. The requirement for dramatic tension does not apply to other narrative forms; novels and short stories do not need to have a conflict or crisis.

Mackendrick notes that the main difference between writing for print and writing for film is that in scriptwriting the author himself has to be removed (Mackendrick, 2004 p. 16). Audiences look for the conflict that needs to be resolved. The most convincing changes in character are the resolution of conflicting personality elements. In many films a character represents the audience. This character will ask questions and seek the answers that the audience needs to find. He represents the audience's 'view' of the narrative. In terms of writing structure, Mackendrick writes that audiences will not know the exact details of the story being told, but they do have some idea of the formula being adhered to, or broken (Mackendrick, 2004 p. 30).

Back-story is essential to convey to the audience how the character has arrived at this point in the story. It must be conveyed succinctly, giving as much information as the audience needs, without creating a new story arc. Both the director and actor consider the script together to explore and make manifest the writer's intention. They interpret the original text, extract its meaning and make creative decisions as to how the work should be brought to the screen. Following their collaboration, the editor, when working with the audiovisual materials they have produced must continue their work to capture the 'still evolving make-believe' (Mackendrick, 2004 p. 67).

After the script has been shot, the film can be edited in a variety of ways, allowing the director space to reinterpret the text. The visual edit can even work against the spoken word to emphasise the subtext of the scene. The script is the first stage of three broad stages of making a film: script, shoot and edit. The script is the framework around which the actors and director create the footage (principal photography). Mackendrick compares the relationship between the script and the completed film as being similar to an architect's plans and a building. He believes that a good script should be easy to read fast.

There is room for interpretation in the casting of individuals and groups of actors; 'characterisation in film is not nearly so concerned with appearances and physique as it is with motives and temperament' (Mackendrick, 2004 p. 74). A character's actions, as they play out within the 'story beats', characterise them within the story much more than their physical appearance. An actor can be physically unsuited to a role, yet temperamentally perfect. A dynamic relationship between (miscast) actors will create a much more interesting story than slavishly casting according to the script's character descriptions. A strong script will have elements of the 'feeling' needed by the actors to make the words come alive. When the script is too descriptive the writer is relying on the talent of the actor to make the words work. The script should be able to convey its own emotion through the text.

INTERPRETING THE AUTHOR'S INTENT

The relationship between text and cinema was explored by the Russian literary theorist Viktor Shklovsky. In his view, the translation of a work from print to screen affects our interpretation of the author's original intent. When reading, the positioning of words on a page communicates one perspective on their meaning, whereas listening to the voiced delivery of the text as dialogue, presented alongside cinematographic visuals, builds into something quite different. The logic of the original (written) sequence collapses; 'at first, literature seizes upon cinematic devices and imitates them ... Maybe literature will move into a purely linguistic sphere and relinquish plot' (Shklovsky, 2008 p. 73).

NARRATIVE REALITY VERSUS AUDIENCE REALITY

William Goldman discusses the differences between the reality that we live in and the reality created by film-makers. Goldman points out that the reality created by a movie is not grounded in our real world and therefore the movie's characters are not restrained by this reality (Goldman, 1989 p. 139). If events in the film make sense in the world created by the film story then they will be acceptable to the audience. However, in the world that the screenwriter creates, the 'reality' must conform to established audience preconceptions. These include the fact that the story must take the audience on a journey and provide entertainment. Certain junctions in the story will leave the audience questioning what will happen next. But they will already have some idea of what 'could' happen next within the 'standardised' reality of film texts (Goldman, 1989 p. 139). For the writer to do something completely different and unexpected (in other words something that goes beyond known film text realities), there is real danger that the immersive nature of the story will be broken and the audience will withdraw from the narrative, retreat to the real world, and try to 'figure out' the story as it is being told.

> But every movie – from a Robert Flaherty documentary to *Raiders of the Lost Ark* – sets its own special reality. And once those limits are established, they may not be broken without the risk of fragmenting the entire picture.
>
> (Goldman, 1989 p. 139)

Some directors work film history into their texts. Martin Scorsese often plays around with established film conventions. He tweaks them slightly to present the audience with a fresh, new perspective. In *Mean Streets* (1970), the character Johnny Boy, played by Robert DeNiro, suffers an unexpected and violent death during a car-chase shoot-out. His character had previously provided some light entertainment for the audience and characters alike. The drawn-out death scene has Johnny Boy screaming loudly, a disturbing wail. His tough guy image evaporates and we are left with the new reality of an immature 'kid' out of his depth. The vocalised suffering brings pain to empathic listeners (Sonnenschein, 2001 p. 139).

In *Casino*, characters narrate parts of the story through voiceover. This technique was used in an earlier generation of gangster films, but *Casino* depicts a new generation of criminal. The old rules no longer apply and the director conveys this effectively by modifying the genre's narrative conventions. Through voiceover, Joe Pesci's character, Nicky Santoro, talks the audience through the events that led up to a meeting of opposing gang members. We see the characters arrive and Santoro himself is present at the meeting. Shockingly, he is ambushed and beaten to death by club-wielding thugs. His voiceover, describing the meeting as it was about to take place, led the audience to assume that he would certainly live through this event. Characters do not usually narrate their own story diegetically or non-diegetically (on-screen or off-screen) if they are just about to be killed. Yet, in *Sunset Boulevard* (1950) Joe Gillis, the story's narrator, is introduced floating face-down in a pool at the beginning of the film. We know he is dead throughout the movie. With *Casino* (1995) Scorsese has updated the genre conventions while still working within the narrative context. Everything that happens is believable in that it could happen in this story. He has reworked and updated the genre, but in the context of the story being told, he has stayed within the rules.

In *American Splendor* (2003) the actor Paul Giamatti plays comic book writer Harvey Pekar in a staged re-enactment of Pekar's life. Yet the film cuts back and forth to the real Pekar commenting on the original events while we watch Giammati's performance. In *Marvellous* (2014), Toby Jones plays Neil Baldwin, a man with perceived learning difficulties who has lived a life full of achievements and without boundaries. Baldwin actually appears in the film several times to discuss his optimistic view of life with his fictional self. This apparent break with the narrative reality of the film is potentially disruptive, yet the execution is ingenious and serves to enlighten the audience as to the nature of Baldwin's eccentric personality. *To Walk Invisible: The Brontë Sisters* (2016) is a dramatic account of the Brontë sisters' life in Haworth Parsonage, West Yorkshire in the 1840s. The Brontë house and surrounding landscape is fundamental to the story, and in the closing scene, director Sally Wainwright 'walks' us through Haworth Parsonage as it is today. This offers the audience a poignant reflection on the literary influence and impact of the sisters' work.

TEXT ON SCREEN

Atom Egoyan and Ian Balfour consider the use of subtitles in various international films. They examine the role of the subtitle writer and translator, who must interpret the text of a film and communicate it to multinational audiences. This requires both fluency and creativity in the languages involved if the subtitles are to elucidate the film text, instead of becoming an inconvenient and distracting parallel storyline. Atom Egoyan laid the text from Russell Banks' original novel over stills taken during principal photography of *The Sweet Hereafter* (1997). The stills were used to create an alternative narrative, telling a similar story to the film but which was not part of the film. The result was a new interpretation of the same story. The stills/subtitles version created a new perspective on the narrative without affecting the plot. In one scene in the film *Friday Night* (2002) by Claire Denis there are two people talking through a glass window. Denis wanted the subtitles to be misprinted to reflect the difficulty the characters were having in communicating with each other. The subtitler responded that this could not happen with subtitles; either you use them or you don't. This does not replicate the difficulty the characters were experiencing in hearing each other talk. The subtitles do not correctly replicate the level of comprehension that was in the original scene. Henri Behar points out that a subtitler goes through the problems experienced when translating languages for subtitles. Some colloquial phrases have no translation (Egoyan & Balfour, 2004 p. 82). The subtitler must choose an approximate phrase that somehow conveys a similar meaning. Therefore, the original meaning has been lost and replaced by a proxy. In this way the subtitler becomes part editor and part director, changing the text and changing the dialogue as uttered by characters.

BORGES RETROSPECTIVE NARRATIVE

In 1936 Jorge Luis Borges, writing in *Sur*, commented on the potential of rearranging time within the narrative, editing scenes to play out-of-sequence (Egoyan & Balfour, 2004 p. 114). He is talking of retrospective narrative, a narrative device used by Joyce in *Ulysses* (1993). Retrospective narrative allows characters to introduce themselves, then 'tell' a story that has happened previously. Retrospective narrative allows significant scope to alter the timeline. In Shakespeare's plays, the passage of many years are presented in a couple of hours, whereas Joyce's *Ulysses,* which depicts just one day, takes much longer to read due to its tremendous detail and focus on internal monologues.

According to Allardyce Nicoll, the retrospective narrative is more dramatic than cinematic (Nicoll quoted in Egoyan & Balfour, 2004 p. 114). The timeline is flexible and must not get in the way of telling a good story. Orson Welles' masterpiece *Citizen Kane* (1942) does not play out in chronological order. Retrospective narrative is used to show the dying media mogul's final words and their interpretation by the executors of his will. They sift through historic evidence and meet acquaintances to better understand the significance of his last word, 'Rosebud'.

When text is used onscreen during films, Hamid Naficy points out that the audience is forced to undertake the simultaneous activities of 'watching, listening, reading, translating and problem solving' (Naficy quoted in Egoyan & Balfour, 2004 p. 146). The resultant 'asynchrony and critical juxtaposition' makes a coherent interpretation difficult to achieve. There is simply too much to do in order to follow the narrative. Poorly subtitled films mask the true narrative and leave the audience with only the bare bones of the real storyline. Subtext and subtleties of performance may be lost altogether. It is the role of the subtitles' writer to summarise the translated text and present it both spatially and temporally so that the new localised text (which includes subtitles) faithfully represents the true spirit of the original.

B. Ruby Rich notes that trailers may be released without dialogue to fool audiences into thinking the film dialogue is actually in English (Rich quoted in Egoyan & Balfour, 2004 p. 157). American audiences consider the 'interactivity' of reading subtitles as not complementary to being lost in the story. They see reading as work and subtitled films do not perform as well in the American box office as their unsubtitled counterparts. 'Monolinguism posits a monocultural world, one where "our" values are not merely dominant but genuinely shared and undisputed' (Egoyan & Balfour, 2004 p. 165). How can we use text in computers, phones etc. so readily and not read subtitles? Rich suggests the subtitles reference a bigger world that we want to avoid. Subtitles let us subjectively interpret the original performance of the actor.

Ameresh Sinha writes that a good translation is one that does not appear to be a translation at all. The meaning has been conveyed in another language without losing its original essence or value (Sinha quoted in Egoyan & Balfour, 2004 p. 189). Negar Mottahedeh notes that as Iranian modesty laws forbid images of women not wearing a veil, some Iranian film-makers have responded by moving female characters to outdoor locations where the veil looks natural (Mottahedeh quoted in Egoyan & Balfour, 2004 p. 310). *Through the Olive Trees* (1994), the third film in Kiarostami's Koker trilogy, appears to document the making of the previous film in the series. Characters break the fourth wall by staring into the camera, and establishing shots are eliminated to disorientate the viewer's perspective. Kiarostami seeks to develop a film language 'to make Iranian cinema principally national; a cinema that speaks with a dialect in the global context' (Egoyan & Balfour, 2004 p. 326). By averting its gaze, this cinematic language ignores closure, which Kiarostami recognises is an impossible outcome in a 'decontextualised cinema'.

The Wind Will Carry Us (1999) is referred to as his half-made film. Kiarostami talks about elements being left out to 'invite the viewer's imaginative participation ... what we see with a modest and an averted gaze' (Egoyan & Balfour, 2004 p. 327). Kiarostami's 'camera frames and fabulates peripheral movement as the object of fascination, ignoring its contemporary audience's naturalised quest for the forward push of the narrative' (Egoyan & Balfour, 2004 p. 329). Like the audiences of primitive cinema, his audience is less immersed in the story and is more of a curious spectator whose interest has been piqued.

CONSTRUCTING A STORYLINE

Edward Branigan states that:

> The impetus for creating a story time does not derive in any simple way from the running time of the film – screen time – but rather from top-down processes seeking a new order which will be sensitive to other constraints on the data, e.g. presumed causality and event duration.
>
> (Branigan, 1992 p. 45)

The audience engages in an interpretative analysis of the film structure, unpacking the story into a meaningful, coherent narrative construct.

The format of the audiovisual product impacts on the audience. The medium itself has a significant bearing on content reception. Each one requires a different application of spatial and temporal deconstruction skills. Various media systems will engage the audience in an immersive experience, holding their attention within the narrative so that they will follow the story arc, and participate in a perspectival reception of the work. We may feel empathy with a character, or their situation, but the story must remain possible within the reality of the world that has been created by the narrative. Going beyond this world will lead to audience disengagement and a complete lack of immersion. The audience cannot become aware of the system during the narrative; 'engagement is only possible when we rely on the system to maintain the representational context' (Laurel, 1991 p. 115).

Historically, the wide shot was used in film to capture the whole scene, like the storyteller giving just an overview of the narrative, without adding details about particular narrative elements to create a more immersive arc. In *Dr. Mabuse The Gambler* (1922), Fritz Lang used multiple shots where previous film-makers would have used one. The viewer must create a mental picture of the space within which the action takes place, to follow the sequence of shot perspectives. This innovation in film-making helped to create a new language of film where audiences were 'invited' into the action, to view the narrative from the inside.

NARRATIVE DISTANCE, DEPTH AND ALIGNMENT

Narration can be calculated in literal measurements: 'distance' (from our commonsense beliefs and knowledge of film conventions); 'depth' (subjective/knowledge presented to spectator) and 'alignment'. The audience knows that there is more going on in the story than that which is on the screen at any one time. The spectator is making calculations on the narrative arc trajectory based on previous films, stories, narrative conventions etc. What is presented on the screen may be more concerned with maintaining the immersion of the piece that is driving the plot forward. In Hitchcock's 'bomb theory' there is a bomb under the table, the audience knows about it but the characters in the film do not. 'He realised that there is a close relationship between a spectator's wish to know, and his or her wishful involvement with situations and persons in a film' (Branigan, 1992 p. 75).

BAZIN'S INVISIBLE WITNESS

Some film-makers reject the use of point-of-view shots. They are too literal. Cinematic photography does not capture the unconscious; it records the real world. Therefore, the point-of-view shot does not fully realise the expressive potential of the camera, it limits the story to the perspective of single characters. But the printed word can capture the unconscious; therefore it is often considered the most suitable medium for first-person narration. André Bazin 'disliked "Lady in the Lake", German Expressionism, and Eisenstein's montage effects' as he believed they were a manipulation of the reality being recorded which deliberately favoured the author's vision (Branigan, 1992 p. 144). Bazin proposed that the author of the work should not fix an interpretation of the text or impose their view on the audience but instead let them experience the story themselves and form their own opinion; 'a good adaptation should result in a restoration of the essence of the letter and the spirit' (Bazin, 2005a p. 67). Yet the author exists no matter how a film is made, the world must be created within which the plot will play out. The author may stand back and invite the audience to participate in the construction of the narrative by filling in the temporal gaps that have been deliberately created. These spaces in time are separate from the projection order and refer to the chronological time frame of the story. When the narrative invites interpretation at various levels of open complexity it becomes chameleon-like. The more latitude allowed for spectator interpretation, the more spectators will participate. Bazin noted the influence of 'literature, theatre and music' on the evolution of cinema, like a child imitating an adult (Bazin, 2005a p. 56). He believed that cinema had made good progress on achieving independence from these traditional arts up until 1938. They had succeeded in exploiting new technical resources including artificial lights, increasingly sensitive film emulsions, sound, montage effects and new camera techniques; 'film-makers discovered original themes to which the new art gave substance' (Bazin, 2005a p. 73). Bazin considered the relationship between text, theatre and cinema, describing 'drama' as the soul of the theatre which is capable of inhabiting 'other bodies' (Bazin, 2005a p 81). The drama of the text is first adapted for the theatre where the text is synthesised into its 'crystalised essentials'. If commercially successful, it is these elements of the text which are reworked for the cinema; 'a novel is rarely made from a play. It is as if the theater stood at the end of an irreversible process of aesthetic refinement' (Bazin, 2005a p. 83). Writing during the classical age of cinema and prior to the dominance of television, Bazin in fact believed cinema to be the 'totalising art form, replacing opera as the culture's *Gesamtkunstwerk*' (Ryan, 2004 p. 381).

Sculpting In Time (1989) by Andrei Tarkovsky was written over an extended period of time to outline his approach to film-making. Tarkovsky was the son of a poet, and he himself approached film as an artist; the film-making process was his artistic medium. He worked with the same team on several films, but the vision they created was always his.

> All this proves yet again that cinema, like any other art, is created by the author. What the director can be given by his colleagues in the course of their work together is inestimable; but all the same it is his conception alone that finally gives the film its unity.
>
> (Tarkovsky, 1989 p. 33)

Tarkovsky's films approached time with a fascinated gaze; the camera hangs on characters and settings, looking to find their true meaning through intensive observation. 'Time cannot vanish without trace for it is a subjective, spiritual category; and the time we have lived settles in our soul as an experience placed within time' (Tarkovsky, 1989 p. 58).

Like poetry, Tarkovsky believed that film could convey an inner truth, a conceptual beauty that is more than the sum of its parts, initially created in the mind of one person, the director. This person will work with others, including actors and composers to create the texture and aesthetic of a film, then transfer this vision onto the screen for an audience to both engage with and interpret. Tarkovsky compared the essence of the director's work to that of a sculptor. Instead of marble, the director works to fashion a period of time, 'an enormous, solid cluster of living facts', and carefully removes the features that are not 'integral to the cinematic image' (Tarkovsky, 1989 p. 63). Tarkovsky called this process 'sculpting in time'.

STORY RHYTHM: THE HAIKU

The Japanese haiku is a poetic form which is at one with its subject, and this purity appealed to Tarkovsky. Eisenstein used the haiku as an example of how three separate elements, when combined, create something unique and fundamentally different from each single unit. Tarkovsky's film texts were poetic, he strived to remove artifice from his work. He believed each scene should stand alone, representing actual fact both functionally and expressively. The interpretation of these images is subjective, and changes over time. Successive readers interpret even classical narratives subjectively and uniquely. The film-maker creates art by stripping the text of all extraneous meaning, leaving only the component parts that the audience will use to interpret. Tarkovsky references Japanese poets' protracted observations of reality, represented in three lines of text. A film is first shot to create the working model, and is then trimmed into shape, removing everything until all that is left is that which is required to create true meaning. The shots have their own inherent pacing and this dictates the rhythm of the film. Tarkovsky tried to hide the process of film-making, avoiding montage and working with long shots that required few edits. He rejected montage cinema as it prevented the audience from using their personal experience to explore the film. For him, montage cinema used too many effects and symbolism that created a barrier to meaning. He brought the audience into the experience of the narrative, to feel what he felt as the director, the power of the story translated into another medium and distributed to all.

The story will progress with its own internal rhythm intact. This rhythm will hold the audience in an immersive experience that creates highs and lows, alternating periods of intensity and lifelessness, humour and drama. Rhythm is within the narrative of each scene, and is not dictated by time lines. Tarkovsky supported the use of extended shots, unedited scenes. He believed edits interrupted the natural rhythm of the story, to create an artificial pattern. Tarkovsky did not support the traditional focus on colour and form in film. He believed that colour should be neutralised to reduce its 'painterly' effect on the audience. Like photographers who use lenses that do not replicate the human eye's angle of view, film-makers present the story from an angle that the audience does not expect to be in, an angle that they would not see from even if they were there. This focuses the story perspective in line with an 'angle of view' as chosen by the director. Shape, audio, colour and form are also selected in this way, 'Strangely enough, even though the world is coloured, the black and white image comes closer to the psychological, naturalistic truth of art, based as it is on special properties of seeing as well as hearing' (Tarkovsky, 1989 p. 139). The black-and-white 'image' is not replicating the truth of the real world. For the viewer it is very much a memory of what has happened. Therefore, black-and-white images allow the viewer to suspend real life and enter the narrative's own reality. Tarkovsky believed in the process of film-making, the process of an artist creating. This process must be kept fluid and alive, the production takes on an organic life of its own, guided by the director, fuelled by the cast and crew. Actors who assume they fully understand their character from reading the script undermine the process of film production. The characters and plot form their own dynamic and must not be too influenced by potential audience reactions. Creating an end product purely for audience consumption will detract from the truth of the original vision. The concept is supported by economical use of diegetic and non-diegetic music. Tarkovsky noted that music can be used 'to prompt the emotions of the audience in a particular direction, by widening the range of their perception of the visual image' (Tarkovsky, 1989 p. 158). Music alters the appearance of visuals and distorts how they are perceived.

SILENT-ERA TECHNIQUES

Christian Metz identified syntagmatic and paradigmatic structures as theoretical constructions (Metz quoted in Monaco, 2000 p. 420). Syntagma relates to the linear structure of the narrative, paradigmatic structures are vertical and relate to choice. Syntagmatic and paradigmatic categories replaced montage and *mise en scène* (the visual style of the scene). Metz defined film as a series of codes, which could be broken down into sub-codes. These codes included every element of film including genre, character and technique. In *Film As Art* (1957) Rudolf Arnheim assesses the impact viewing conditions and distance from the image have in greatly affecting our interpretation. From a distance, a grainy image will appear as continuous tone with high contrast, yet in close up, the detail is lost in the fragmentation of grain. Smaller images are higher contrast and tend to be more pleasing to the eye. Larger images lose contrast and need to have a stronger composition. Carl Dreyer's silent film *The Passion of Joan of Arc* (1928) was based on actual transcripts of the trial of Joan of Arc. In the film, the spoken word is represented visually by an unending series of cuts, different shot angles attempting to hold the audience's interest in place of the dialogue. This is described as 'form for form's sake'. Arnheim notes that many sounds can be left out of the film audio-mix as long as the essentials are present. The audio does not have to be real; it has to fit with the visual information the audience is receiving. On the intelligibility of the film image, Arnheim compares film to music, where the use of pre-defined musical scales allows specific patterns to be created. The formalised structure of black-and-white film places white on black or black on white to create striking visuals, avoiding 'indeterminate tones'. Silent-era techniques transcended simple visualisation of the narrative and included the superimposition techniques to convey abstract concepts.

The reality created within the text of the film, as opposed to everyday reality, is based on the perspectival choice of the director, what they want us to see, the story they want to tell us. The director can choose to leave out and include elements without altering the reality. The director is telling the story using available perspectives, made up of scenes shot and audio recorded. Time can be fragmented, slowed down and speeded up to emphasise elements of the reality in the text. Not all advances in technology advanced the [film] storytelling form. Sync sound recording changed the direction of the universal language of film. Before the introduction of sound, film was a global art. Sound made films culturally specific and promoted the commercialisation of the product.

BONITZER ON HITCHCOCK

Writing about Hitchcock's film *Notorious* (1946) Pascal Bonitzer notes that Hitchcock's films were:

> characterised by a 'dryness' ... his was an art of structures, which demanded that 'cinema' take precedence over all else, over any notion of realism, and certainly over any existentialist effusions on the part of the protagonists.
>
> (Bonitzer quoted in Žižek, 1992 p. 152)

These 'structures' are the building blocks of film narrative. Hitchcock created a filmic experience that immersed the audience in a familiar narrative space, a recognisable situation created by the work of the auteur film-maker. External demands of realism and pragmatism are not related to Hitchcock's narrative. The film is a construction of parts, driving forces on the narrative that suspend reality and absorb the audience into the storyteller's world. Bonitzer comments on Hitchcock's style:

> Suspense is thus indeed achieved through editing, but Hitchcock, in contrast to the Griffithian acceleration of parallel actions, employs an editing of convergent actions in a homogeneous space, which presupposes slow motion and is sustained by the gaze, itself evoked by a third element, a perverse object or stain.
>
> (Bonitzer quoted in Žižek, 1992 p. 29)

THE MACGUFFIN

Hitchcock's films promote audience engagement resulting in a greater interaction with the narrative. The audience is not a passive observer, but actively investigates the frame both spatially and temporally, responding to the tension created within the narrative space. In this way Hitchcock the film-maker could connect directly with the audience. His stories became familiar and reassuringly recognisable within a finely woven yet formulaic space. Hitchcock often used a plot device called a 'MacGuffin'. A MacGuffin is an unidentified object that a plot centres on, while its purpose and meaning is not explained. The MacGuffin's existence and significance drive the story, and distances the narrative reality from the real world inhabited by the audience. This reduction of dramatic exposition leaves more time for character and plot. A MacGuffin was included in *Mission Impossible III* (2003) where the protagonists seek and fight over the unidentified 'rabbit's foot'. It is never explained what the object is or what it can do, it is just emphasised that it is of extreme importance.

ŽIŽEK ON HITCHCOCK

Slavoj Žižek writes that 'Hitchcock's films ultimately contain only two subject positions, that of the director and that of the viewer – all diegetic persons assume, by turns, one of these two positions' (Žižek, 1992 p. 218). Hitchcock created an intimate cinematic style that invited the audience into the familiar world of his stories. He treated his audience like a familiar acquaintance, who could be pushed and cajoled within certain boundaries, but who also had certain expectations of his work. Hitchcock used this familiarity to create films that audiences could appreciate for their complex subtleties, respecting their ability to decode and deconstruct the narrative based on previous experiences.

MANIPULATING TIME WITHIN THE NARRATIVE

Structural/materialist film stresses the process of creating the audiovisual product (Heath, 1981 p. 165). A one-to-one temporal relationship would result in a film the same length as the timeframe it depicted. The audience is the spectator who follows the film's pacing to view time speeding up and slowing down. Expanding time through delay (Van Sijll, 2005 p. 70) slows down the sense of time for the spectator, allowing concentration on one time-period within the narrative. Similar conventions can be used to increase the speed of time, bring the audience through the narrative at a greater rate, driving the story relentlessly forward. The physical manipulation of the pace of time reflects the spectator's perception of reality, where periods of boredom seem to play out endlessly, and periods of excitement feel rushed. Time can be oriented to be geometrically circular and linear. Circular narratives loop the action in a cycle of repetition, trapping the characters in their own lives. Linear patterns use devices like crossroads, representing decisions that must be taken in the characters' lives (Van Sijll, 2005 p. 38).

Many interactive texts are print-based; the emphasis is on the author. For interactive titles to work the author should not be so significantly present. Mackendrick's emphasis on the use of narrative conflict also presents an opportunity for user interaction. The conflict promotes active thinking about the text; this will lead to natural interaction as the audience attempts to 'reach out' and change their perspective, as if they were studying a work of art in a museum, walking around it, discovering its elements when viewed from different angles.

In this chapter I noted that William Goldman considers that the immersive nature of film replaces the reality of our real world with the reality created within the text. When the film edit, performance and directing techniques are correctly executed there is no reason why this immersion should not last for the duration of the film. The challenge facing the interactive developer is how to maintain immersion while getting the audience to physically react in their real world, in order to interact with the world created by the text. The use of subtext does help to promote active thought in relation to the work. With proper handling, a thought-provoking subtext can initiate interaction as the user adjusts perspective to learn if their speculation on the story is correct. The speculation includes their conclusions on the events that have taken place during temporal gaps in the narrative progression.

The use of text alongside visuals is used extensively in the form of subtitles. However, with interactive texts, there is also the possibility of using hypertext links embedded within the visual sphere. The interface needs to be intelligent to understand various user interactions and respond to them accordingly.

The great challenge in the development of interactive titles is that the interaction will create new edits not decided on or controlled by the director. The time-period required to allow the user to select their interaction is the same time period within which an edit can happen. This means edits created by the use of additional spatial presentations will appear at any time over a predefined time slot. The edit, which was once sacrosanct, is now a moveable feast.

The traditional linear film text provides a comfortable experience for the audience. With advances in technologies, particularly in relation to distribution, film-makers can now consider adding interactivity to their works. The level of interactivity will dictate how immersive the experience of watching the film will be. At this stage in the development of an interactive film paradigm, I believe that the realist approach, utilising an uncomplicated navigational system, will be the most successful. The interface will be a means to an end, not a fundamental part of the creative work in itself. Through the incorporation of traditional storytelling techniques, along the lines of Aristotle's *Poetics,* the audience will recognise familiar narrative devices that are widely used in linear texts. The interactivity will extend and broaden the use of traditional techniques without losing the audience in technology. The user experience within the interactive environment will need to be closely monitored in order to match the sophisticated level of editing we are used to in linear films. Walter Murch's theories in this regard are an excellent starting point for creating and understanding the editing conventions that apply to both linear and interactive narratives. His work is focused on audience reaction and interaction with the text, and it is the audience that the developers of interactive films need to concentrate on rather than on the technology itself.

NOTE

1 Fabula: 'a series of logically and chronologically related events that are caused or experienced by actors' (Bal, 1985 p. 52).

3

Subjective Interpretation

Context influences the interpretation of narrative texts. Audiences will endlessly reinterpret films during repeat viewings if the work has substance enough to promote critical analysis. Knowledge of the text, gained through previous viewings, enables a subjective re-interpretation of the story. This chapter considers subjective interpretation of both traditional and new narrative formats.

NARRATIVE PERSPECTIVES

By manipulating perspective in interactive stories the author enables the viewer to observe a narrative from multiple viewpoints. Although these viewpoints are created by the author, their order of presentation is 'edited' by the viewer. Perspective in storytelling has a long history. Perspective enhances the interactive elements of the story by presenting alternative viewpoints both spatially and temporally. The panorama paintings of the late eighteenth century were 360° images which surrounded the viewer (Rieser & Zapp, 2002 p. 28). These immersive art pieces were an early form of interactive narrative where the viewer 'engaged' with the painting to create a story. Like a gallery, the panorama allowed the viewer to move back and forward through time, establishing temporal links between narrative elements. These pieces were designed to be engaging and were a precursor to modern interactive narrative systems. Such narrative systems demand an active reader. The viewer must appropriate the work by forming an implicit relationship with the text. The difficulty of interactive texts is that they require a two-way flow of communication between viewer and author. The author can create a work containing various narrative pathways and then hand over authorial control to the viewer. The viewer navigates a pathway through the narrative, creating an individual perspective that can be recounted to other audience members. Retelling the story in this way allows the audience to become aware of multiple perspectives of the story. The 'triangulation' of information results in a new meta-perspective where many members share knowledge of various perspectival approaches to the same narrative.

ENTGRENZUNG: THE DISSOLUTION OF PERSPECTIVAL BOUNDARIES

James Joyce employed the strategy of *Entgrenzung,* or dissolution of boundaries, to bring separate experiences together. The stream of consciousness technique allows the reader to view the internal and external with reality being dependent on the point of view of the observer. The audience is encouraged to create new realities. In *Ulysses* (1993) the identity of the narrator is not always clear. When Molly Bloom speaks in the final chapter she may be speaking directly to the reader, or her voice may be the internal thoughts of her husband Leopold Bloom. The thoughts are about her, and what she had been doing that day, but the narrative works on both levels, as it is the level of passion that engages the reader. In *Ulysses,* Joyce has not represented reality; he has created a work that generates a reality in the eyes of the individual, a reality that will be different for each reader. Similarly, Maya Deren's *Meshes in the Afternoon* (1943) 'created new time-space-relations, thereby generating worlds instead of depicting them' (Rieser & Zapp, 2002 p. 32). According to Anthony Burgess, Joyce was most certainly a 'class 2' writer for whom:

> it is important that the opacity of language be exploited, so that ambiguities, puns and centrifugal connotations are to be enjoyed rather than regretted, and whose books, made out of words as much as characters and incidents, lose a great deal when adapted to a visual medium.
>
> (Burgess, 1975 p. 15)

Joyce's art was created to be read, it is not cinematic, an idea supported by Viktor Shklovsky who said that 'there is almost nothing in a novel that can be transferred to the screen – nothing, that is, but the bare plot' (Shklovsky, 2008 p. 24). In 1952 André Bazin wrote that American crime novels were increasingly being written with a view to being adapted into Hollywood format movie scripts, and suggested that novels would in future be written as films. While the spectacle of theatre lends itself to film, Bazin noted that 'the novel at least calls for some measure of creativity, in its transition from page to screen' (Bazin, 2005a p. 54).

LINGUISTIC FLEXIBILITY: BLENDING WORDS INTO CHORDS

Joyce did however recognise 'the close kinship between music and poetry' (Burgess, 1975 p. 90). Burgess noted that he was capable of 'blending words boldly into genuine chords. The words of *Finnegans Wake* are nearly all chords. Instead of merely juxtaposing *thorns* and *thoughts* ... Joyce was able, if he wished, to combine them into *thornghts*' (Burgess, 1975 p. 92). Joycean text is a participatory experience, where one must give thought to the references to Joyce and his life experiences, as well as semantics.

> The language of *Finnegans Wake*, on the other hand, justifies its difficulties and unprecedented complexities in terms of its subject-matter. Joyce, having exhausted the potentialities of waking English in *Ulysses*, was compelled, in his next book, to 'put the language to sleep'. Freed by sleep of the rigidities of daytime modes of interpreting time and space, language becomes fluid.
>
> (Burgess, 1975 p. 138)

Joyce skilfully exploited the linguistic flexibility of cross-language phonetics, positioning words which, when spoken, communicated multiple meanings in different languages. This layering of denotation and connotation requires a high level of engagement with the text, to unpack both its meaning(s) and the writer's intention. Yet his aim was not to be obtuse, his description of food being eaten in *Work in Progress* reflected the chewing of food by literally breaking down the language used, yet 'the *masticated* words can easily be reconstructed by the reader' (Gilbert, 1934 p. 191).

NARRATIVE DECONSTRUCTION

Michael Buckley's interactive story *The Good Cook* (1998) invited the audience to view it several times to 'get to know' the main character. Buckley taped audio recordings of the 'Cook' and added visuals, graphics and animations. He unveiled the 'Cook' to us over time. But the pre-recorded, time-based media are not presented to us through a director's 'gaze'. The audience is provided with the opportunity to discover the character by exploring the narrative elements that make up *The Good Cook*.

> Deconstruction theory suggests that a text constructed by an author, whose life contains a definite history and clear bias, is reconstructed by a reader whose life differs from that of the author and whose perspective is framed differently. The text in fact becomes different to that which the author intended through the action of the viewer.
>
> (Rieser & Zapp, 2002)

THE LOOP: IF, THEN, GOTO

Manovich identified the 'loop' as a new narrative form appropriate to the computer age. Basic computer programming languages use loops to perform the repetitive routines on data arrays. 'IF/THEN' and 'GOTO' statements manipulate the control flow of program code to execute run-time instructions as a non-linear sequence. The loop is also extensively employed in cell animation. Walking characters are achieved through a series of repeating cells. This technique was also employed by the film-maker Zbigniew Rybczyński in his film *Tango* (1982). Rybczynski 'loops' live action footage to move repeating characters through a fixed spatial location. The characters are placed so skilfully that they never occupy the same spatial or temporal space. While we can view the loops as repeating information, their juxtaposition with other narrative elements allow the audience to create a new version of reality with each iteration. The screen is at one stage so overcrowded that it seems impossible that the film-maker could be working with a fixed area of focus, a fixed point on the screen where he expects his audience to be looking. In other words, the author has created the work and then given authorial control to the audience to establish their own perspective on the story.

CAUSE AND EFFECT

Creating interactive works for public/private consumption will be successful if the works make the viewer comfortable with the navigation. Ken Feingold developed the interactive title *The Surprising Spiral* (1991). The work runs on a computer-controlled videodisc and is built around a cause-and-effect structure. Sounds and images are the general responses to user interaction. Feingold's research into how audiences used this system led him to the belief that audiences are not comfortable being participants in public interactive works where the objective is unclear. Users found that while they could initiate responses from the system, they had no real control over it and could not navigate to a place where they wanted to be. The frustration experienced by the audience resulted in short interaction times and few repeat plays. Feingold also questions the process of interaction. A simple cause-and-effect system lacks mystery and complexity and results in a rather bland narrative. Feingold strongly resists the 'user-friendly' approach in interactive narrative works as they do not raise questions in the user and do not promote innovative thought. This 'dumbing down' of the product is symptomatic of popular media. The lowest common denominator approach creates a simple product that is accessible and interesting to a wider audience. However, the simplicity of successive products means that there is little difference between them, and their ability to hold audience attention is severely compromised.

RELINQUISHING AUTHORIAL CONTROL

Jon Dovey states that a successful interactive narrative works on both the spatial axis and temporal axis (Dovey quoted in Rieser & Zapp, 2002 p. 138). Time must progress regardless of user interaction to allow the viewer to relax and not feel compelled to interact for the story to continue. In games design, where branched narrative structures are employed, the story may stop completely while the system waits for the user to make a decision. Dovey believes it is more satisfying for the user if the responsibility for narrative progression does not reside solely with them. A continuously progressing narrative that offers, and reacts to user interaction will let the audience become an observer, rather than an author. It is not that the viewer wants solely to be entertained; rather they do not want to have to work too hard. Eku Wand suggests that this emphasis on the viewer driving the narrative can be resolved by employing traditional storytelling techniques, particularly the art of rhetoric (Wand quoted in Rieser & Zapp, 2002 p. 164). Their 'manner of interrupting a narrative by asking the listeners questions, by rhetorically deviating from the main plot, by inserting theatrical pauses, were means to the end of building up tension, of involving the listeners, of captivating them' (Rieser & Zapp, 2002). The cause-and-effect 'pauses' can be built around rhetoric, natural pauses in the narrative. Wand observes that the 'back story' used by popular soap operas to guide story writers with regard to the histories of individual characters, could also be used in an interactive narrative. This backstory affects character behaviour but is not explicitlyreferenced in each episode. Interactive narratives will produce a proportion of content that will not be viewed by all audience members. Narrative sequences will be viewed depending on the 'perspective' of the user. Wand also points out that it is always most important to drive the plot forward. As with the Aristotelian perspective, characters exist only to further the plot.

ATTENTIONAL BLINK

Advertising industry research seeks to analyse and assess audience responses to television adverts. Researcher Jane Raymond has considered how people's attention can be easily distracted. She describes it as 'a quirk in the brain's attentional system' (*New Scientist,* 24/31 December 2005). Raymond conducted an experiment where people were shown a stream of alphanumeric characters and were asked to look for 'a white letter or an X'. When the white letter and the X were presented in close proximity, people failed to see the second character. Raymond called this phenomenon 'attentional blink'. The brain is blind to new information while it processes the data of the previous significant information packet received. This is important for content creators who are using fast edits to grab attention. Fast editing may move the narrative along at speed, packing more story into a short timeslot, but it may also ensure that the audience loses track of the plot. Attentional blink is also another reason for using long-duration shots in interactive stories. Fast editing will work against the interactive points within the script, and information overload will lessen the inclination to interact. Raymond has also conducted research into whether the attentional state can influence a response to a brand. She found that if a person is 'distracted by an image or brand when performing an intellectually demanding task' they tend to have an unfavourable response to it regardless of its emotional value to them (Fisher, 2005). The distraction is designed to draw attention towards the brand. It may be an interstitial page, an autoplaying social media ad, or the blatant and unjustifiable placement of a branded product within a film. Both serve to disrupt narrative engagement and take the person out of the story. This undesired break in concentration and intellectual absorption may result in the brand being blamed for ruining a rewarding experience.

CONFABULATION: EMOTIONAL EXPERIENCES WITHOUT CONTEXT

Jim Coan created *Eye & I* (2005), an art installation that was designed to measure people's response to facial expressions. The piece featured:

> a darkened room with slots about the size of letterboxes randomly arranged on the walls. Behind the slots were actors making facial expressions reflecting anger, sadness, happiness and so on. People who went into the room could only see the actors' eyes.
>
> (*New Scientist*, 24/31 December 2005)

This research into the relationship between facial expressions and emotions required the actors to hold specific expressions for an extended period of time while being viewed by an audience. The actors reported that holding these facial expressions made them emotional. The emotion they experienced conformed to the expression they were performing. Coan noted that the facial expression had created a 'context-free emotional stimulus' which is not how our brains normally process emotion. We usually have an emotional experience with context. To compensate, the actors invented for themselves an imaginary context called a confabulation. This created for them a justification for their emotional experience. Going further with this research, Coan has also explored how people experience images when they are with someone else and whether holding hands with this person alters their experience.

EVOLVING LANGUAGE

Henry Hitchings notes an anecdote of Dr Johnson's childhood which tells how, as a child, Johnson intensely read the play *Hamlet*, and at the ghost scene he ran to be near other people.

> His communion with the text was so complete that he took it for reality, and in those words 'got the play ... in his father's kitchen' there is a nice suggestion of the accidental unpurposed nature of his reading.
>
> (Hitchings, 2005 p. 15)

In the early part of the eighteenth century there was a significant increase in printed materials. Johnson mocked this, claiming that everyone now believed themselves to be an author. He argued the need for a definitive version of the English language to be fixed forever. His contemporary, Chesterfield, favoured the 'propriety of usage' of polite society, that this version of the language should be fixed forever as the gold standard.

> Linguistic conservatives like Chesterfield were afraid that unchecked changes in general usage would cause the English of the eighteenth century to become as bewildering to its inheritors as the language of Chaucer was to them.
>
> (Hitchings, 2005 p. 68)

When defining certain words Johnson invoked actual experience, such as the meaning of 'salt' as that which tastes of salt. Eventually Johnson felt that language was a living entity that must grow in order to stay alive. Additions to language are used to express the culturally specificities of each generation, to cultivate and present their identity in words. Without these added extras, language would become staid and unexpressive.

CALVINO: THE MALLEABLE RELATIONSHIP BETWEEN READER AND NARRATOR

Interactive narratives certainly create new possibilities for the narrator/reader relationship. If the interaction is part of the authorship of the text, then the reader becomes the narrator. *If on a Winter's Night a Traveller* (1982) by Italo Calvino explores the ambiguous relationship between reader and narrator and allows their identities to cross and merge. The story arc allows the reader to have a single perspective on the narrative; it navigates a single pathway through the text. Yet, the metanarrative of any text is infinitely broader than what we are offered and encompasses parts of other texts and scenarios that are not immediately relevant:

> I'm producing too many stories at once because what I want is for you to feel, around the story, a saturation of other stories that I could tell and maybe will tell or who knows may already have told on some other occasion, a space full of stories that perhaps is simply my lifetime, where you can move in all directions.
>
> (Calvino, 1982 p. 109)

Therefore, Calvino has obliterated the story 'arc' of the traditional text, the arc that follows a pathway recognised by conventional readers. The arc may have twists and turns that surprise and delight the reader, but it is still linear, still generic. Calvino treats the reader as a contemporary in the text-creation process. The reader may be a third-person character from a previous chapter. Calvino proposes that the author does not write directly to the reader, but communicates via a proxy, another author invented by the writer as a communicator of ideas. This creates a new level of separation between author and reader, maximising the potential of the fabula.

Calvino considers the writing of *The Koran*, 'the holy book about whose compositional process we know most'. In the seventh century, Muhammad verbally received the word of Allah and he in turn dictated this text to several scribes so that it could be written down. Once, when Muhammad did not complete a sentence, a scribe called Abdullah instinctively offered a conclusion. Muhammad 'absently' accepted this text which was not the original word of Allah. The scribe was 'scandalised' and later 'abandoned the Prophet and lost faith'.

> He was wrong. The organization of the sentence, finally, was a responsibility that lay with him; he was the one who had to deal with the internal coherence of the written language, with grammar and syntax, to channel into it the fluidity of a thought that expands outside all language before it becomes word, and of a word particularly fluid like that of a prophet.
>
> (Calvino, 1982 p. 182)

The process of creating the text that includes several mediations and interpretations is true of all texts; a relationship is formed between the author and the reader and this relationship is malleable. It changes over time, particularly with successive visits to the text. The emotion felt during a previous reading becomes a memory that colours future interpretations.

SUBJECTIVE RESPONSES TO COLOUR AND FORM

Chiaramonte & Tarkovsky examined Tarkovsky's Polaroids, taken between 1979–1984 in Russia and Italy. These images possess the same poetic aspect as his films, 'an instantaneous mirror of memory, every photograph leaves a motionless trace of what has been' (Chiaramonte & Tarkovsky, 2006 p. 123). The images are thoughtful and invite the viewer to peruse form and colour. They are very 'Tarkovsky' in style and content. They empower the viewer towards a subjective interpretation of the text to work with the author to understand the message. They speak to the viewer in order to communicate something more than visual texts; 'the image, then, creates, includes, and brings together in a single spatial and temporal place its creator, the object represented, and the observer over the course of time' (Chiaramonte & Tarkovsky, 2006 p. 125).

Eisenstein observed that while audiences may have generally similar responses to colour, the more subtle use and juxtaposition of colours produced subjective responses that could not be codified into any meaningful order.

> We cannot deny that compositions of this kind evoke obscurely disturbing sensations – but no more than this. But to this day attempts continue to be made to arrange these subjective and largely personal sensations into meaningful relationships, that are, frankly, just as vague and remote.
>
> (Eisenstein, 1986 p. 95)

Eisenstein considers the theory that specific colours influence the audience in specific and codifiable ways. As with the relationship between visuals and music there are some fundamental facts that have to be accepted. Also, certain colours evoke blunt emotional and physical responses, such as the association between the colour red and heat.

ACTIVE AND PASSIVE COLOURS

Eisenstein noted that the writer Goethe divided colours into 'active and passive groups'. Active colours appear closer to the viewer and passive colours appear farther away. This division is like the association with warm and cold in cinematography. Red implies heat and warmth in film, blue implies cold and is primarily used as a night-time colour. Blue is also used to desaturate the image of colour to make it look 'washed out'. Eisenstein rejected the notion of an 'all-pervading law of absolute meanings and correspondences between colours and sounds – and absolute relations between these and specific emotions' (Eisenstein, 1986 p. 122). Colours and sounds are to be employed to serve the emotion of the story as and when they are most suitable. Context is critical, the spatial and temporal location of story elements significantly affects their interpretation.

EMOTIONAL RESPONSES TO COLOUR

Patti Bellantoni examines emotional responses to the use of colour in film. Colour works on our subconscious, signifying emotions via instinctive and learned associations. Some colours result in basic emotional responses like love and hate, while others, when juxtaposed with other colours (including geometric shapes and form) can give much more complex interpretations of their meaning:

> Red light is like visual caffeine ... red can activate whatever latent passions you might bring to the table ... Because we tend to see it first, red gives the illusion of advancing toward us. Due to this, it can manipulate our sense of time and space.
>
> (Bellantoni, 2005 p. 2)

Other colours give more subtle responses. Pale colours are not so powerful; they lack any visual punch and can be used to suggest weakness and limitations. Yellow is a contrary colour. It is 'visually aggressive' and appears to move towards you. It has a 'powerful life energy' and draws attention to itself. It can 'be a scene-stealer' (Bellantoni, 2005 p. 42). Conversely, Bellantoni also claims that yellow is anxiety-producing and a stressful colour that may signify obsession. Orange is close to yellow in the visual palette yet it is more cheerful and less complicated. The effect of colour can be tempered by its tone and saturation, for example Bellantoni looks at the use of yellow in the films *Chinatown* (1974) and *Rosemary's Baby* (1968):

> To take a color that is the brightest in the spectrum and desaturate it down from noisy to a murmur is understatement personified. It becomes more delicate, and it perfectly reflects the essence of Mrs Mulwray: chic, enigmatic, and vulnerable. She is a fragile woman with a dark secret, and an obsession.
>
> (Bellantoni, 2005 p. 64)

Yellow has been used to 'colour' our subjective interpretation of the characters and plot. Its juxtaposition with corresponding and opposing colours become part of the narrative arc. In *The Talented Mr. Ripley* (1999), 'The bright yellow bathing suit he wears reveals Tom's character ... Bright yellow calls attention to itself. A strange choice for someone who is trying to blend in' (Bellantoni, 2005 p. 77). Bellantoni conducted a broad array of experiments to measure their effect on her students; these ranged from painting the room to working with coloured props and costumes. 'Blue can be a tranquil pond or a soft blanket of sadness ... color investigations show that in a blue environment, people become passive and introspective' (Bellantoni, 2005 p. 82).

In *The Shipping News* (2001), blue is used effectively to slow down our responses, in line with the location. This adds to the melancholy feeling of the Newfoundland geography. Perhaps this blue is tapping into our memories of cold, wet days and the emotions that went with the experience. Bellantoni describes orange as being a positive influence on our emotions, an upbeat colour that lacks drama. Bellantoni conducted experiments with colour that focused on the juxtaposition of several colours. In *The Godfather* (1972), Michael Corleone's fiancée Kate is first seen wearing red-orange, a colour that gives a powerful reaction. According to Bellantoni, the colour orange is simple, warm and welcoming.

Cinematographers play with colour to draw on our previous experiences and also to suggest new relationships between colours. Nuances in the script and in performances can be reflected by nuances in colour sequencing and concurrence. Cinematographer Edward Lachman made colour choices for the film *Far From Heaven* (2002) to deliberately contrast warm and cool colours. If the scene was 'predominantly cool' then he used warm highlights and if it was warm then the reverse. Lachman was using the complex interplay of light to convey the complexity of characters' emotions (Bellantoni, 2005 p. 136).

Primary colours result in an immediate and clear response; red and black register as 'evil'. These fundamental responses continue with the colour green, an ambiguous colour that can represent both freshness and decay. Green liquid is often used as the colour of poison.

Bellantoni considers the colour purple to have the greatest significance in film narrative. 'Purple is a color that inspires associations with the non-physical. It sends a signal that someone or something is going to be transformed' (Bellantoni, 2005 p. 191). Purple light is often seen just before the death of a character or a major change in direction of the story. Its use reflects its association with other worldly events and spirits. Bellantoni makes associations between colour and form in film. Colour may be used to convey emotion and inner feelings, but spatial movement can indicate the passage of time, where moving and looking left indicates 'the past'.

DIGITAL AND ANALOGUE COLOUR PALETTE

Manovich considers modern film-making technologies that are used to create seamless and invisible effects; 'cinema works hard to erase any traces of its own production process, including any indication that the images we see could have been constructed rather than recorded' (Manovich quoted in Lunenfeld, 2000 p. 178). Ironically, documentaries and online training materials educate the public on the film-making process, its technologies and the latest techniques of modern film-making. The colour palette of scenes created using digital effects composited into live-action footage (shot on film) once betrayed their artificiality. They were unable to blend seamlessly with the photographic image. Now the typical film colour palette is being edged into the digital space and many large-budget movie images (live action and CGI) look 'digital.'

INSTINCTUAL RESPONSES TO GEOMETRIC FORMS

Photographer William Mortensen states that an image impacts on our consciousness to produce a 'deep-lying instinctive response' which 'is purely biological in its effect' (Mortensen, 1948 p. 25). In his book *The Command to Look* he identified four basic geometric picture patterns that exploit our instinctual fear responses and which allow a photograph to 'demand' attention. The emphasis is on form not content; 'the looker participates in the picture and makes it part of his experience' (Mortensen, 1948 p. 51). The eye travels along the rhythmical *contours* and *outlines* which the image creates, successively promoting and hindering movement, engaging the viewer. The four patterns are:

1 diagonal – representing movement, something that passes through our field of vision;

2 S-curve – a furtive movement, suggesting danger;

3 triangles (in combination) – sharpness, a potential threat;

4 dominant mass – an obstacle to movement.

When working, Mortensen carefully examined all of his images to satisfy himself that these geometric criteria had been met. He destroyed all images that did not conform to his rules of image construction. He also rejected photos that carried what he called a 'date line,' as this anchors an image to a particular place and time, the here and now. He believed that *realism* should be avoided as it prevents the image from effecting a profound visual experience, one that does not fade over time.

THE WILL-TO-ART

In *Monsters and Madonnas,* Mortensen referenced Alois Riegl's idea of *Kunstwollen* (the will-to-art), that which makes a culture or period produce art works of a particular style (regardless of technology or trends) to create a crystallisation of 'the instinctive geometric ornament' (Mortensen, 1936 p. 12). Mortensen believed that the imagination needed to be freed from the 'officious' conscious mind. He said that a meticulous, organised approach to image creation produced 'tight, hard, smug' images, whereas 'improvisation on a well-established basis' opens the way to spontaneous creativity, allowing the image to reveal itself. Competency with technology and workflows allows the full exploration of emotions. The creative mind is free to express itself, to make manifest artistic works without the hindrance of conscious thought, obligation and doubt.

KNOWING YOUR AUDIENCE

Narrative worlds depend on the words used to describe them. For example 'Texas' transports us to the place. Yet some texts (like poetry) do not naturally create a virtual world. Evocative language can be used as building blocks of the alternative reality that the writer is creating. Certain words give specific responses, but others are more generic. This reminds us of Eisenstein's attempts to codify responses to montage and colour which ultimately turned out to be too subjective and too dependent on individual experience. The word 'Texas' 'creates a reservoir of ready-made pictures; place names offer compressed images and descriptive shortcuts that emulate the instantaneous character of immersion in the space of visual media' (Ryan, 2001 p. 128). Readers might generally accept that 'Texas' is a big place with lots of desert land, but is it good, bad, kind, inviting etc? This depends on reader knowledge and experience. Most film viewers are reasonably well informed about the plot before they view a film. This makes for a more satisfying experience as they have some idea where the journey is taking them and are content to make the journey to see the final outcome (the ending should not be so predictable that the viewing experience itself is made redundant). Films with complex plots that are difficult to follow, such as Brian DePalma's *Mission Impossible* (1996), often alienate the audience who find the journey too difficult and unrewarding. Richly layered films can be viewed again and again to be reinterpreted as more information is garnered about subplots, character development, character relationships etc.

At any point in the presentation of a linear film the audiences 'place' in the story timeline should sit slightly behind the current onscreen temporal position of the narrative. If the audience is still considering story elements that took place some time ago, it means they are confused, still trying to 'catch up' to follow the story thread and the immersion is lost. If they are ahead of the narrative position on screen, the story has become predictable and no longer holds their attention. Again, the immersion will be lost. I find that stand-up comedians provide good examples of audience immersion while maintaining a steady rate of narrative progression. Ronnie Corbett always told a long meandering joke at the end of each episode of *The Two Ronnies*. The joke would feature many sidebar and off-point references, yet narrative progression was always maintained and the story moved forward at a rate that was just sufficient to hold your interest. In other words, he could read the audience's attention and move and increase/decrease narrative progression as needed to build up and deliver the punchline.

Clive James' position as a TV critic allowed him to make obscure televisual references within the context of his reviews, safe in the knowledge that the audience would 'get the references' as they knew the 'text' as well as he did. He notes Edward Crankshaw's review of a book about Stalin where he had to devote a good part of the text to the history of the Soviet Union in order to provide his readers with adequate context. James' reviews on television shows were aimed at a readership who 'already knew what I was talking about'. This allowed him a great deal of freedom to be 'as allusive as I liked' (James, 2007 p. 112). He could be literary and obscure, include in-jokes that drew on the audience's specialist knowledge. This can also be seen in episodic televisual content where references to character histories must always be accurate within the context of the meta-narrative, despite the fact that many viewers no longer remember what is correct or not. The viewing experience is much richer and more rewarding for those who can appreciate subtle references to distant characters and stories, no matter how insignificant. They are reminded of the real scale of the story, even though it is delivered one small part at a time.

CONTROLLING THE NARRATIVE/OWNING THE TEXT

G.H. Hardy considers the work of the creative artist and declares that 'good work is not done by "humble" men'. He states that it is important to overstate or exaggerate both your subject and one's own status in relation to it. 'A man who is always asking "Is what I do worthwhile?" and "Am I the right person to do it?" will always be ineffective himself and a discouragement to others' (Hardy, 1992 p. 66). An audience will more readily accept a narrative delivered in a confident, self-assured voice. Indeed, one must own the text. Hardy's approach reinforces the argument for the author maintaining control of the narrative and never giving navigational freedom to the reader to the point that it is the reader who decides the ending, not the author. The latter approach creates a game, an arc with multiple endings, with one chosen by the reader to satisfy their personal requirements of the text. The author must create the world within which the reader may navigate, but navigation will be within the parameters of the arc set out by the author. The created work has, in its concept, a basic message for the reader. Decoding the text through navigation will lead the reader to the message. Therefore, the communicated message should have an inherent value and meaning, which necessitates an ambition in the author.

> Ambition is a noble passion which may legitimately take many forms; there was something noble in the ambition of Attila or Napoleon: but the noblest ambition is that of leaving behind one something of permanent value.
>
> (Hardy, 1992 p. 77)

A narrative can be openly navigated, yet still contain a fixed message or communication to the reader. While a perspectival approach to the strands of a narrative leads to interpretation, a broad space for the reader to 'create' their own narrative from the author's work:

> A mathematician, on the other hand, is working with his own mathematical reality. A chair or a star is not in the least like what it seems to be; the more we think of it, the fuzzier its outlines become in the haze of sensation which surrounds it; but '2' or '317' has nothing to do with sensation, and its properties stand out the more clearly the more closely we scrutinize it.
>
> (Hardy, 1992 p. 129)

Hardy compares real and imaginary universes, where the latter are much more beautiful than the former. Much of the imagined universe in the applied mathematician's mind does not fit the real world and must be discarded. Like mathematics, subjective interpretation works within the parameters of the narrative context.

KANDINSKY'S CHAIN OF RELATED SENSATIONS

Wassily Kandinsky notes that Debussy was often classed with the Impressionist painters due to the fact that he used natural phenomena in his work. Kandinsky believed that artists are influenced by their contemporaries whatever medium they worked in. The influence of paintings on music suggests a spiritual association that crosses media. Kandinsky developed a theory on the psychology of colour. For him, looking at colour produced a dual result. First, a short-lived physical impression, an initial reaction to the warm or cool colours. Following this, there is what he calls a 'chain of related sensations' (Kandinsky, 1977 p. 23). The initial superficial reaction acts as a catalyst for the recall of associated memories related to the viewed colours. Red may cause a sensation of dangerous heat, pain or blood. Kandinsky notes that chromotherapy experiments have shown that exposure to red light stimulates the heart, while blue light has a calming effect. However, the theory of association does not apply to animals and plants, which probably suggests that the association must be learned through experience and referenced by recall. Kandinsky may have been a synaesthete and have applied colours to each note in the musical scale. Theodore Gracyk notes that the Russian composer Alexander N. Scriabin produced a chart matching musical pitches to colours. Kandinsky attributed spiritual values to combinations of form and colour (Kandinsky, 1977 p. 25). He believed they could 'hamper' and 'nullify' each other when employed as inharmonious arrangements. Certain combinations drew strength from each other to evoke emotional responses. Kandinsky promoted the primacy of the 'meaning' and 'idea' of art, rather than its physiological and psychological effects on the viewer. He encouraged the artist to work towards achieving a pure artistic language that spoke directly to the viewer, without the need of formal artistic training and technical knowledge.

* * *

This chapter has looked at audience interpretation of the narrative elements of a story. Interactive works are often viewed more than once. The navigational pathways invite multiple screenings to test alternative progressions through the narrative. In the development of the interactive narratives it is clear that the audience's perspective on the story is of paramount importance. Repetition of narrative sequences creates new subjective interpretations. Each viewing adds to the user's knowledge of the text and influences their understanding of the meaning of the work. As we have seen, the subjectivity of interpretation can be predicted in very broad terms, but audience responses cannot be accurately foreseen. The possible interpretations of a story are increased substantially when interactivity is added. Interaction alters the subjective response of each viewer due to the uniqueness of his or her experience. Raymond's identification of 'attentional blink' may influence how quickly spatial screens are presented in an interactive text, but not their content or storyline. Bellantoni's research into colour responses indicates that the use of colour is complex and highly subjective. While colour does exert a strong influence on the audience, it does this in union with other elements such as storyline, pacing and performance. Hardy noted the importance of the authority of the author, not giving away full narrative control but simply giving greater options to the reader. Even with an interactive work there is still a distinction between the storyteller and the audience.

4

Sound Design

Our visual perception is limited to what is before our gaze, whereas hearing is 'omnidirectional' and thus fundamental to achieving a sense of presence (Collins et al, 2014 p. 215). Many years ago, I went on a scuba diving course in a flooded quarry somewhere in the UK Midlands. It was an unfortunate experience as I could not equalise the pressure and ended up with a splitting headache, an ear infection and eventually lost all hearing in my right ear. The result of this is that I cannot localise sound sources, everything happens to the left of me. The brain calculates the direction of a sound by the minuscule time difference it takes to reach one ear, then the other. In my case, my left ear registers everything both louder and more clearly and I instinctively look left in response to nearly all sounds. In everyday experience, crowded rooms are particularly difficult as I cannot separate the multiple voices and sometimes have to lip read to follow a conversation.

PRIMAL RESPONSES TO SOUND

Certain sounds elicit a primal response in the audience. Sound designers change the pitch and pace of the sounds and mix and match them until the aural response enhances the visual. Engine sounds may have lion roars and monkey screams added. The boxing scenes in *Raging Bull* (1980) wove in animal sounds, jets, arrows and the 'ripping, tearing and stabbing' of beef

(Sonnenschein, 2001 p. 191). Dialogue can be mixed with other sounds and altered to evoke a specific response in the listener.

Music works within a narrative to convey the inner thoughts of characters and to represent their emotions. On film, it is presented in parallel with the dialogue and sound effects. The audience triangulates these sonic elements to interpret the story. Music in film narrative has evolved from simple denotative sound on screen to offer an additional level of connotation. It can represent the complexity of the subconscious. Musician and composer Mica Levi soundtracked the profound emotion of 'overwhelming grief' for the film *Jackie* (2016), reusing the glissando effect she had employed previously in *Under the Skin* (2014) (Lobenfeld, 2016). The 'glooping and distortion and morphing' of sound served to create a transition from 'blissfulness to grimness throughout the film'. The seamless blending of music and film resulted in an aural experience that accurately communicates the lead character's traumatised emotional state. In *Dunkirk* (2017) Hans Zimmer used an audio illusion called the Shepard tone to create a ticking score, a 'continuing ascension of tone ... a corkscrew effect' which both increased the intensity and complemented the mathematical complexity of three interweaving narratives (Guerrasio, 2017). The script's unusual structure is amplified by music. A single, rhythmical track of percussion recurs back and forth throughout the film, the invocation of divine intercession within the minds of desperate young men.

The Witch (2015) is the tale of a banished puritan family living at the edge of a haunted forest in 1630s New England. Composer Mark Korven created a unique musical score by using only instruments that were 'old and archaic'. These included a Swedish nyckelharpa, an instrument which dates back to 1350 (Spurrell, 2016). The result is a soundscape that is both unfamiliar and disquieting. It emphasises the family's isolation and promotes a sense of foreboding. The family is utterly alone, far away from the general community. I found this to be profoundly moving and it brought back a childhood memory of an early morning walk down a remote country lane where I could not hear identifiable sounds of anyone, anywhere. For several anxious minutes, I felt completely and utterly alone.

CLASSIFYING HARMONICS IN TERMS OF EMOTIONAL RESPONSE

In the eighteenth century Friedrich Marpurg attempted to 'categorise definable mood states and emotions according to musical rhythms, tonal progressions, and harmonies' (Sonnenschein, 2001 p. 107). Musicologists have classified the characteristics of our conscious and physical responses to various harmonics. A perfect fourth conveys serenity, a major second happiness, and a major fifth the demonic (Sonnenschein, 2001 p. 121). All locations have a unique sonic landscape. The sound of trains, cars and streets are specific to each place. Generic sounds that are similar to the original, but not actually accurate, can contradict the visuals. Car engines and police sirens are common faults. In 2011 I shot a photo essay in New York. Some months later I watched Scorsese's *Gangs of New York* (2002). During the end credits, after the title music stopped, the film's audio track featured only the idiosyncratic sound of New York city streets. I was immediately transported back to the photo locations; the soundscape was appropriate and evocative of the location.

NARRATIVE SOUNDSCAPES

Spatialised sound and auditory cues positively influence the sense of presence and immersion within a narrative (Collins et al, 2014 p. 223). The multimodal nature of human experience necessitates a clear correlation between audio, visual and haptic stimuli. A reduction in the quality of audio produces a perceived reduction in the quality of visuals. Sound is temporal. In a story world, visuals can become static and unchanging whereas sound is always 'ongoing and alive'. In an interactive narrative where input is required to navigate the plot, narrative progression is at times temporarily halted. A rich soundscape with texture and detail can ensure the audience stays immersed within the fictive reality while they contemplate their response to narrative options. Sound designer David Sonnenschein states that music lowers our critical faculties to create a 'suspension of judgement and a lack of intellectual resistance' and is a key factor in immersing the audience in the 'illusion-reality' (Sonnenschein, 2001 p. 105).

When working on soundscapes for films Sonnenschein views film footage at different speeds and even in reverse in order to consider its 'pure structure' (Sonnenschein, 2001 p. 26). Literal sound or audio recorded on location often does not fit with the emotional content and intention of a story scene. Most onscreen elements have some form of sonic character, even dead bodies (Sonnenschein, 2001 p. 182). Sound must be built from scratch. If a character is close to the screen, the voice must be recorded close too. With a close voice we can 'hear effects of breathing, lip and tongue movements, and enhanced high frequencies that give greater presence (Sonnenschein, 2001 p. 26). The sound designer can choose what the audience hears and thus control what they are focused on.

AFFECTIVE AUDIO

In interactive narratives music 'creates and supports mood, tone, tension, pacing' and the emotion of an experience (Collins et al, 2014 p. 419). Interactivity must influence the music or the user experience will be diminished. Do compositions have inherent characteristics which evoke a particular emotional response, or does the story context more influence an audience's reaction? Affective audio systems modify musical accompaniment to reflect the current status of a character or the plot content. Increased tempo indicates excitement or danger, whereas a more ominous tone suggests impending ruin. The Algorithmic Music Evolution Engine (AMEE) monitors the user's experience and mood in order to create appropriate musical accompaniment from its library of sound elements. Dynamic composition based on story synthesis and modelling techniques will create a hybrid model of sound creation that reinforces the 'interactive experience by leveraging the inherent dynamism of simulations' (Collins et al, 2014 p. 505). Generative music, created in real time, will allow music to interact with various inputs, with a fluid movement between segments (Collins et al, 2014 p. 565). Jazz musicians agree 'to some basic common agreements on form, chords, tempo, and basic melody' then follow the lead musician's harmony and rhythm (Collins et al. 2014 p. 566). This could work in interactive stories where the generative music follows the lead of the story agent and narrative point. Markov Chains can be used to create generative music; a probability index selects the direction of musical progression within a piece.

BBC Research and Development have released *The Mermaid's Tears* (2017), an interactive object-based radio drama. This was created as part of their involvement with ORPHEUS, an EU project to produce 'an end-to-end object-based broadcast chain for audio' (Baume, 2017). 3D immersive audio enables an individual listener to follow the drama from a particular character's perspective. Metadata describing the appropriate mix for each character is broadcast along with all the individual audio objects, and the sound is mixed on the listener's device. Following different characters, the audience's opinion of what actually happens in the story will be influenced by their unique perspective.

CUEING-IN EMOTIONS

When working on a film soundtrack, composer and sound designer Ciarán Hope studies the energy of each scene to consider what is going on inside each character's head (Hope, interview 2017). He uses the precise placement of key sound elements as a storytelling device to cue in emotions, to aurally suggest their existence before the audience is aware of them. A distant car alarm or a dog barking can irritate the ear and prefigure an argument on screen. A soundtrack should accurately represent locational features and unique characteristics. An open window suggests an outside world, perhaps represented by the distant sound of passing cars and children playing. For *Screw Cupid* (2008), Hope constructed a highly accurate quadraphonic sound recording of an LA rooftop in order to build an authentic soundscape. This sound was critical to immersing the audience in the story location. In developing a sound design and musical score, Hope states that he seeks to return the story to the script, to build a soundscape that both references and recalls the emotion of the original text.

SEPARATING DIALOGUE FROM BACKGROUND NOISE

Film-score composer Neil O'Connor uses a spectral analysis technique to separate film dialogue from sound effects and room tone (O'Connor, interview 2017). A common issue with recorded audio in media projects is that two sounds may have the same frequency and thus both are unclear during playback. When an actor's voice shares the same audio frequency as a sound effect, the voice becomes indistinct and the dialogue difficult to follow. O'Connor selects and reduces the volume of specific audio frequencies in the effect, then boosts those same frequencies in the dialogue. The result is that both sound elements can be heard clearly as they have a different frequency range and playback in separate parts of the speaker.

PROSODY AND SYNTAX

English psychiatrist Anthony Storr explores the development of music as a function of communication through language. He notes that the prosodic elements of speech are distinguishable from the syntactic. Prosodic features include 'stress, pitch, volume, emphasis, and any other features conveying emotional significance' whereas syntactic features refer to 'grammatical structure and literal meaning'. Storr notes that prosodic communication is similar to music (Storr, 1993 p. 9).

Prosodic features enhance speech, giving greater complexity than syntactic elements used alone, much like the difference between a single note and a chord. In storytelling, this level of detail can greatly inform the audience about the character's' subconscious, conveying information that cannot be acted or spoken. Prosodic elements of speech may also exploit our responses to specific harmonics.

Storr looks at the origins of speech as a communication tool and references Herbert Spencer writing in *Fraser's Magazine* in 1857 (Spencer quoted in Storr, 1993 p. 10). Spencer noted that emotional speech has a wide tonal range and its sound is closer to music. Considering the impact of emotion on language, Spencer observed that eventually 'the sounds of excited speech became gradually uncoupled from the words which accompanied them, and so came to exist as separate sound entities, forming a *language* of their *own*' (Spencer quoted in Storr, 1993 p. 10). This is seen in the film *Quest for Fire* (1981), where the characters communicate through a primitive language. This language was specifically devised for the film by the writer Anthony Burgess. The musicality of the prehistorical characters' language enhances the depiction of their basic emotions. While their language does not have a recognisable structure, we interpret emotion through the prosodic elements of their speech. Storr notes that the eighteenth-century Italian philosopher Giambattista Vico believed that, 'men naturally embodied their feelings, attitudes, and thoughts in symbols' and that 'the metaphorical use of language ... preceded the literal' (Storr, 1993 p. 12). In Greece, music was considered to be a natural accompaniment to the 'subjective language of poetry' rather than intellectual argument (Storr, 1993 p 14).

MUSICAL MOTIFS

Musical motifs enable the audience to have informed expectations as to what is going to happen. People respond to music in a similar way when in groups, which explains its power to draw audiences together. The musical motif is used to 'anchor' an audience to parts of the story. It directs the audience's attention to what the director wants them to concentrate on at any particular time. In some films, characters will have a musical motif assigned to them, or a specific emotion may have its own chorus.

Music can streamline interpretations if it is allowed to have its own voice. Where music is presented with a multitude of background noises, dialogue and effects, it can get too confused with other sounds. The effect of music is more pronounced on those who are actively listening and concentrating. This arousal can lead to finger tapping and foot tapping which leads to a greater level of immersion on the part of the listener and ultimately creates a 'percussive barrier' to the outside world. Such immersion within the 'reality' of the film is important for the audience to fully appreciate the audiovisual aesthetic created by the author/director. '[Wilhelm] Worringer claimed that modern aesthetics was based upon the behaviour of the contemplating subject. If the subject is to enjoy a work of art, he must absorb himself into it, make himself one with it' (Storr, 1993 p. 39).

As a film-maker, I have often recognised the primacy of audio over visuals. Sounds trigger a series of memories in the audience which allow complex interpretations of scenes. The emotional impact of sound is greater than the visual. Therefore what cannot be achieved by performance or writing can be achieved through music. The palette of musical styles understood by the audience allows them to piece together the information the music is giving them and to juxtapose this with the visuals.

Using music in this way in film is similar to how we consider sound in everyday life. Ambient audio reminds us of the world around us and everything that exists in it. Ambient music tracks can subtly take us from one scene to another, incorporating their respective changes in pace and mood. This helps to create seamless edits where we are not aware of scenes changing but instead perceive only a single sequence. Music can enhance the rhythm of a film sequence and help it flow more smoothly. Music may even have originated to increase work efficiency through rhythmic organisation. However, music can conflict with demanding tasks that require concentration. It can distract and disrupt.

Separating music and dialogue in film is representative of human physiology. Storr states that the brain divides the processing of language and music 'not so much between words and music as between logic and emotion' (Storr, 1993 p. 35). Emotional content is dealt with by the right hemisphere of the brain and conceptual thought is processed by the left. Film-makers are appealing to both right and left hemispheres when they incorporate both music and dialogue into a single scene.

REPRESENTATIONS OF EMOTIONS

Over-emphasis on music can lead to blunt, unsophisticated responses. Music videos emphasise sound over visual content and action scenes are often accompanied by loud music. Music can be used to heighten crowd emotions and 'can powerfully contribute to the loss of critical judgement' (Storr, 1993 p. 46). In the cinema, the resonating effect of a 'turned-up' bass line vibrates the seats that audiences are sitting on. The crowd experiences a single universal response to this direct assault on their senses. Various sound devices and musical techniques have been used to promote political propaganda such as Hitler's incantation/musical-style delivery at the Nuremberg rallies.

Yet different cultures will respond to music in different ways. Latin-American films released in the West may deliberately include a soundtrack of music that is more western than Latin. This increases audience identification with the music, and therefore with the film itself. A culturally specific soundtrack would alienate those who are not familiar with the music, they would need time to learn its subtle details.

> The universality of music depends upon basic characteristics of the human mind; especially upon the need to impose order upon our experience. Different cultures produce different musical systems just as they produce different languages and different political systems.
>
> (Storr, 1993 p. 64)

Foreign films and their soundtracks may require repeat viewings: 'unfamiliar music may induce different intellectual and emotional reactions on a first hearing from those experienced subsequently' (Storr, 1993 p. 68). As independent non-US-based films become more popular, audiences are becoming increasingly aware of their music and its forms. After several viewings, their interpretation of the film will be closer to the author/director's original vision. Storr even suggests that music is a clearer form of communication than the spoken word: 'some writers suggest that music conveys the same meaning to different listeners more accurately than a verbal message; that music is less likely to be misinterpreted or variously interpreted than words' (Storr, 1993 p. 70). But this clarity of interpretation can only go so far. Specific responses will vary considerably due to the subjective nature of story interpretation. General responses with regard to comedic/tragic content may tally, but nuanced and finely tuned responses will differ.

UNIVERSAL 'PALETTE' OF SOUND

Some codification has been achieved in music interpretation. With regard to the classification of musical notation in relation to specific responses

Deryck Cooke notes that there is an increasing consensus amongst Western composers and the musical devices they use to 'represent particular emotions' (Cooke quoted in Store, 1993, p. 73). He gives as an example 'the interval of the major third commonly expresses joy; whilst the minor third is generally associated with grief' (Cooke quoted in Storr, 1993 p 73). The flawed sound of the augmented fourth is often used to depict dark, hellish content and was called *diabolus in musica* by medieval theorists (Cooke quoted in Storr, 1993 p 73). There are musical arrangements that inspire melancholia or light-heartedness. The writer Anthony Burgess posited the idea that a formal relationship would be developed between the written word and musical notes to create a new language allowing emotions, ideas and feelings to be expressed through a more sophisticated communication medium, where the complementary nature of words and music could be codified and 'alphabeticised' (Burgess, 1987 p. 429). While no such schema is available for this relationship, it is true that to a certain extent some note structures evoke particular responses.

Perhaps these generic responses are due to a universal 'palette' of sound, a common interpretation within Western society. This consensus on 'musical devices' has created a standard response to sound sequences. While this codification enables musicians to build sophisticated musical forms that produce complex emotional responses, it also discourages experimentation outside the existing palette. If the audience cannot 'hear' familiar elements in the music, they may be put off.

MEMORIES OF FEELINGS: THE LIMITS OF THE CODIFICATION OF MUSICAL FORMS

Storr notes Hindemith's point that reactions to music are not feelings themselves but the memories of feelings (Hindemith quoted in Storr, 1993 p. 76). This is useful in creating film narratives; the camera's images are presented on screen, whereas images inspired by the music are replayed in the memory of the audience. The feelings that music can inspire are limited to those feelings that have already been experienced by the listener. This highlights the limits of the codification of musical forms and their ability to provoke specific emotional responses. If the viewer has not previously experienced a particular emotion then their emotional range is simply not extensive enough to exploit the potential of the musical device. There is no reference point in their memory between what they are hearing and what they have previously experienced. Audience diversity will result in differing responses to film music, where individual musical memory creates alternate perspectives and interpretations of a scene.

Music is an important feature of interactive stories due to the fact that it is constantly moving forward: 'Music more aptly represents human emotional processes because music, like life, appears to be in constant motion' (Storr, 1993 p. 79). It is very easy for interactive titles to 'loop' at a decision making point in the story and become entangled, with no way forward. If a navigational decision must be made for a story to progress, then the narrative may simply stop. In that instance the author/director has essentially given authorial control to the audience. Neil O'Connor notes that the rhythmical aspect of music promotes narrative progression and that classical music is useful as it has an implied progression (O'Connor, interview 2017). Therefore, music can provoke forward motion and encourage user input to enable an interactive story to advance.

ANTICIPATION AND RESOLUTION

Storr suggests that typical story and musical patterns are hard-wired into our brains.

> It is not trivialising either literature or music to point out that conventional forms in both arts are based on archetypal patterns of a simple kind which are probably encoded in the brain. Symmetry is one such pattern; stories are another.
>
> (Storr, 1993 p. 83)

Therefore musical forms which follow basic symmetrical rules produce responses based on standard codifications that exist in us all. Storr notes Leonard Meyer's suggestion that music arouses and inhibits emotions and that the great composers are expert at controlling anticipation and resolution. In film, the composer is juxtaposing our responses to both story and music. Musical symmetry may run slightly in advance or behind the actual onscreen story, acting as an indicator of what is to come, or as a memory/reminder of what has just happened. In the same way that an editor can take the viewer back and forward from shot to shot, controlling what you are seeing and in what order, the composer can control how the audience focuses on film elements by structuring story and musical symmetry in a specific order. Hans Keller links 'compositional skill with the listener's expectations ... an experienced listener is able to make judgements and comparisons within a particular stylistic context' (Keller quoted in Storr, 1993 p. 85). Like film genres, the audience's familiarity with the content allows the film-maker flexibility in terms of the presentation of the story. In fact, the audience expects to be taken into unfamiliar territory, away from what they know, to where they can no longer predict with any degree of certainty what is going to happen. This unpredictability keeps the audience in their seats. When the story plays out along predictable lines the audience gets 'ahead of the story' and they simply do not need to stay to the end.

With regard to the level of music employed over dialogue and within different types of scenes, there are various approaches among film-makers. Some prefer to let dialogue exist in its own auditory space with only ambient sound as a background. Others mix music and dialogue, like competitors constantly vying for the audience's attention, each driving the narrative through character development and emotional recall. Yet audiences are divided on which approach works best: 'Some people cannot bear trying to conduct a conversation through background music; others apparently do not notice it, or can even cut it out of their perceptual field' (Storr, 1993 p. 102). Much is dependent on the content of the scene. Driving a fast-paced narrative like Meirelles's and Lund's *City of God* (2002) incorporated a fast mix of music and dialogue, while Kieślowski's reflective film *A Short Film About Love* (1988) used just one or the other.

It is the job of the sound editor to 'filter' sound on behalf of the audience. In real life, the audio pattern of stereo sound makes it possible for the human brain to filter out wavelengths that are not important to us. By doing this for the audience, the sound editor is replicating the typical human response when listening to audio. In *Timecode* (2000) the screen is split into four segments, each showing a single, unedited, 90-minute shot. Director Mike Figgis edited only the sound, to move the audience's point of focus from screen to screen. Francis Coppola used the media presentation software Isadora to tour a 'live remix performance' of his experimental horror film *Twixt* (2011), allowing him to change the experience based on the audience response within each venue.

RHYTHMIC ORGANISATION AND 'PERCUSSIVE BARRIERS'

Music can shield the audience from unwanted interruptions. It creates a narrative reality much like that of a text-based story or film. While we are 'participating' in that reality it becomes our first world, the reality in which we are temporarily living; 'When we take part in music, or listen to an absorbing performance, we are temporarily protected from the input of other external stimuli. We enter a special secluded world in which order prevails and from which the incongruous is excluded' (Storr, 1993 p. 105). This might also explain why some people tap their fingers while concentrating. The music they are creating drowns out the other stimuli and helps to create an internal world of rhythm and beats. 'Music, according to Schopenhauer, is understood immediately without any need to give account of it or from any abstract conception of it ... What music expresses is the inner spirit' (Storr, 1993 p. 140). Music can perfectly capture and communicate the mood of a scene in a film and promotes story development and progression. It can be used to convey the inner thoughts of characters as they speak. In this way, music can enhance an actor's performance. It can communicate the emotional meaning of spoken words when running parallel with them.

PSYCHOLOGICAL AND ONTOLOGICAL TIME

In music, as with the narrative, time can be divided up between the story characters' perception of time and real time. The perception of time relates to how the story is being told, how the author focuses on key points in the narrative. Stravinsky distinguished between what he termed psychological and ontological time (Stravinsky quoted in Storr, 1993 p. 85). Psychological time refers to the subject's mood and emotion, how they perceive time passing according to their emotional state. Time will pass quickly during periods of excitement and more slowly during periods of boredom. Ontological time is time as it is, as a measurement (Storr, 1993 p. 185). The difference in perception of time is also exploited by the film editor who can speed up or slow down time according to the requirements of the telling of the story. It is more important to maintain the interest of the audience by effective retelling, than to adhere slavishly to a fixed time base.

MUSICAL NOTATION

Composer Howard Goodall examines the origins of music and the development of musical notation. Neumatic notation was an early system used by cantors to 'dictate' notes to the choir as they followed the cantor 'by watching his hands. He would indicate the movement of the tune by gesturing his hand about into various positions' (Goodall, 2001 p. 17). However this system was flawed due to the fact that it was 'still handicapped by the reliance on one singer knowing his chant, successfully transmitting it a split-second in advance to his colleagues, and in his memorising the whole repertoire and not dropping dead before an assistant can be trained up' (Goodall, 2001 p. 17). Goodall explains the difficulties experienced in creating a workable system of notation that could transcribe emotions onto paper. Greek musicians first used musical notes in sequences to create feelings and emotions in the listeners. Eventually a system was developed that allowed music to be transported in its original form around the world. Guido d'Arezzo designed a 'workable system of writing music down ... He offered a model for the modern *scale*, or musical ladder, made notes easy to identify and follow' (Goodall, 2001 p. 31). Previously, music had to be memorised by ear and thus 'endlessly recycled and repackaged' in order to share it. Written musical notation created a permanent, historical record of sound and enabled the creation of uniquely individual works of art.

ACCIDENTAL COUNTERPOINT

Goodall considers accidental or improvised counterpoint where two or more pieces of music are played at once. It is found in Indian music and is 'limited to what can be imagined and played there and then: what one's hands are capable of doing without too much interference from the brain at any one time' (Goodall, 2001 p. 34). Live performance can only create what the musicians themselves were capable of on the night. While Goodall is improvising at the piano, the chords and riffs of the most recent work he has played often 'creep' into his performance and this makes the composition less original than work created using visual notation (Goodall, 2001 p. 35). He compares this method of composition to the work of early architects; complex structures would have been impossible if they had been designed through trial and error instead of using plans. Early chord structures in Guido's age were very simple with only about five combinations of two notes together; it took some time for musicians to begin playing three simultaneous notes at once.

Music vocabulary was created between the years 1000 and 1400 AD. Therefore we do not know what Roman music sounded like; we can only guess the type of music they created. The system of notation developed by Guido was open to interpretation. Reading and writing of music is a subjective process. When music is read and played it is the performer's version of the composition that we hear. They interpret what is written down. With the development of new technologies that read music for us, there is less need for some musicians to develop skills in this area. It seems as though we are reverting to a time when only a few people possess the ability and learning to decode music. New technologies may make music accessible to a greater number of people, yet they may also reduce the skillset normally required within the music-making process to create sophisticated works.

In 1640 Gregorio Allegri wrote *Miserere Mei, Deus*, a significant work featuring Renaissance ornamentation techniques. The Pope considered the work so powerful, so close to the divine, that he allowed only the choir at the Sistine Chapel to perform it, once a year during Holy Week. However, Goodall states that the experience of listening to this music was greatly influenced by the time and the place, and that the majority of moving musical experiences are felt while listening to 'live' music (Goodall, 2001 p. 48).

COMMUNICATING EMOTION THROUGH MUSIC

Goodall makes an interesting comparison between Shakespeare's writing and the functional elements of opera. He compares Shakespearean monologues to a sung aria, which is heavily stylised, with internal character thoughts vocalised for the audience (Goodall, 2001 p. 55). In *Poetics*, Aristotle made the distinction between retelling the 'true' elements of a story and the story itself, arguing that it is preferable to manipulate the truth in order to create a better narrative (Aristotle, 1996 p. 1). Known as 'effects', the ability of music to convey heightened emotional states like jealousy and anger was used extensively by Shakespeare to represent man's inner mind. Goodall considers other groups including the Camerata, which was made up of artists and scientists. Their aim was to create a visionary movement that fused all the arts. This group was effectively pre-empting the age of multimedia with its fusion of multiple media streams into a single entity.

In support of the theory of 'words sung' dominating 'words spoken', Goodall believes that the 'filtered medium' of singing allows more powerful thoughts and emotions to be formulated and expressed (Goodall, 2001 p. 68). Speech is too raw and limited in comparison. Operas used song to achieve greater freedom of expression than was possible with the spoken word of a play. An emotional delivery of the spoken word conveys melodrama, while singing adds colour, clarity and aural emphasis to a character's speech. In other words, highly emotive words delivered naturally through music were more believable than forced dramatic speech.

Goodall's composition process involves revising the work again and again. Each revision adds another conscious level of experience and feeling to enhance the work. It is this tinkering with the text that creates a layered, nuanced piece. It becomes more refined, more direct and focused. This transcription is affected by the location of the work done. The locale influences the mood of the composer and ultimately impacts on the style of the finished piece. Therefore, one can almost 'hear' where the piece was written; it is a characteristic of the work. Goodall believes that the 'time and place' affect the experience of both writing and hearing music. Textual analysis of works is much informed by historical knowledge as to the period and place of writing, to fully understand the intentions of the author.

Goodall examines the technical structures of Western music. 'Equal temperament is the tuning system by which practically all the notes in our Western music are organised and structured' (Goodall, 2001 p. 101). Stringed instruments, which are essentially 'free', have had strict rules of notation imposed on them.

Musical history reflects the history and development of other art forms: Renaissance artists' experiments with perspective are reflected in music by the combination of notes used to make chords. Each art form was both influencial and influenced by others.

SYNCOPATION

Significant technical leaps were made with the introduction of jazz. Syncopated piano playing, as developed by the ragtime player Scott Joplin, was fundamental to early jazz music. Syncopation is delaying or anticipating the beat, the 'busy approximating of several melody instruments by the right hand fractures the rhythm, syncopating it' (Goodall, 2001 p. 164). Technological developments, including the editing revolution, led to 'the idea of a definitive performance of a particular piece'. Attempts to accurately recreate the sound of the concert hall were left behind. With the endlessly repeatable experience offered by recorded music, 'an improvised, un-notated performance on one night in one place can be preserved in time, it can and does become a Work of Art' (Goodall, 2001 p. 206). This extends to unique 'edits' and various production additions. Recordings allowed composers to listen to the music of remote ethnic groups, to break it down, study its parts and incorporate this new knowledge into their own compositions.

Theodor W. Adorno and Hanns Eisler bemoan the uninspired use of music in early Hollywood films. The imposition of melody held back the development of complex and ambitious soundtracks. They believed that an opportunity for creative progression in musical development had been lost in the use of accompanying music; 'the disparity between symmetry and asymmetry becomes particularly striking when music is used to accompany natural phenomena, such as drifting clouds, sunrises, wind, and rain' (Adorno & Eisler, 2005 p. 13).

Adorno and Eisler believed that music should be used as an explicit element within the audiovisual framework, but was being wasted as a simple accompaniment. They felt that music was not being given its rightful place in film: 'musical illustration should either be hyperexplicit itself – over-illuminating, so to speak, and thereby interpretative – or should be omitted' (Adorno & Eisler, 2005 p. 46). They believed that the influence of music is so significant, if it is not going to be used to its full creative potential, it should not be used at all. They indicate that the potential of film and music association is not being fully exploited; film is being left in 'pulp fiction' territory. Merging the two could create something that the other arts have not yet achieved.

During their careers they fought for recognition of the importance and potential of music in film: 'motion-picture music, however, suffers from a particular handicap: from the very beginning it has been regarded as an auxiliary art not of first-rank importance' (Adorno & Eisler, 2005 p. 71). They worked within a Western system with people who did not have their formal training. They were disappointed with the colour/sound associations being created that reduced the artistic potential of the medium. They questioned the reasons for reproducing the same idea in two different media when something much more powerful and complex could be achieved by paralleling separate statements in sound and vision. Drawing on Eisenstein's theory of montage they proposed a new relationship between film and music; 'montage makes the best of the aesthetically accidental form of the sound picture by transforming an entirely extraneous relation into a virtual element of expression' (Adorno & Eisler, 2005 p. 71).

Ultimately constrained by the motion-picture system, they were expected to create music that related directly to plot and characters. The referential nature of this form of music creation negates the possibility of music meaning something itself; it only exists in relation to the visual.

THE SOUNDTRACK

Pauline Reay assesses the score for Eisenstein's *Battleship Potemkin* (1925). She notes that Edmund Meisel worked closely with Eisenstein on the score; they were trying to prove 'a formal correlation between the montage of a film and music' (Reay, 2004 p. 11). She reiterates Adorno and Eisler's observation on the standardisation of film and music, its effects on audiences and their belief that these prejudices held back progress in film music. The standard practices being used throughout the industry led the audiences to 'expect' a formulaic soundtrack which used 'leitmotif, unobtrusiveness, visual justification, illustration, stock music, clichés and standardised interpretations' (Reay, 2004 p. 15). Film composer Aaron Copland also criticised the leitmotif as being formulaic and predictable (Copland quoted in Reay, 2004 p. 16). In 1949 he suggested five general areas in which music serves film. It should convincingly add to the 'place and time' of the film and reflect the 'unspoken feelings or psychological states of characters'. It can function as a background filler, add to the sense of continuity in the edit, emphasise the 'theatrical build-up of a scene' and add a sense of finality (Copland quoted in Reay, 2004 p. 32).

Music is given its own weight as a functional part of the audiovisual experience. Early cinema was plagued by musical accompaniments that added nothing to the audience's interpretation or understanding of a story. The visual aspect of the experience dominated. Claudia Gorbman also identified several principles of composition: non-diegetic sound sources should be invisible; music should not be heard consciously; music 'first and foremost' signifies emotion; music cues in new narrative settings and characters; music interprets and illustrates events; music creates rhythmic continuity to help construct narrative unity (Gorbman quoted in Reay, 2004 p. 33). Gorbman's principles bring to mind Murch's 'rule of six' criteria for making a good cut. She also observes that these rules are a guide only and can be broken if it serves the film to do so.

Counterpoint is the melodic interaction of independent notes. Eisenstein employed counterpoint as a central aesthetic element in his films to create conflict within montage sequences. This complex process was not popular in Hollywood where music budgets were kept under tight control.

CINEMATIC ALLUSIONISM

Reay notes the distinction between the perceived 'high-culture' of the orchestral score and the 'low-culture' of the pop score (Reay, 2004 p. 38). The orchestral score is constantly moving with the story. Pop songs are developed independently from the visuals and often they do not fit. This is particularly true when a character sings a song onscreen and also for songs sung non-diegetically. Kathryn Kalinak notes that pop songs pose particular difficulties due to their structural unity and integrity (Reay, 2004 p. 38). They cannot be segmented like themes and leitmotifs. Rock music fails to support the story and mood in film because this genre of music is the story and mood itself. It is an independent entity in its own right. Also, songs are usually chosen for their relevance to a film rather than being composed specifically for it. Martin Scorsese, Quentin Tarantino and Paul Thomas Anderson write songs directly into the screenplay. Scorsese uses cinematic allusionism (alluding to film history) as a storytelling device. He references the audience's knowledge of film history and plot structures. Alluding to these structures he can suddenly shift the story by straying from the predictable story arc and character development. Scorsese sometimes puts the lyrics of songs between lines of dialogue so they appear to comment on the action. Reay notes that 'since the 1970s there have been examples of sound effects used as music and music used as sound effect' (Reay, 2004 p. 32). A good example of this is Walter Murch's use of helicopter engine noise (effect) to replicate an orchestra strings section (music) in *Apocalypse Now* (1979). In *The Graduate* (1967) Simon and Garfunkel's music is mainly presented non-diegetically and in isolation. The song *Scarborough Fair* acts as an interior monologue for the lead character Benjamin. In *Magnolia* (1999), each song moves the plot forward. Aimee Mann notes that director Paul Thomas Anderson 'understands that the lyrics substitute for narration or dialogue' (Mann quoted in Reay, 2004 p. 68). The film was shot using Mann's music as the inspirational source.

SOUND ELEMENTS OF FILM

Sound editors break scenes down into 'four sonic elements: dialogue, effects, music and Foley' (Kisner, 2015). Sound editor and designer Skip Lievsay has created audioscapes for Scorsese and the Coen brothers. He has a particular affinity for 'how the brain converts sound into information'. Every sound detail must be considered in terms of its influence on, and interpretation by an audience; it is 'one of the most visceral, subtle tools available to filmmakers' (Kisner, 2015). The sound design team often experience issues with regard to the articulation of their ideas. It can be difficult to clearly communicate a complex and subjectively interpreted aural experience, to describe to others (in words) the sound needed. Foley work involves the manual addition of everyday sounds such as footsteps, to create the aural space that a narrative takes place in; 'the impact a tiny aural cue can have on the brain's understanding of narrative is astonishing' (Kisner, 2015). Lievsay uses software called Altiverb to calculate the reverb pattern for a wide variety of rooms. This pattern (known as the 'delta') ensures the sound, as heard within the scene, exists naturally in that location. The delta is a finely tuned effect added to a sound element, that produces a specific emotional response; it is 'sound plus feeling.'

The formulaic use of music in film now extends to the marketing department. Films are produced, high-profile bands/songs are selected and material is released as a soundtrack album. Not all songs in the film are on the soundtrack album and not all songs on the soundtrack album are in the film. In some cases, the music on the soundtrack album is simply associated with the film in terms of genre and style, but is not actually used in the film itself, 'Russell Lack suggests that film music survived its earliest beginnings due to its effectiveness as a marketing tool' (Reay, 2004 p. 89). *The Blair Witch Project* (1999) had an accompanying music soundtrack album but there was no music in the film. *Down From the Mountain* was a series of tracks recorded by the performers in the film *Oh Brother Where Art Thou?* (2000).

It was Henry Mancini who initiated recording film music for soundtrack albums in the early 1960s. He criticised soundtrack packaging, believing many of his contemporaries only established a main theme and that the rest of their soundtracks were bits and pieces:

> by the end of the 1980s the trend for marketing films through music had become institutionalised in both the mainstream and underground. This was to continue throughout the 1990s with the increasing fragmentation of the market and the development of niche audiences.
>
> (Reay, 2004 p. 101)

In fact:

> the 1990s also saw three major developments; firstly the emergence of the soundtrack as a cultural product in its own right; secondly, the diversification of the soundtrack genre; and thirdly, the increasing fragmentation of the market into niche audiences.
>
> (Reay, 2004 p. 102)

Trainspotting (1996) was marketed almost like a band or an album including a series of posters featuring band-like shots of the leading actors, photo studio images that were not taken from the film. Future experimental films may allow the user to choose or create their own soundtrack to films.

Reay notes that postmodern culture:

> has been described as a culture of 'intertextuality' – rather than original cultural production there is a cultural production born out of other cultural production. This is demonstrated in film music by scores partially born out of other film scores.
>
> (Reay, 2004 p. 115)

When film audiences know the same films as film composers, music can be referenced and sampled endlessly. They know where the composer is going with the score; they know the genre and the style. This idea was extended by Roland Barthes who 'proposes the notion of the death of the author, making the viewer the most important interpreter of the text' (Reay, 2004 p. 117).

Claudia Gorbman states that music in film creates a struggle between the explicit content of the shot, and the musical codes. This is a struggle between filmic discourse (irregular rhythm) and musical discourse (regular rhythm). 'Music, indeed, is constantly engaged in an existential and aesthetic struggle with narrative representation' (Gorbman, 1987 p. 13).

Standardisation of form has made music subservient to film narrative. It is deliberately composed in short, flexible phrases using compositional devices such as 'modulations, *sostenuti* [sustaining a note beyond its full value], and sequence-progressions'. By employing these devices the composer forces the music to accommodate itself to the narrative with 'minimum adherence to musical syntax' (Gorbman, 1987 p. 14).

IMITATIVE-DENOTATIVE INSTRUMENTATION

The film composer works thematically, within the context of the narrative, augmenting the visual story. Imitative-denotative instrumentation (known as mickey-mousing) is where the music simply parallels or mirrors the visual. It produces a comedic effect and is often used in animation. Manipulating the rhythm and articulation of the music affects how we interpret diegetic information (Gorbman, 1987 p. 17). The function of music in film varies from creating a parallel interpretation, to building on the dominant reading of the audiovisual text, like a Greek chorus commenting on the story.

LIMITATIONS OF VISUAL AND DIALOGUE

Visuals and dialogue in film are constrained by pacing and synchronicity; their interpretation is conceptually limited and they present a fixed interpretation of reality. Music has a greater degree of flexibility with regard to film narrative and can function at a number of levels including 'temporal, spatial, dramatic, structural, denotative, connotative – both in the diachronic flow of a film at various interpretative levels simultaneously' (Gorbman, 1987 p. 22).

LEITMOTIF

Musical themes are used in film to circumvent establishing shots and scene setting; they are used more than once during the film and their repetition brings with them an emotion or idea that has been developed earlier in the story. Some themes feature in multiple genres to indicate a single connotation: 'rhythmic repetition in groups of four with accented initial beat, and predominance of open intervals of perfect fourths and fifths – already signify "Indian" in the language of the American music industry' (Gorbman, 1987 p. 28). The leitmotif, as employed by Wagner, functions as an evocation of a memory, a character's memory. The 'nonverbal and nondenotative status' of music enables it to flexibly move across 'levels of narration (diegetic/non-diegetic), between narrating agencies (objective/subjective narrators), between viewing time and psychological time, between points in diegetic space and time' (Gorbman, 1987 p. 30).

Silent films manipulated time with the use of long close-ups, unrealistically long, where the drama was postponed to concentrate audience attention on one character. Time in silent films was flexible; time could speed up, slow down, and move forward and backwards to support the rhythm of the scene without disturbing narrative conventions. Musical accompaniment was essential to narrative continuity, carrying the audience over from scene to scene and focusing its attention despite the temporal manipulation. 'Music removes barriers to belief; it bonds spectator to spectacle ... Like hypnosis, it silences the spectator's censor ... it makes us a little less critical and a little more prone to dream' (Gorbman, 1987 p. 55).

In film, music draws on our basic emotional experiences – some relate to our early development. Simple musical codes are used in many genres, referring to the audience's knowledge of film texts and music conventions. Film music is influenced by musical forms from other traditions. 'Musical "meaning" was codified and institutionalised well before the coming of sound. In turn, these meanings were inherited from a long European tradition [including] theatrical, operatic, and popular music of the later nineteenth century' (Gorbman, 1987 p. 85).

EMPATHETIC/ANEMPATHETIC SOUNDTRACKS

Music as simple accompaniment adds little in terms of textual representation. Hollywood composer Max Steiner worked on many films including *King Kong* (1933). Steiner's scores were hyper explicit, catching every movement and emotion presented on screen with a burst of music. Music in film has since achieved much greater complexity.

> Michel Chion distinguishes three types of soundtrack music, the third of which is the heedless music of the organ grinder: (1) 'empathetic' music, the sort most frequently heard on soundtracks, which participates in the characters' emotions, vibrates in sympathy with their actions; (2) music of didactic counterpoint – nondiegetic music to signify a contrapuntal idea, demanding to be read and interpreted; and (3) 'anempathetic' music, in relation to the intense emotional situation on screen (death, crisis, madness).
>
> (Gorbman, 1987 p. 159)

The subjectivity of musical interpretation forces the audience to anchor its meaning within the text. The story offers a perspective but also narrative facts; '[t]he ambivalent function of music is possible because it can easily move back and forth across the film's narrational boundaries' (Gorbman, 1987 p. 161).

* * *

This chapter has dealt with the expressive power of sound design and music in storytelling. Music helps to 'level out' the narrative disruption of interactivity. Music tracks that are not affected by user interaction will ensure a narrative progresses smoothly. Music reminds us that time is passing whether the user interacts or not. This is important to user immersion in the text. Goodall traced the development of music and identified several concepts that are important to interactive film. The addition of varying levels of conscious experience when writing and rewriting music reflects the multiple perspective experience of the interactive film viewer. Repetition in this world should make the viewer feel more at home with the text, developing a greater understanding of its subtleties. The freeform nature of jazz music echoes the freedom created by interactive texts to navigate a pathway through the narrative. Adorno and Eisler recognised the explicit nature of music in film. They understood the potential of music to convey its own meaning, yet it continued to be used as an accompaniment. Interactive films make use of dynamic music creation; sometimes constructed 'live' according to user interaction while the film is playing. Popular music tracks and orchestral scores are still being used in interactive film, but their position in the timeline will be controlled by algorithms. Intelligent and dynamic application of non-standardised musical form enhances the experience of the viewer, giving a truly unique experience in the form of a feedback loop that creates music according to their interaction. Some interactive titles use music to create a relaxed ambience to encourage the user to interact with the interactive clips. Music always moves forward and this prompts the viewer to make a decision at branch points within the narrative. Music helps to smooth over the disruptive influence of interaction by providing a seamless aural 'flow'. It represents character subconscious and unifies multiple narrative threads within the metanarrative. It reflects the relaxed attitude of the interactive viewer while immersed in the story, allowing music to carry them along a non-linear narrative path. Music can organise and control emotions, allowing a viewer to experience a single story with multiple perspectives.

5

Visual Montage

Visuals presented in montage format can include several images on screen at the same time, arranged into a pre-specified order along a timeline. Their relative position and juxtaposition indicates their spatial and temporal relationship. Spatial montage editing is now much easier due to the availability of digital editing tools. Traditional optical effects created photographically are complex, costly and time-consuming and are comparatively limited when compared with digital workflows. As interactive titles can include an array of story elements including text, stills, video and graphics, it is useful to consider the impact of spatial arrangement in storytelling and to look at some historical works of note. With interactive narratives, the spatial arrangement can be a function of the navigation system. It can be dynamic or passive. Multiple narrative viewpoints presented as spatial montage allow an audience to navigate a story visually. Each sub-screen indicates a narrative option, making each reading of the story unique. Examples of spatial montage include Joel Schumacher's *Phone Booth* (2003), Lars von Trier's *Europa* (1991) and David Hockney's photographic 'joiners.' Temporal montage presents images as an edited sequence. The presentation order influences the audience's interpretation of the author's intention. Relationships between story elements are created and sustained. In film, temporal montage moves an audience through the narrative at a fixed rate of 24 frames per second. Navigation is limited as the sequence relentlessly moves forward. Viewers will consider some story elements to be more important than others. These are used to both comprehend the narrative and to piece together an interpretation of the story. In this way, audiences already selectively navigate stories on an individual basis, some parts of the temporal sequence are remembered and others are forgotten. When retelling a story, viewers typically recount their own 'version' of the narrative, highlighting only the parts that are relevant to their interpretation.

This chapter explores the visual organisation of narrative elements within various film, photographic and literary works and considers the impact of montage on the reading of a text.

MONTAGE: JUXTAPOSING VISUAL ELEMENTS

Eisenstein states that the juxtaposition of shots in sequence 'resembles not so much a simple sum of one shot plus another shot – as it does a creation ... in every such juxtaposition the result is qualitatively distinguishable from each component' (Eisenstein, 1986 p. 17). While each shot has its own content and meaning, it is the 'montage' or sequencing and placing of shots that creates meaning to the viewer. Shots in a film are viewed as a combined sequence and not as a series of individual elements. The film-maker aims to evoke an emotional response in the viewer which replicates the original emotion they felt as they conceived their story idea. They attempt to manufacture on film 'partial representations which, in their combination and juxtaposition, shall evoke in the consciousness that same initial general image which originally hovered before the creative artist' (Eisenstein, 1986 p. 33). Particular tools are available to recreate this emotion including the choice of visuals, their order of presentation and juxtaposition to other 'plastic' elements. The meaning of each montage sequence is subjective. Yet Eisenstein stated that their interpretation brings the viewer as close as possible to the original thought process of the film-maker. In other words, the viewer does not just reach similar emotional levels, but also travels a similar pathway to get there. They become a 'creating spectator', a participating author in the construction of the artist's representation.

AFFIDAVIT-EXPOSITION

For Eisenstein, the opposite of the emotionally charged montage sequence is 'affidavit-exposition' where a single unedited shot simply presents what was there, without any attempt to manipulate the viewer's experience and their subsequent response (Eisenstein, 1986 p. 36). Steve McQueen's *Hunger* (2008) features a 17½-minute shot of a Catholic priest (Liam Cunningham) trying to talk Irish republican prisoner Bobby Sands (Michael Fassbender) out of going on a fatal hunger strike in the Maze prison, Northern Ireland in 1981. McQueen intended that the intensity of this unedited scene would make people 'physically lean forward, their ears become more sharp, their eyes become much more attuned to what's going on' (Olsen, 2009). The real-time scene creates a triangular relationship between Sands, the priest and the audience. McQueen states that the resulting engagement forces the audience to 'become part of it physically' (McQueen quoted in Olsen, 2009). Fassbender notes that the rhythm of this scene is created by the 'dance' the characters are doing; to have edited it would have imposed the director's interpretation and reduced its dynamism (Fassbender quoted in Olsen, 2009). In comparison, director Michael Bay tends to edit all scenes in his films into shots of three seconds or less. In fact, I have found that it is impossible to count three seconds between edits while watching a Bay movie, no matter how dramatic or profound a scene is intended to be. The result is that there is little or no time to consider the content or meaning of each scene. The story appears to be dynamically moving forward at high speed, yet the narrative is relatively static.

Classical artists manipulated both spatial and temporal perspectives to enhance the narrative complexity of their paintings. The still photograph can be seen as an affidavit-exposition equivalent to their work. A photograph is taken in a fraction of a second and is shot from a single perspective. This limits the artist's ability to manipulate the visual content and its subsequent interpretation. Composition and timing are certainly considerations for the photographer to exploit, but the spatial elements are fixed, seen at a single moment from a single point of view. In recent years artists have often used photographic stills as source images for their paintings. By recreating this still image, often shot with a 50mm lens on a 35mm SLR camera, they have managed to drain the detail and life from the painterly work. Rather than explore multiple interpretations and perspectives, all the drawbacks of stills photography are transferred onto the canvas without the spatial energy that rescues a temporally redundant image.

Eisenstein recommends the reading of Milton's poem *Paradise Lost* (1667) in the study of audiovisual montage; 'our first and most spontaneous perceptions are often our most valuable ones, because these sharp, fresh, lively impressions invariably derive from the most widely various fields' (Eisenstein, 1986 p. 62). Therefore, in approaching the classics, it is useful to examine not only finished works, but also those sketches and notes in which the artist endeavoured to set down his first vivid and immediate impressions. 'Making-of' documentaries and vignettes dedicated to the craft of film production are widely available. Initially these materials were used as 'fillers' to increase the amount of footage being added to distribution products to make them more attractive and increase sales. Supplementary materials bundled into re-released units encouraged members of the public who had already seen a film in the cinema to pay for it again as an online download or streamed file. As audiences were exposed to greater levels of behind-the-scenes footage they became more knowledgeable of the production process. For films such as the often re-edited and re-released *Blade Runner* (1982) and *The Matrix Trilogy* (1999–2003) it was as important for film fans to know the background story of the production as it was to know the film story itself. Film websites now review both cinematic releases and their subsequent iterations as they become available on various distribution platforms. Presentation restrictions are prompting film-makers to optimise the product with each release. For example, films intended for a small screen size such as a smartphone or tablet tend to include a greater number of close ups.

VERTICAL MONTAGE

Eisenstein compares 'vertical montage' to music in written form; only here the montage includes visuals. Musical notation is written so that multiple notes played by various instruments stay in sync. 'Double-exposed' images are also a form of montage and are used in film as cross-fades. Eisenstein notes that 'we have only to glance at a group of cubist paintings to convince ourselves that what takes place in these paintings has already been heard in jazz music' (Eisenstein, 1986 p. 82). He identified and explored the complex musical forms that were developing. Musicology was being extended beyond the traditional, to create a new 'formless' style that evoked tremendous emotional responses. Eisenstein unsuccessfully attempted to codify these responses in much the same way as he attempted to codify audience responses to colour and montage.

> Each time these traits reappear in history, one finds them aspiring towards a unified whole, a higher unity. It is only in periods of decadence in the arts that this centripetal movement changes to a centrifugal movement, hurling apart all unifying tendencies – tendencies that are incompatible with an epoch that places an over-emphasis on individualism.
>
> (Eisenstein, 1986 p. 84)

This emphasis on individualism was evident in many early online broadcast scenarios. Entrepreneurs sought to compete with existing national and international broadcasters by announcing the imminent arrival of wide-ranging and diverse audiovisual content for online broadcast. Inexperience led many of these initiatives to fail as they often neglected to research and consider the objectives of traditional content distributors. Public-service broadcasters on radio and television initially focused on news and light entertainment. Their range of content developed over time, when brand loyalty had been firmly established and they had secured their core audience. Many online broadcasters produced audiovisual product with no target audience. The result was that they failed to achieve market share as the public did not fully relate to, nor show any interest in the content they were offering.

Eisenstein states that an image without motion exists only spatially, without any order of time. There are no identifiers to establish temporal distance within the shot. The musical stave orders the image in a specific time framework. As Terence Davies suggests in his film *Distant Voices, Still Lives* (1988) the 'left' represents 'before' and the 'right' represents the 'future'. Therefore as the camera moves right to left the audience identifies this as going back in time, or looking into the past. *Distant Voices, Still Lives* is part of Davies' trilogy about growing up in post-war Britain.

PHOTO MONTAGE: HOCKNEY'S JOINERS

David Hockney created the 'joiner' montage of still images to breathe life into the medium of photography. Previously, he felt that stills photography could not hope to compete with the representative potential of painting. The photograph recorded just a fraction of a second whereas a painting could convey a period of time. One could potentially observe a temporal sequence of events, from multiple perspectives, within a single spatial space (the painting). While documenting some of his works for an exhibition, Hockney used a Polaroid camera to take photographs of the inside of his home. He used multiple images to make up a single 'joiner' of each room. He found that when the images were laid out in a rigid grid they made up a larger more complex image that represented a single physical space over an extended period of time. In short, his 'joiner' had begun to close the divide between the photographic 'instant' and the slower-paced, more thoughtfully selective medium of painting. The joiner was a visual representation of temporal space, a series of images shot from multiple perspectives, a spatial representation of time-based narrative. His work was later published as the book *Cameraworks*

(1984). This photo-montage technique was successfully used by various artists including Katerina Jebb who has produced life-size body scans. Jebb was in a car accident in 1991 and her right arm was paralysed. She could not fully use a camera and turned to using and modifying scanning technologies to create large-scale photographic montages. Her work parodies contemporary commercial advertising concepts, yet she has been commissioned to produce campaigns for many international brands (Hodgkin, 2015).

Hockney describes the work of Picasso as more real than naturalism. Picasso's profound use of time and perspective shows both the front and back of a figure, from various positions over time, within a single painting (Hockney, 2002 p. 102). Hockney believes the edges of the photograph create the composition, allowing you to 'see' the middle. He used this technique to make his joiner images 'in which you could alter the edges a great deal' (Hockney, 2002 p. 103). He no longer recognised any separation between representation and abstraction: 'the more you go on the more you realize there's actually only abstraction. The photograph is a refined abstraction' (Hockney, 2002 p. 126). Composition can create order from disorder. When creating his joiners, Hockney looked for a perspective on a scene or group of objects, then chose the edges that bordered a composite image, framing the selected scene elements to produce a coherent narrative. This narrative communicates his response to what he saw, his experience.

BURROUGHS'S LITERARY CUT-UPS

The writer William Burroughs appropriated existing visuals to create his own collages; 'it was precision with intent: by rearranging different images, Burroughs sought to create new visual connections and establish new meanings' (Malkani, 2014). He used the juxtaposition of images to produce a form of language. Burroughs also worked with literary 'cut-ups' to reorder printed words on a page, unlock new meanings and to allow him to consider the author's original intent. Burroughs believed he could detect the 'voice' of Shakespeare by pulling apart his sentences and rebuilding them into new word arrangements. His cut-ups brought together varying cultural elements and would 'incorporate pop culture, advertising and celebrities, but they also demonstrate his appreciation of what Allmer calls "the infinite reproduction of reproduction"' (Malkani, 2014). Similarly, the nonlinear structure of interactive stories and contemporary 'mash-ups' require a form of reading where meaning is constructed subjectively, through the interpretation of both original and appropriated recombinant art elements.

THE LETTRISTS

The multi-disciplinary avant-garde movement called the Lettrists began in 1946. Its members announced 'Lettrism' to be the successor to figurative and abstract art. Lettrism aimed to turn everyone into a creator. Instead of using letters and writing as a means of communication, the Lettrists perceived them as aesthetic art objects. Later, they used real and invented scientific notation and symbols from all cultures of the world to create Hypergraphics, often unrecognisable works made up of found films and materials, scratched and distorted until they were undecipherable. Lettrist poetry was a performance art of flatly sounded letters, without pitch or semantics, deliberately disregarding linguistic conventions to create 'the new'. They worked in all art disciplines, aiming to free the individual from the tyranny of established traditions and influence. In pursuit of this cause, the Lettrist artist Maurice Lemaître stated that he preferred to read 'manuals and condensed works' due to the fact that 'their determined spareness saves the reader from ... "stylistic" coatings, and tasty exclamations which ... only blur it and discourage the enthusiasm of the impatient searcher' (Lemaître, 1954 p. 2).

BRUEGHEL'S MICRONARRATIVES

Manovich considered the use of spatial montage in the paintings of Brueghel and Bosch. These 'micronarratives' allow the paintings to show 'events that form one narrative but are separated by time' (Manovich, 2002 p. 322). This spatial narrative was further developed in the form of comics. Framed drawings on the page do not conform to any preset dimensions or size. The visual communication of the page moves with the narrative flow. During action scenes the viewer must scan the images quickly to gain some sense of the visual continuity and pacing. Manovich points out that:

> spatial montage can accumulate events and images as it progresses through its narrative. In contrast to the cinema's screen, which primarily functions as a record of perception, here the computer functions as a record of memory.
>
> (Manovich, 2002 p. 325)

Spatial montage involves a number of different-sized images appearing on screen at the same time. These can be faded in and out at separate intervals or left on screen throughout the narrative. Each image has its own position on screen and embedded audio. A number of images may appear in succession or as an amalgamation of onscreen clips. The order of the clip presentation and their timing and position on screen invoke a unique audience response and narrative interpretation.

Manovich uses the term 'micronarratives' for visuals that play out on screen at the same time in the form of 'sub-screens' presented in full-motion video yet not full-screen. The advantage of this display methodology is that the sequence of events can be played out much faster than with traditional linear presentation of scenes and clips, yet without any loss of audiovisual information to the audience. Like a gallery, the audience can 'read around' the visuals which are now interconnected using sequential diagetic and non-diagetic audio. The audience's natural tendency will be to look at the most recently 'arrived' clip on screen. However, over time their eye will go back to clips that have been there for some time, thus revisiting visual information for confirmation of its subject matter or in an attempt to cross-reference audiovisual content. The result is a continuous sequence where multiple elements of a scene can be played out at the same time. In this sense, shots which are normally reserved for 'setting the scene' can be overlapped with actual dialogue sequences or sequences presenting specific action.

MARKER'S *LA JETÉE*

Chris Marker's film *La Jetée* (1962) uses visual montage to tell the story of a man who, as a child, observed a woman's reaction to a violent incident at Orly Airport, Paris. Forever haunted by this memory, the striking image of her stays with him all his life until he finally meets her during a series of time-travel experiments conducted by post-apocalypse scientists, hoping to save their dying world. He later realises that the woman was watching his adult self being killed, the incident at Orly was his own death. *La Jetée* is a sequence of black and white still images. These images are on screen for two or three seconds each. Marker used the stills to recreate movement by placing the camera where the audience wants to be. In one sequence he 'tracks' around the young couple as they sit chatting on a park bench. The sequence conforms to film production conventions such as 'crossing-the-line' so that the viewer forgets they are viewing a series of still images sequenced together using cross-dissolves and hard edits. It leaves us with a memory of having watched a short live-action scene. This audiovisual deception is further developed by the use of a three-second film clip showing the woman lying in bed, staring at the camera. In a sequence of still images, we see her move just slightly between frames, as she listens intently.

Suddenly, she blinks her eyes in full-motion. The result is so visually smooth that often the audience does not notice. Yet even if they have not realised the use of film in this sequence of stills, there is something quite chilling about the subtle return to continuous temporal movement.

SPATIAL REPRESENTATION OF TEMPORAL SEQUENCES

Lars Von Trier's film *Europa* (1991) employs complex spatial montage to allow the audience to view several scenes from different viewpoints. In one scene, a man is shot while travelling in the overnight compartment on a train. The viewer sees the gun, the victim and the murderer on the screen at the same time. The shots overlap both spatially and temporally. There is a slight delay between shots that allows the viewer time to 'go back' and rewatch the event from a different perspective. The resulting increase in tension is due in part to the fact that Von Trier has shown us all the angles we would have viewed the scene from (or wanted to view it from) if we had actually been there. Although this is the goal of traditional linear editing it is generally not possible without overlapping the temporal space of juxtaposed clips. *Europa* is also very interesting in that the visual effects were created optically using a classical back-projection system as this film predated any widely used digital-effects technologies. Actors interact with characters on several projected images on a screen behind them. In Ang Lee's *Hulk* (Lee, 2003) spatial montage is used throughout the film to reflect the comic book origins of the story. Split-screen effects are used extensively. As the story intensity builds, 'subscreens' travel across the field of view in order of importance, creating an innovative temporal sequence in a comic book style. Lee developed a complex backstory for the Hulk. The spatial montage conveys a large amount of story data – including the development of the technology that created the Hulk, presented in tandem with the mental and emotional deterioration of his scientist father.

MULTIPLE NARRATIVE PERSPECTIVES ONSCREEN

In Zbigniew Rybczyński's *The New Book* (1975), the screen is spatially divided up into nine equal parts, each concurrently showing the story location from a particular perspective. The main character (wearing a distinctive long red coat) manoeuvres his way through the nine parts of the segmented screen as the story unfolds. While editing, Rybczyński had to change the timing of some of the screen views to avoid the character appearing in more than one perspective at the same time. A slow motion effect delays his movement toward the end of several segments. This perspectival representation of the film narrative using spatial montage risks having the audience gradually interpret the sub-screens as self-contained stories. Rybczyński resolved this by including several moments in the film where all the characters in all nine screens react to a single event at the same time. A plane flies overhead and everyone looks up; the man in red drops a book on the ground, there is a loud noise and all the characters stop what they are doing for a moment, apparently responding in unison to his mistake. Similarly, in Mike Figgis's *Timecode* (2000), a tense Hollywood-based story plays out in real time, using split-screen to show the narrative from four different perspectives at once. Figgis employed a narrative device to remind the audience that the multiple screens were perspectives of a single story. Several earthquakes take place at random points within the narrative. Each of the screens shake violently and all the characters seek cover. Again, having everyone and everything within the multiple perspectives react to the same event, the viewer is reminded that the multiple screens are all part of a single narrative. It does, however, indicate that if spatial montage is used in the development of interactive narratives, then the issue of each screen taking on an unintended degree of independence will need to be considered and carefully avoided.

VERTOV'S KINO-EYE

The Russian film-maker Dziga Vertov had another view about the use of montage in cinema: 'Montage means organizing film fragments (shots) into a film-object. It does not mean selecting the fragments for "scenes" (the theatrical basis) or for titles (the literary basis)' (Vertov quoted in Michelson, 1985 p. 88). Annette Michelson notes that the film *The Man with a Movie Camera* (1929) is the visual representation of the Marxist project. In Vertov's own writing he says 'The kino-eye lives and moves in time and space; it gathers and records impressions in a manner wholly different from that of the human eye' (Vertov quoted in Michelson, 1985 p. 15). He describes how he wanted to work towards the ideal visual aesthetic of visual survey, joined through montage. Vertov intended to create a language of film that did not depend on the use of titles, to allow an uneducated audience access to the meaning of the film. However, the absence of explanatory intertitles put more pressure on film-makers to produce meaningful visuals that were both coherent and truthfully represented their vision. Vertov sought to develop a unique aesthetic by creating a universal language of film that would unite people of the world around communist ideals:

> Instead of surrogates for life (theatrical performance, film-drama, etc.), we bring to the workers' consciousness facts (large and small), carefully selected, recorded, and organized from both the life of the workers themselves and from that of their class enemies.
>
> (Vertov quoted in Michelson, 1985 p. 50)

Vertov wanted to avoid a technocentric approach to film-making. He believed many of his contemporaries were using unnecessarily complex techniques which he felt were distanced from reality and unlike the qualities of human observation. Vertov believed that 'Kino-eye uses every possible means in montage, comparing and linking all points of the universe in any temporal order, breaking, when necessary, all the laws and conventions of film construction' (Vertov quoted in Michelson, 1985 p. 88). Vertov voiced his frustration about the difficulties in setting up this new methodology of audiovisual communication, complaining that administrative and funding issues kept him from completing his projects. He summed up his difficulties:

> The problem lies not in separating form from content. The problem is one of unity of form and content. Of not permitting oneself to confuse the viewer by showing him a trick or technique not generated by the content and uncalled for by necessity.
>
> (Vertov quoted in Michelson, 1985 p. 187)

Vertov was constrained by the rules associated with the Kino-eye. His language of film became more abstract. He ignored the techniques that his contemporaries explored and experimented with, thus losing the potential to develop the language of the people that others were working towards.

Interactive film texts will employ spatial montage arranged temporally over a flexible navigational structure. The spatial layout of the visuals may depend on the level or timing of user interaction. Directors of interactive films do not create fixed works. The traditional system of 'locking' an edit weeks before a film's release is necessary to allow distribution of a single uniform product. If a film is not properly locked, it is possible that several final versions could be released at once, each one featuring some minor changes in colour grading, editing tweaks etc. Locking an interactive title will fix the shots and scenes but not the edit process. The user will create some of the edits while viewing.

Interactive titles will require some user knowledge prior to viewing. For the user to make informed interaction decisions, they must know something about the text already. This is quite common in today's film distribution cycle as films are endlessly reviewed, critiqued and judged prior to release. Film sequels work with the audience's in-depth and intimate knowledge of the story world and are careful not to contradict or simply repeat the original.

While interactive films may be viewed in small groups, allowing for all audience members to interact, they will also be viewed by individual viewers. The shared element of the experience will take place during intervals or after the film where users speak to each other and share and debate their perspectival knowledge. Spatially developed stories will ensure that users will be given multiple perspectives of the narrative; too many for one person to view in a single sitting but enough for a group to discuss the various permutations in a post-viewing discussion. Eisenstein identified the subjective audience responses to colour and form that made codification impossible. Vertov attempted to build a universal language of visuals without intertitles. This in itself limited the interpretative potential of the film. Its meaning was fixed for the audience, making it a less satisfying experience to watch. A cinema audience's shared experience is made up in part by the process of decoding the meaning of the text. Post-viewing discussions and argument allow individuals to gradually make up their mind as to the meaning and the impact of the narrative. Fixed visuals presented a static and unrewarding viewing experience. The dynamic spectacle that is interactive film laid out temporally in spatial montage can potentially be a more satisfying experience than traditional film. The spatial layout and navigational interface are guarantees to the audience that the work has been created for them to 'experience'; it has been created for their intellectual synthesis and subsequent response. The viewer as co-author of the text is a fundamental shift away from the passive, inert and powerless reader. The reader can now do more than simply interpret; the reader can 'see' around the text, into the world created by the author, making reality-style decisions such as following specific narrative pathways and ignoring others.

6

Codifying Story Elements

The codification of audiovisual content allows an author/director to signify meaning within the narrative through the quantification and classification of story elements. The narrative can be structured according to a predetermined arc using codified clips that can be viewed across multiple navigational pathways. Codification of story elements enables the author to create a narrative that is archived as a database of clips. These clips are accessed sequentially via an interactive user interface and their narrative order is influenced by viewer interaction. The codification criteria are story dependent. An interactive horror story will probably quantify story elements according to their level of blood, gore and fright potential. A romantic tale will emphasise more thoughtful criteria such as emotion, level of sacrifice and dialogue. This chapter looks at the classification and archiving of traditional narrative elements and considers their relevance to interactive storytelling. It goes on to explore the database as a repository for story texts and the use of algorithms in narrative construction.

PROPP'S *MORPHOLOGY OF THE FOLK TALE*

Vladimir Propp states that 'function is understood as an act of a character, defined from the point of view of its significance for the course of the action' (Propp, 1968 p. 21). Propp sought to codify the elements of Russian folk tales and create a scientific breakdown of their narrative components. He considered folk tales to be the textual archive of the country's cultural history and a record of times gone by. He noted that folk tales can be deconstructed to reveal the patterns of life that existed at the time of their writing. At some stage in the evolution of social groups, a religious belief system was constructed which was based upon people's daily lives. This belief system reflected their everyday life in much the same way that the folk tale does. However, Propp observes that 'a way of life and religion die out, while their contents turn into tales' (Propp, 1968 p. 106).

Propp states that the creators of folk tales were writing down what they saw, they did not invent the stories. They observed the world around them and adapted what they saw into folk tales. By deconstructing the tale, we can identify social patterns in the lives of the writers. Propp believed that there were a fixed number of folk tales. All were simply variations of single themes. The structure and incidentals could be changed, but the story remained the same:

> The entire store of fairy tales ought to be examined as a chain of variants. Were we able to unfold the picture of transformations, it would be possible that all of the tales given can be morphologically deduced from the tales about kidnapping of a princess by a dragon – from that form we are inclined to consider as basic.
>
> (Propp, 2001 p. 114)

Propp also noted that tales that have been written down for us to study are relatively recent phenomena and this collection of work only began after the stories had begun to break down and fragment. He discovered that there were periods of great creativity and development, and periods of stagnation. Although Propp was convinced of their existence, the texts of the periods of creativity were not recorded or written down and we can only speculate as to their origin and content.

NARRATOLOGY: HOW NARRATIVE STRUCTURES AFFECT OUR PERCEPTION

Mieke Bal states that interpretation of the text is open-ended and that meaning is fully dependent on the relationship between the author and the work. Meaning is derived from the process of writing and reading; 'once we acknowledge both the necessity and the strategic nature of limits to interpretation, we move from the question of the author back to the question of interpretation' (Bal, 1985 p. 17). This challenges the notion of the author/director as undisputed controller of interpretation and the meaning of a text. The meaning is derived from the audience's interpretation. However, Bal goes on to note that this process should become a method of exclusion, where the act of interpretation becomes a privilege only available to the few.

Bal uses formulaic elements to codify the content of the text: she refers to the EN (External Narrator), CN (Character-bound Narrator), CF (Character-bound Focalizor). These elements are used to create formulas that allow analysis of the text, e.g. in a text where an irritating character is speaking, it is the speaker who focalises the event. The conversation can be represented as: EN [CF (character angry) – other character]. The narrator, the focaliser and the actor are each of different identity. The narrator is EN, the focaliser is 'character angry' and the actor is 'other character'.

NARRATOLOGY TERMINOLOGY: SYNECDOCHE, CONTIGUOUS, METONYM

In narratology theory, the term synecdochical is a figure of speech where the name of a part is used when referring to the whole; using the whole for a part, using the general for the special, using the special for the general, calling the thing the name of the material that makes it (using the word 'steel' when talking about a 'sword'). Contiguous refers to touching, neighbouring, adjacent. A metonym is a figure of speech in which a word is substituted for another word that it is closely associated to (using the word 'Washington' when talking about 'the United States').

Embedded narrative texts are used in the story *Arabian Nights,* a story about Scheherazade who tells stories to the king to prevent her husband being killed. Embedded narratives run contiguously with the primary narrative. In narratology theory, the fabula is defined as the content of the story, a series of logically and chronologically related events that are caused or experienced by actors. A story can be made up of a primary fabula and several embedded fabulas. The syuzhet is the presentation of those events told through form, the form being camera angles, narration etc.

EMBEDDED NARRATIVES: FABULA AND SYUZHET

Embedded narratives are usually non-narrative embedded texts. They are mostly dialogue, yet they can take any form including discussions, descriptions, and confidences. With this dialogue, it is the actors, not the primary narrator, that utter the language. In 'dramatic texts', the whole text is spoken by actors, who together through their interaction, produce meaning. The meta-narrative is an untold story that unifies and totalises the world, and justifies a culture's power struggles, i.e. what is really going on. In the text it is also known as the framing story.

In my own interactive film *The Little Extras* (see Appendix 1) the audience was given the opportunity at various points in the narrative to change their perspective on the story. This allowed them to choose to focus more on the experience of a particular character. The story itself could not be altered, just the viewer's perspective. This resulted in varying interpretations of the text. The meta-narrative was presented as a combination of primary narrative and embedded narratives, navigated by the audience via an interactive interface. The interaction and perspective-altering navigation differentiated the experience of viewing. Bal writes that narrative perspective in literature has become increasingly important. It has been the 'prime means of manipulation' for over two centuries, 'the point of view from which the elements of the new fabula are being presented is often of decisive importance for the meaning the reader will assign to the fabula' (Bal, 1985 p. 79).

A PERSPECTIVAL APPROACH TO NARRATIVE

Narrative perspective positions the audience relative to the text. It creates a uniquely singular observational viewpoint with regard to characters, plot and story. With this approach to storytelling it is possible that the chronology can be represented out of order, enhancing its impact, yet still maintaining narrative coherence. While written linguistic text is linear, in a narrative text it is possible to speak of a 'double linearity', that of the text, the series of sentences, and that of the fabula, the series of events. Altering the sequential ordering can focus the reader's attention on specific story elements, 'to emphasise, to bring about aesthetic or psychological effects, to show various interpretations of an event, to indicate the subtle difference between expectation and realisation' (Bal, 1985 p. 82).

The differences between the chronology of the fabula and the arrangement of the story are called chronological deviations or anachronies. The beginning of *The Iliad* is made up of five units numbered one to five. Chronologically the order is 4, 5, 3, 2 and 1. The anachronies can be presented – A4, B5,

C3, D2, E1. Anachronies are separated from the reader's timeline, 'an event presented in anachrony is separated by an interval, large or small, from the "present"'. If we compare the time of the fabula to story time, their differences become clear, 'a truly synchronic scene in which the duration of the fabula coincided completely with that of the presentation in the story, would be unreadable' (Bal, 1985 p. 106).

SUBJECTIVE RETROVERSION

Retroversion within the text is moving back in time. Bal gives the example sentence 'Last year I went to Indonesia for a month' where the span of time is a month yet the distance of the time is one year. With 'subjective retroversion', time is slowed and every nuance is described. In Lars Von Trier's *Europa* (1991), tense moments are presented from different visual perspectives onscreen at the same time. Shots are repeated spatially, out of sync, allowing the audience to witness an event several times. This enhances the emotional intensity of the scene and allows the audience to recover from the effects of attentional blink.

Repetition, accumulation, relations to other characters and transformations are the four principles which work together to construct the image of a character; 'When a character appears for the first time we do not yet know very much about it. The qualities that are implied in that first presentation are not all *grasped* by the reader' (Bal, 1985 p. 125). When a character is presented by means of their actions we deduce from these actions certain 'implicit qualifications'. The reader will perceive the character by what they see them do. Yet what they see may be contradictory, a virtuous character may commit a seemingly unvirtuous act. These implicit qualifications are open to reader interpretation and can be used within the text to uncover secrets; the reader has to search for the truth. An explicit qualification is more absolute and less open to interpretation; a character that commits a murder is explicitly qualified as a murderer.

The space defined and created within the text is expanded through references to distant objects, to suggest a world beyond the immediate position of a character. 'Point-of-view' and 'narrative perspective' do not distinguish between the character vision presenting the elements and the identity of the voice that is verbalising that vision. There is no distinction between those who see and those who speak. In principle, all actants (a villain is both a character and an integral structural element) are represented in each fabula: without actants there are no relations, without relations there is no process, without process there is no fabula. Coincidental events may take place within the narrative across multiple story sequences; 'the elaboration of parallel strings of one fabula makes it difficult to recognise one single chronological sequence in that fabula. Several events happen at the same time' (Bal, 1985 p. 273).

THE PHOTOGRAPH: A MESSAGE WITHOUT A CODE

Photo essays are a good development tool for storytelling. Like the act of paraphrasing, a photographer must select only the most pertinent still images from a period of time to communicate the essence of the story and to move the narrative forward. Roland Barthes examines 'the special status of the photographic image: it is a message without a code; from which proposition an important corollary must immediately be drawn: the photographic message is a continuous message' (Barthes, 1978 p. 17). Barthes explains that describing a photograph is an impossible task, as the process of description changes the sense and adds meaning to the photograph. The act of creating the image from composition within the viewfinder, recording a latent image in silver halide crystals, development/ enhancement of the grain size to make visible, fixing the 'exposed' image and printing the negative using various techniques of dodging and burning all add to the image's message. The image connotes different meanings at the different stages of production. The description of the image will be different depending on the person describing it, the circumstances surrounding their viewing of the image and their perspective. Each has a number of different possible readings and interpretations built into it; 'all images are polysemous; they imply, underlying their signifiers, a "floating chain" of signifieds, the reader able to choose some and ignore others' (Barthes, 1978 p. 39). Text used with images 'anchors' the meaning of the photograph and 'directs' the audience towards a particular interpretation. Text is perceived to be more concrete and less plastic in its potential interpretation, text positions the image absolutely in one perspectival orientation. The photographic image is immediately perceived to be a supporter of the meaning as defined by the dominating text. Non-photographic visuals have a different relationship with the text, called relay. In comics the image and text are complementary. In film texts the dialogue gives additional meaning to the image, meaning that could not be conveyed by the image itself. Dialogue enhances the perception of complex relationships between characters and their motivations within the text.

WAR PRIMER: BRECHT'S PHOTO-EPIGRAMS

In his book *War Primer* (1955), Bertolt Brecht juxtaposed cut-out newspaper photographs (collected over many years) with his own text, to create 'photo-epigrams'. Each piece of text is a four-line poem and together with the image it offers an alternative view of the war to the traditional Western outlook. Brecht was unhappy with how photography was used as a propaganda tool during World War II. The photographers Adam Broomberg and Oliver Chanarin created the limited edition *War Primer II* (2013) with photo-epigrams depicting the 'so-called War on Terror' made up of images appropriated from the Internet.

TALKING PICTURES: PHOTOGRAPHIC STILLS AND AUDIO VIGNETTES

Photographer Daniel Meadows began his short-form narrative series called *Talking Pictures* in the north of England in the 1970s. Meadows photographed members of the public and recorded the voice of each person on audio tape, allowing them to tell their own story. Up to 40 years later, he revisited his archive and the audio and still image were stitched together as an audiovisual vignette of his subjects' lives. These wonderfully evocative pieces are a poignant reminder of people and place – in the style of Perec's 'infra-ordinary'.

PEREC'S 'INFRA-ORDINARY'

In Paris, 1969, the novelist and essayist Georges Perec determined to visit two locations each month, to write a description of them onsite, and to then write another when he was somewhere else 'to evoke all the memories that come to me concerning it' (Perec, 2008 p. 55). Perec would ask a photographer to capture some images of the places, which he would seal in an envelope with wax, having never looked at them. He included other paraphernalia from the visit including Métro tickets, bar slips and cinema tickets. The following year, on a different month he would revisit each place and describe it again; 'what I hope for from it, in effect, is nothing other than the record of a threefold experience of ageing: of the places themselves, of my memories, and of my writing' (Perec, 2008 p. 55). Perec described his work as an attempt 'to try meticulously to retain something, to cause something to survive; to wrest a few precise scraps from the void as it grows, to leave somewhere a furrow, a trace, a mark or a few signs' (Perec, 2008 p.92). Stephen Shore's photo book

Uncommon Places (1982) features his symmetrically organised photographs of 'the everyday'. Travelling across America in 1973, he shot on a 10" × 8" plate camera, all the time documenting in a diary 'what he ate, how long he drove, what he saw on TV and at the movies, how many photographs he took' (Shore, 2007 p. 10). Photographer Henri Cartier-Bresson walked the streets of Marseille with his Leica camera, 'to seize, in the confines of one single photograph, the whole essence of some situation' (Cartier-Bresson, 2004 p. 22). In doing this, he was capturing the 'decisive moment', an instant within a given period of time that represents both the immediate past and the future of a temporal event, observed in the 'search of objective chance' (Cartier-Bresson, 2004 p. 67).

In his book, *The Present* (2012), photographer Paul Graham sought 'the breaking down of the decisive moment, not allowing life to become this single frozen shard, trying to reflect something of the flow of time in the work' (Graham quoted in Jobey, 2012). Graham photographed each scene twice, a short time apart, and paired the images together for exhibition. His intention was to capture 'the way life comes at us, unbidden, and without perfect little narratives' (Graham quoted in Jobey, 2012).

DE QUINCEY'S RECORD OF REGENCY LONDON

In 1821 the writer Thomas De Quincey had imagined himself 'writing at a distance of twenty – thirty – fifty years ahead of this present moment' to create the detailed recollection *Confessions of an English Opium-Eater* (De Quincey, 1994 p. 168). He believed that in the future, someone would be interested in some aspect of his work, but first it must be written down. De Quincey included a poignant memory of his life in London. At one point, he was almost destitute; unable to afford lodgings he resided temporarily at a vacant house on Greek Street, Soho which he shared with a 'poor, friendless child, apparently ten years old'. At night, the child 'crept close to me for warmth, and for security against her ghostly enemies' (De Quincey, 1994 p. 120). This delicate description of an obscure act of human kindness invites the reader to forensically deconstruct, then reconstruct an experience which, without his archival record, would simply have been lost in time.

THE PHOTOGRAPH: FLAT ANTHROPOLOGICAL FACT

The photograph presents what was actually there, not an illusion (such as drawing). This reduces the level of possible interpretation. Real-time features such as frame rates and the visual perception phenomenon called persistence of vision (where a succession of stills images are perceived as smooth motion) do not inhibit the interpretation of the photograph. The photograph can be read in stillness or within the context of linear time, always moving forward, always changing; 'the photograph must be related to a pure spectatorial consciousness and not to the more projective, more "magical" fictional consciousness on which film by and large depends' (Barthes, 1978 p. 45). The level of manipulation required to create any moving image adds meaning and adjusts perspective; the photograph as a fragment of time taken from one perspective can be seen as more absolute in its meaning. Barthes describes photographs as being 'flat anthropological fact ... messages without a code' (Barthes, 1978 p. 45) containing an 'obtuse meaning' that 'appears to extend outside culture, knowledge, information' (Barthes, 1978 p. 55). Barthes believed that there is emotion in this obtuse meaning.

Barthes examined the meaning of film. He believed the filmic elements in film were those that could not be described, that the filmic begins 'where language and metalanguage end' (Barthes, 1978 p. 64). This places film outside the descriptive power of traditional texts, enhanced with a third meaning that cannot be described. This suggests that film is a more emotional experience than the printed text or the photograph. Its active and immersive nature creates a symbiotic relationship whereby attentive film viewing results in emotional satisfaction; and the activity of viewing connotes additional meaning within the narrative. The still image dissociates the 'technical constraint' from the 'indescribable' meaning and institutes 'a reading that is at once instantaneous and vertical, [and which] scorns logical time' (Barthes, 1978 p. 68).

BRECHT'S THEORY OF DISTANCIATION

The actor too must function primarily as an element of the narrative, and not be held back by 'reality', to become a sovereign power within the text, able to move freely to convey the meaning of the text, as in Brecht's theory of 'distanciation'. Distanciation is the term used to describe the effect of distancing the spectator through the use of non-traditional form/techniques or textual content. Barthes describes narrative progression as a three-dimensional construct that needs to be 'read' in both horizontal and vertical axes:

> To understand a narrative is not merely to follow the unfolding of the story, it is also to recognise its construction in 'storeys', to project the

horizontal concatenations of the narrative 'thread' onto an implicitly vertical axis; to read (to listen to) a narrative is not merely to move from one word to the next, it is also to move from one level to the next.

(Barthes, 1978 p. 87)

The text is understood by both reading the words and by comparing and connecting elements within the narrative. Character relationships and plot developments take time to create. The reader's access to the intellectual property created by complex narrative elements, does not relate to the narrative in a linear way. Rather, narrative progression results in 'bursts' of narrative constructs that become clear to the reader when their description is complete.

The description of these constructs is broken down into narrative indices and informants. Indices refer to character identity, feelings, atmosphere; informants locate the story in place and time. Informants 'are pure data with immediate signification. Indices involve an activity of deciphering, the reader is to learn to know a character or an atmosphere; informants bring ready-made knowledge' (Barthes, 1978 p. 96). Informants reference the prior knowledge of the reader. This knowledge brings with it a range of related text that broadens the character of the text being read. As the narrative unfolds, each character takes a perspective on the sequence of actions they are involved in. A charlatan may charm the young woman. From his perspective she is naïve and foolish to believe him, yet from her perspective she is trusting and virtuously innocent.

PRIMACY OF LEXIS OVER PLOT

Barthes suggests that the narrator can be described as the person who is writing the story; an omnipresent consciousness with a superior perspectival position; or a person relaying the story using only what the characters can know. He argues that modern texts are no longer concerned with conveying inner thoughts, accessing the mind of the character, but instead create a present that focuses on its own delivery. This suggests that the creation of the virtual worlds in interactive texts is part of a trend of the primacy of world (lexis) over plot (logos). Interactive narratives are known for their attention to detail in creating a world outside reality, not for their ability to verbalise complex reasoning and emotive experiences.

In relation to the narrative, experience equips the audience with the necessary faculties to access the text. Audiences seek out explanations and enlightenment from the author of the text, the person who is seen to be the ultimate authority on its meaning and interpretation. Yet the meaning of the text is derived from the work of the author and the work (interpretation) of the reader. The meaning of the text would not exist without either. Therefore, traditional texts already offer an interactive environment, inviting the reader to create meaning through interpretation. Barthes points out that 'classic criticism has never paid any attention to the reader; for it, the writer is the only person in literature' (Barthes, 1978 p. 148).

The modern narrative is doing something to inject new life into the lethargic approach to textual consumption, an approach which has resulted in increasingly bored audiences, unable or unwilling to open the text's meaning. Revitalising the audience's perspective on the narrative will generate new audiences, creating a new, shared experience.

Certain constraints still exist within contemporary narratives. In the quest for new narrative forms and approaches, the text cannot be allowed to become so obtuse that it creates a barrier to its interpretation. In virtual worlds, the complexity of the technology, the conceptuality of interactivity can create this barrier. Yet whichever approach is used, speech cannot be retracted, except by saying that one is retracting it. Once the word has been uttered in the text, it becomes part of the story lexia (constitutive elements or unique units of meaning within the text). The tacit contract that is established between people to regulate relations is often not respected. This also applies to the contract between author and reader. If modes of authorship, textual representation and analysis are established and then contravened, the relationship itself breaks down, and the text cannot be accessed.

VISUALISATION OF LARGE DATA SETS

Lev Manovich's team at the Software Studies Initiative and Cultural Analytics Lab visualise quantified data in order to research and exhibit visual culture; 'media visualizations methods give us new ways to understand the history of photography, to compare content and aesthetics of millions of photographs being created today' (Sutton, 2011 p. 19). Manovich considers the process of digital image creation and storage, and the skill set and knowledge that is required to work with digital data:

> if we want to think about photography today, we should consider its new condition as data organized in data structures and databases, and the interfaces and the logic of popular software used to access, edit, and distribute this data.
>
> (Sutton, 2011 p. 19)

His team create these visual artefacts using a process they call *mediavis* to 'democratise data mining' where specialist knowledge of statistics is not required to visually represent the patterns that are found within large data sets. This computational analysis of media data allows us to consider cultural memory. Vast stores of information, generated for both local and global consumption, framed and reframed by social and economic context, a manipulation of the historical record.

METADATA: TAGGING ARCHIVED CONTENT

Software interfaces use a common architecture. This ensures users can adapt quickly to new functionality that is embedded within a recognisable display. Digital images are tagged with metadata that describes and classifies them; 'all media now share the condition of "searchability". The degree of searchability depends on the type and amount of metadata stored with the objects' (Sutton, 2011 p. 19). The person tagging the data is making informed choices on the relevance of their selections, personalising the process and leaving their archival mark for future researchers. Digital images have a high degree of 'remixability'. Elements can be isolated and combined with other media. Even traditional photographs, shot on film, are digitised for curation and exhibition so that they eventually become digital artefacts which can be incorporated into *mediavis*. Manovich questions the definition of photography that includes both the traditional and new media:

> it is hard for me to accept that Daguerreotypes and contemporary photography belong to the same medium. Perhaps there was never such a thing as photography. It was just a series of different media lumped together.
>
> (Sutton, 2011 p. 20)

The metatagging of traditional photographic images is different to the capturing of digital images where metadata is attached at the moment of creation.

THE PHOTO ARCHIVE

The Magnum photo agency was founded in 1947 and has since created a significant image archive of contemporary culture, important events, news stories and celebrities. Both the archival database of images and new photographs are metatagged with descriptive data to allow future researchers to discover and digitally mine their content. However, the creator of the metatags will exert great influence over this research as it is their perspective of the image object that the tags 'describe'. Therefore, 'the resulting narrative is a construct, created by a storyteller to suit contemporary political and commercial needs' (McErlean, 2014).

In 1859 Oliver Wendell Holmes 'envisioned libraries of images – images of everything, a record of every architectural detail, where the original object is no longer needed' (McErlean, 2014). He proposed that the knowledge detail of important objects could be made available in multiple centres around the world. The photographs, drawings, descriptions and measurements of the works would provide an alternative experience to the original, one that is not unique, but that was certainly more accessible. 'Authentic recreations' of Tutankhamun's sarcophagus and replicas of treasures taken from his tomb recently toured Europe, offering the 'experience' of closely viewing this archaeological discovery. The Metropolitan Museum in New York exhibits a late sixteenth-century carved oak panelled room from Great Yarmouth in Norfolk, England which was taken apart and shipped to the US in the early 1900s. The display allows one to walk around and touch the original wood walls, yet the sense of 'presence' is diminished due to the fact that the room is no longer in-situ. You are inside it, but it is not in its original geographical location. The experience of visiting the room creates an approximation of Walter Benjamin's 'aura' which described art's 'unique existence at the place where it happens to be' (Benjamin, 1999 p. 214). In 1998 I stood in Potsdamer Platz, Berlin and listened to a street-based sound installation which played audio recordings dating back to the 1930s – live recordings of political speeches, public gatherings and incidents which had taken place on or near that spot. It was the sense of presence that made the recordings so profound. I was listening to an aural perspective of an historical event that had taken place in that same spatial location.

PHOTOGRAMMETRY: CYBER-ARCHAEOLOGY

Information held on databases can be exploited to create new digital versions of any object. In the Universidad de Murcia (Murcia, Spain),

Project Mosul is collecting crowd-sourced images of rare artefacts which have been lost to violence and natural disasters. These 'cyber-archaeologists' use a technique called photogrammetry 'to turn multiple 2D photographs of a single object into 3D images' (Webb, 2015) in order to create a digital facsimile. The researchers have requested that members of the public submit their travel holiday images of specific (recently destroyed) sites. The images are collated, then used to construct a photo-realistic digital version of the artefact, one that could even be used in the future to build a physical copy of the original.

TREND-IDENTIFYING ALGORITHMS

The storytelling app Wattpad allows writers to upload and share stories with a global online community (Laporte, 2016). The app enables users to receive highly responsive and detailed feedback from readers. It is used as a marketing tool. 20th Century Fox and Universal Studios have promoted films on Wattpad, asking contributors to create stories that are related to their latest release. Wattpad authors with significant levels of readership have had stories optioned by film companies to go into full-scale production. The site uses 'trend-identifying algorithms to try and tap new writers and ideas', then partner them with studios and distribution networks. Data analytics produce a 'nuanced data supply' that shows which scenes, chapters and paragraphs resonated most with audiences, and which didn't. Data also includes reader demographics, location, time spent on specific sections, and can be used to spot a career trajectory on the rise. The site's global reach means that they can have 'local writers writing for local audiences'. As the Wattpad community socialises in and around serialised texts, the writers develop a direct relationship with their fans, communicating with them regularly for feedback and comment.

NETFLIX QUANTUM THEORY

'Netflix Quantum Theory' uses tagged film elements to data-mine viewing figures. Algorithms process the data and the statistics are cross-referenced with audience demographics to offer personalised recommendations to individual customers. 'Netflix has created a database of 76,897 micro-genres that offer a peek into the American psyche' (Angelica, 2014). The information is also used to identify a particular demand for audiovisual content that can be commissioned or purchased from local and international production companies.

Contextual operating systems will data-mine so much information about your online habits and preferences that they will pre-empt user choices and make decisions on your behalf to search the web, launch apps, even before you make the decision yourself. In other words, your operating system will know you intimately.

AUTHORING MULTIPLE NARRATIVE TRAJECTORIES

A database of audiovisual clips can be presented in any order using both linear and nonlinear access. Clips can be 'navigated' by the user via screen-based, tactile or gesture-controlled interfaces. Navigating the narrative enables different viewers to gain different perspectives on a single story. These perspectives are what make interactive film fundamentally different from linear film. The word 'interactive' has many different meanings in new media discourse. What is often referred to as interactive is seldom anything more than user choice, i.e. the user can decide to pick a navigation route marked 'a', 'b' or 'c'. While this choice affects the resulting navigation of the story it is difficult to argue that the viewer has actually interacted with the narrative. The narrative already exists as written by the author. The narrative options may be varied but the user interaction is not 'creating' narrative pathways. Instead, interaction allows the user to navigate various pre-existing options.

Lev Manovich refers to these pathways as 'multiple trajectories'. He notes that allowing the user the option to select one of these multiple trajectories does not constitute the development of an interactive narrative: 'the author also has to control the semantics of the elements and the logic of their connection so that the resulting object will meet the criteria of narrative' (Manovich, 2002 p. 228).

THE DATABASE

The database holds the 'content' that the reader will observe as they navigate the story. Deleuze and Guattari call the database either a striated place to travel through or a smooth place to be explored for pleasure and discovery (Ryan, 2001 p. 47). Manovich calls a database a 'structured collection of data'. Different types of database have been developed by the IT sector including hierarchical, network, relational and object-oriented. These are selected according to the system being developed, e.g. library lending system, traffic flow, aviation, and command and control systems. Complex database models can cross-reference information in order to present new data that has been developed 'on-the-fly'. In most new-media projects the database is a simple one that calls single database elements according to the user's selections. The Internet is a simple database model which presents images, text and downloadable files according to an HTML document. This document provides layout information that indicates the relative size and position of each element: 'a web page is a sequential list of separate elements' (Manovich, 2002 p. 220). HTML is a universal protocol that all web browsers can work with. This ensures that web pages written in HTML will be presented as intended, no matter what part of the world they are being viewed in.

Many new-media objects work as databases; 'they appear as collections of items on which the user can perform various operations' (Manovich, 2002 p. 219). Web pages are continually updated, so this presents new problems in narrative terms. A new approach to narrative structures must be employed if a website is to be seen as a story and not simply a collection of data elements. This highlights 'the anti-narrative logic of the web' where 'the result is a collection, not a story' (Manovich, 2002 p. 221). Manovich identifies several examples of database narratives including Chris Marker's *IMMEMORY* (1997) and George Legrady's *Tracing* (1997) and *Slippery Traces* (1996). 'As a cultural form, the database represents the world as a list of items, and it refuses to order this list. In contrast, a narrative creates a cause-and-effect trajectory of seemingly unordered items (events)' (Manovich, 2002 p. 225).

HYPERNARRATIVE

Manovich defines hypernarrative (interactive narrative) as 'the sum of multiple trajectories through a database' (Manovich, 2002 p. 227). He gives an example of this in the online narrative *My Boyfriend came Back from the War* (1996) by Olia Lialina. This story offers multiple non-linear narrative threads through the conversation between a boyfriend and girlfriend when they meet after some time apart. Here, basic use is made of web technologies to offer an interactive narrative.

Manovich states that the author has to control the trajectories in terms of semantics and logic. Randomly chosen elements may not form a narrative. The author must identify narrative pathways and write around them. In this way, the author will have travelled every route that the potential audience may travel. Some narrative pathways may be redundant in that they do not progress the story. The author will probably remove these, as they would result in the reader losing interest. The database of narrative nodes, or pre-scripted chapters which the audience can navigate between, has been written in advance. The navigation of the individual reader is in flux, yet the database elements are static; 'the narrative is virtual while the database exists materially' (Manovich, 2002 p. 231).

Spatialised narrative was once the dominant form of European visual culture. It ended up only in comics and technical illustrations. New media presents information on the screen simultaneously. When physical interaction is built into an interface it takes the form of interaction between the user and the computer at the expense of psychological interaction. Icons are presented on screen to represent elements of data that can be retrieved in full by clicking on the link. Data is retrieved in its original form without any user-initiated change to its structure. A more sophisticated interaction would allow the user's selections to alter the physical construct of the data being presented. Therefore, the composition of the data (film clip, photograph, sound clip) would depend on the user's input.

Cinema and books are traditionally seen as linear presentations of pre-written texts. New-media content is considered non-linear due to the navigation structure that employs hyperlinks to data elements. However, traditional books can also be accessed in a non-linear mode and still make coherent sense. Readers often revisit chapters and paragraphs for clarification or enjoyment before continuing on with the general thrust of the story. Films in digital format allow non-sequential access to their content that enables viewers to skip back and forward through 'chapters'. Pages in websites that use a 'branch-based-navigation structure often have to be read sequentially before the user can be sure where specific content actually is. After reading everything the site has to offer, the user goes back to the home page to begin a 'nonlinear navigation'.

EXTRACTIVE HYPERTEXT AND IMMERSIVE 3D

Interface navigation is interaction with the text; this cannot be passive, as it requires work on the part of the audience in the form of decisions. Peter Lunenfeld's research into immersive navigation noted two interaction paradigms within the application of database technologies: 'extractive' hypertext and 'immersive' 3D worlds (Lister et al, 2003 p. 21). The database has been created by the author and effectively contains many narrative perspectives and outcomes. The experience is controlled through interaction, which can be dynamic or passive. Interactive texts offer many navigational pathways through the narrative. This makes comparisons of texts difficult. Different readers will have different perspectives on the story depending on their navigational choices, making conceptual and critical comparisons of interactive texts difficult. For many, the only way to discuss such a text is to talk about the metanarrative or world text that encompasses the general story. Specific analyses of character relationships and plot interactions are difficult as readers may or may not have experienced them despite interacting with the text fully. A successful interactive text will leave the reader feeling satisfied, despite having navigated the text through just one perspectival route. If the reader feels the need to continue reading until all database elements have been read, then the interactive text is a glorified linear narrative. The traditional method of comparing notes on the text will be superseded by the experience of 'sharing' textual elements that may have been missed or explored through to navigational decisions. The text has been 'read' but not all the database elements have been visited. Readers will therefore continue to learn more about the story following the reading experience when they talk to other readers who have followed different perspectival routes. This is not so different from the subjective analysis of linear texts. It is common for readers to share their thoughts on significant text elements that may not have been noticed by other readers.

ASSOCIATIVE LINKAGE

The method of accessing the database elements may follow an associative linkage structure. Associative linkage, like hypertext, is how the mind works. Memories are connected by related elements; story elements in an interactive narrative are related by content. Protohypertexts are texts that challenge the linearity of texts – examples are *I Ching*, Sterne's *Tristram Shandy* (1759), Joyce's *Ulysses*, various stories by Borges, Calvino and Robert Coover; in cinema films by Vertov, Eisenstein and Kurosawa. The traditional model is being usurped in the quest to find a new model of storytelling, one that adds to the experience for the reader to make the story come alive, be more memorable and perhaps challenge the passive receptivity of modern audiences. Post-structural literary criticism argues that texts have an 'intertextual character', texts relate to other texts and the reader as much as the author creates meaning. Texts that have been read more than once have an expanded meaning to the reader as relationships between text elements begin to form. These may be the result of more in-depth analysis, or external factors that are now impacting on the reader's interpretation. Books can be navigated more freely, whereas hypertext links must be checked to avoid downloading the same information. In interactive texts, accessing the same content over and over is often seen as a mistake and leads to less satisfaction in the reader who was expecting fresh content leading to new experiences.

GENRE CLASSIFICATION

Data can be categorised according to genre. This has been used to develop virtual radio broadcasters that transmit a series of musical pieces which are connected through history, tempo, artists, format etc. A database of music contains several thousand tracks. Each track is placed in categories and subcategories. An algorithm builds a playlist made up of a musical medley of 'connected' tracks. This is like a physical library where related texts are placed on the same shelf. With the music database, the tracks are selected to gradually change the mood of the music being played to keep the audience interested.

THE CINEMATIC METAPHOR

Interacting with content emphasises the production process. Without interaction, scenes tail off waiting for user input. If a scene reaches the end of its timeline it must repeat, or go to a 'waiting point'. This suspends narrative progress indefinitely while the story engine waits for input. Traditional interactive stories cannot proceed without input, and so the user becomes fundamental to the story (Manovich, 2002 p. 298).

The database is a fundamental component of interactive works. The interactive developer creates a database of story elements, to be accessed non-sequentially via a navigational interface. Adding story elements to the database increases the potential complexity of the narrative, and gives greater choice to the reader. However, the increase in complexity may lead to a directly proportional breakdown in narrative cohesion. Navigation pathways through the database elements should make sense to the reader and follow the rules of semantics and logic.

The database can hold information and simply retrieve it when called; or it can create data spontaneously in response to user interactions. Websites record user navigation and make changes to subsequent pages depending on user input. This dynamic build creates a unique experience for the user that is different from all others. The large volumes of data being made available by national broadcasters is leading to new navigational interfaces being developed to access this content in a logical and informed way. An intelligent interface tracks users' navigational pathways. The database of content will grow exponentially and will reduce the shared experience of televisual and cinematic audiences. The database will allow content to be viewed at the user's discretion, an individualistic approach that is unlike traditional broadcasting. However, current websites that offer video content for download feature ratings systems that are just like the audience monitoring systems employed by traditional broadcasters. Popular files receive the most requests for download in a relatively narrow time frame, which creates a shared viewing experience much like traditional broadcasting. Even the most popular files eventually fade into obscurity, having already been viewed by anyone who was interested. After this, the videos may be watched occasionally, but the elevated interest following their initial 'release' has passed. *The Little Extras* interactive film model created the potential for a database of film clips or scenes to be accessed via a graphic user interface. The organisation of scenes using a database allowed the footage to be accessed in a nonlinear manner. Eventually these clips will be codified and filed according to their content. Viewers will be presented with clips according to database rules and in response to user interaction.

NON-TRADITIONAL FILM: GORDON'S 'TEMPORAL DECELERATION'

Mark B.N. Hansen offers several arguments against many of Manovich's theories on cinematic metaphor and presents several examples of contemporary reworking of traditional films. Hansen opposes many of Manovich's theories and is particularly scathing on 'cinematic metaphor' as applied to new media (Hansen, 2006 p. 1). Hansen rejects Manovich's use of cinematic terms of reference to predict the future of interactive film. He believes that new media, with their computer-based architecture, requires a fundamentally different theoretical approach. Hansen focuses on alternative and non-traditional film works by independent film-makers. *24hr Psycho* (1993) is the original Hitchcock version of the film slowed down to two frames per second so that it takes twenty-four hours to play. Director Douglas Gordon is working with 'temporal deceleration' to focus the audience on the micro details of individual frames. The amount of time available allows greater deconstruction of the frame elements. Gordon also created a 47-day projection of *The Searchers* (1956) called *5 Year Drive-By* (1995) (Media Kunst Netz, 1999).

EMERGENT NARRATIVES

Emergent narratives allow users to configure their own experience within a story world; 'true emergent properties involve a series of interacting, interlocking systems, out of which arise novel solutions that the designer hasn't planned' (Biswas, 2016). With traditional texts, readers engage with a logically structured narrative, discovering and interpreting plot elements. An emergent narrative allows discovery in a 'world pre-seeded with possibility'. Warner Brothers' *Middle-Earth: Shadow of Mordor's* Nemesis system tracks the hierarchical relationships of characters and their 'procedurally chosen personalities'; individual characters remember your interactions with them and react accordingly on subsequent encounters. Sharang Biswas believes that emergent narratives are simply a 'different species' to the more rigidly structured traditional stories. He notes Mark Brown's question on how narrative devices such as foreshadowing and pacing could possibly be replicated in such 'systemic narratives'. Yet, in both story forms the reader 'unpacks' the story, piecing it together to make sense of it and to interpret the author's intention.

TRIANGULATING CONTENT

New distribution channels allow greater monitoring of user access. They offer audiences non-scheduled content targeted towards specific market segments. Twentieth-century mass media standardised 'content, distribution and production' to control and regulate media output and to set 'very clear distinctions between consumers and producers' (Lister et al, 2003 p.31). New distribution outlets enable authors to publish niche content, where the audience can access a range of related materials and triangulate their opinions, drawing on their own experiences and their reading of the text. While these outlets may give voice to many opinions, the boundaries between credible, trustworthy sources and unreliable ones is less clear.

* * *

This chapter has dealt with various methods of codifying texts and has explored the text as an archive. It has also considered the work of storytellers who have organised their work into a searchable database. An interactive narrative will need to codify the content of story elements (video, stills, text, graphics, audio) to coordinate their presentation depending on engagement with the interactive interface. The method of codification and codification criteria may refer to story content; colour analysis of frames; descriptors of atmosphere, mood, tone. 'Describing' the content allows it to be organised within a defined database structure. The creation of a story algorithm will arrange the codified content according to interactivity to build a unique and customised presentation.

The codification of content creates a significant level of work for the author/director. The interface of an interactive text is designed to work autonomously, independent of its creator whose influence ends when the story product is delivered to the reader. Faults in the interface will become features of the narrative; this is already a feature in online games where advanced players exploit bugs in the system. The test for an interactive film text is to create an immersive world that is also challenging and emotive. Where codified content is presented to the audience via an interface, the interface becomes part of the story structure. The interface takes the part of the narrator of traditional texts. Therefore, the interface must have a distinctive 'voice' that is recognisable to the audience as the authority on the story. The level of interface complexity and distinction should not become so distracting that it impedes viewer interaction with the text.

7

Interactive Narratives

Interactive narratives offer the viewer varying degrees of navigational control of the story. Pathways may be formulated and plotted to create new experiences and interpretations of the text. Multiple perspectives create a unique experience for each viewer. In production terms, interactivity within the narrative creates redundant content, scenes that may never be viewed, chapters that may never be read. This has made interactive film costs prohibitive. However, the potential of interactive narratives to create a new storytelling paradigm is both exciting and ambitious. In 2015, film-maker Steven Soderbergh announced an app-based interactive fiction called *Mosaic* (2017) which will allow the viewer to navigate a 'fixed universe'. Typically, the project involved a lot of trial and error to create 'a time-jumping, murder-focused "branching narrative piece" that gives viewers the "possibility of going right or left" after the first chapter and presents similar choices from there' (Canfield, 2017). *Mosaic* is also available as a six-episode series but Soderbergh insists that the interactive version is the 'ideal'. This chapter explores both historical and contemporary interactive narrative texts and theatrical performance. It considers choice-based narratives, virtual and augmented reality titles.

TEXTUAL INTERACTION

Textual interaction includes the act of 'reading' and 'viewing'. 'Interpretative relationships' and 'active material relationships' are created when we cut, tape or write in the margins of traditional analogue texts. With online content, we interpret the meaning of the text by talking about it with other people. Marshall McLuhan and Raymond Williams shared the idea that 'all new media "remediate" the content of previous media' (Lister et al, 2003 p. 77). Williams suggests that all technologies have uses and effects that were unforeseen and unintended by their developers (Williams quoted in Lister et al, 2003 p. 81). In the audiovisual sector the post-production workflow has been streamlined to increase efficiency and reduce costs while new distribution platforms remove market barriers and increase the availability of content to a wider audience. The complexity of technological implementation, experimentation and streamlining of systems, coupled with cultural needs and desires of the audience, makes predicting how technology will develop and be used with any degree of accuracy very difficult. Futurists are always hindered by the fact that they are working today, in the here and now, surrounded by today's needs and desires, and these may not be the needs and desires of future audiences. Williams argues that a technology must be defined as a social function as well as a technical system and the social does not always follow the technical as a matter of effect (Lister et al, 2003 p. 83). Text must be read by someone to be a communicative technology. McLuhan considers technology to be an extension of man; the medium is the message. John Berger states that 'ways of seeing' are shaped by ideas, institutions and technologies at different times (Berger quoted in Lister et al, 2003 p. 81). New technologies and their uses and applications come about when they are needed, not before. Also, new and old technologies exist together, not all are replaced or become obsolete. Television did not create the end of cinema; it just reduced its audience by taking some of its function into the home, where audiences actually wanted part of its function to exist.

CHAR DAVIES: *OSMOSE*

Audiences must acquire new competencies and skills to understand and utilise new technologies. As virtual and augmented reality become mainstream and accessible to all, the new visual culture will include images that are synthetic, created via algorithms independent of objects as referents. Mimesis, the skilful copying of the appearance of nature is giving way to 'simulation'. Virtual reality (VR) systems are not a 'complete sensory experience' but sometimes crude and cumbersome. Some VR platforms aim to produce photorealistic images, to create verisimilitude. Others contend that their remit is to create a fantasy world full of sensory states outside of our real world experience. Char Davies's *Osmose* (1995) created a highly immersive world where the viewer, wearing a VR headset, traversed a virtual world of colour and geometric shapes (Davies, 2008). The system did not feature photorealistic images yet its immersive potential was so profound that users found fifteen minutes overwhelming and reported that it was difficult to 'readjust' to the real world for some time after their immersion.

Many characterise electronic media products as being 'depthless', lacking the charm of traditional models. Popular cinema is thought to be dumbing down, creating simplified products that sell in multiple markets internationally. Digital spectacle has become a dominant feature of films. Audiences never fully suspend belief because they must judge the effect as well as the story. Science fiction creates a particular kind of realism where advances in technology are regularly showcased to audiences. The digital tools for telling stories are continuously evolving and audiences expect regular technological innovation in the film production cycle. In each film the conceptual leaps must first reference previous cinematic experiences then surpass audience expectations to order to be successful. In *The Abyss* (1989), director James Cameron employed digital effects house Digital Domain to make water appear to float and form into various objects including a human face. In *Terminator 2* (1991), Cameron used a considerably enhanced version of the technology to create a fully animated liquid metal cyborg capable of morphing into an infinite variety of complex shapes. It was important that the advance in the digital-effects technology was greater than the audience expected. However, over-emphasis on the 'newness' of technologies brings about a boom-and-bust cycle in cultural and media studies. This cycle prevents critical evaluation of new technologies.

PROPRIOCEPTION

Proprioception is the sense that tells us where the boundaries of our bodies are. Through a combination of physiological feedback loops and usage we become aware of these boundaries. Proprioceptive coherence with objects such as sports equipment makes us feel the equipment is part of our bodies. Reduced kinesthetic feedback loops, experienced when reading, prevent us from feeling attached to a page although we can become immersed in the story. The deeper the immersion the more the printed page is forgotten. Proprioceptive coherence is why spatial layout is so important in hypertexts.

ARTIST AND AUDIENCE: ATHERTON'S INTERACTIVE DISCOURSE

In Kevin Atherton's *Two Places/Two Performances* (1976), the artist repeated a performance art work he had previously presented in another gallery, this time with a video installation of the earlier work in situ. Atherton was exploring 'the idea that what was happening was *actual*, was really happening in the same time and space as the viewer' (Atherton, 2012 p. 34). Immediately after, he engaged with the audience in a discussion on the meaning of the performance, positioning himself as 'both the producer and the consumer of the work'. Atherton explored the potential of 'the vernacular in spoken or written language', favouring literature's 'writer-reader' paradigm to the art world's 'artist-viewer' model as a mechanism to 'step out of the work ... to reflect on the work' (Atherton, 2012 p. 49). In Beckett's *Malone Dies*, the writer anticipated the reader by talking directly to him about the text. This interactive relationship, this discourse between artist and audience, blurred the line between the fictional and the real world. Atherton continued this work with *In Two Minds* where he revisited a series of questions he asked on video in 1978, answering them live on stage 28 years later, to create 'a discourse about work'.

In 2015 Moira Buffini directed *wonder.land* at the Palace Theatre, Manchester, a musical adaptation of Lewis Carroll's *Alice's Adventures in Wonderland*. The staging of the play simultaneously presented multiple locations and events in a theatrical tableaux. Buffini says, 'theatre is more fluid than film. You can be inside someone's head and outside simultaneously; you can be in several different realities at the same time' (Hemming, 2015).

NON-LINEAR TEXTS

A linear text can be followed easily as long as the story does not contradict itself, thereby breaking the immersion. A non-linear text requires close study to ensure a logical story outcome where the viewer is taken on a journey and not led down a meandering 'blind alley'. With non-linear interactive narratives a significant design feature is the system of navigation. If it is over-designed and complex, the audience will take so long learning it, that the freshness of the text will be lost. If it is too simple and immediate, it will lack the sophistication to offer a complex or satisfying user interaction experience. Developing a title to be experienced rather than to educate will ensure the audience is immersed in the story. *Sin City* (2005) and *Hulk* (2003) use a comic-book presentation style where images are delivered as a spatial montage. This offers the viewer multiple simultaneous perspectives of the same scene or concurrent scenes. In *American Splendor* (2003) the comic-book style of spatial presentation used in the film is established during the opening credits. This informs the audience of the film's presentation style prior to viewing. As the opening credits end, the audience is comfortable with this stylistic format and subsequently can easily recognise and understand its use and meaning throughout the film. The self-reflexive nature of modernist works draw attention to the materials that created them (Hayward, 2006 p. 256). Yet the interactive film seeks to present its 'art' as native, with natural points of interactivity presenting, without the need to educate or inform the reader of their presence. The audience should not need to have the navigation interface explained to them; it should be organic and natural, a part of the film structure. Explaining the interface before would focus too much attention on its function and detract from the immersive nature of the film. Immersion allows the audience to concentrate on the reality created by the narrative without interruption from the 'real' world. Therefore, the interactive interface for interactive film needs to be uncomplicated. We can also see elements of non-linear storytelling in other art forms:

> The French garden is the horticultural equivalent of a framed painting; as an emergent landscape choreographed for a wandering eye and a moving body, the English garden is a metaphor for the space management and representation that we find in VR.
>
> (Ryan, 2001 p. 79)

SYNCRETIC AND SYNAESTHETIC LANGUAGE

Ryan notes that modern interactive technologies are not the first to fuse the impact of all media. 'In *Finnegans Wake*, as Donald Theall has shown, James Joyce attempted to create a syncretic and synaesthetic language that involved the entire sensorium and simulated the effects of all media' (Ryan, 2001 p. 55). As technology is becoming more miniaturised and yet more pervasive, computers are in a sense becoming invisible. All the viewer sees is the media, not the technology. The technocentric focus is gradually being replaced with a customer-centred usability. Technical knowledge is no longer a prerequisite for using digital equipment. Digital cameras are marketed towards people who do not have any knowledge of traditional processes. The technologies have a built-in obsolescence that negates the need for 'repairs'. This equipment is designed to be replaced regularly, not upgraded or mended.

THE DISRUPTING EFFECT OF LATENCY WITHIN SIMULATED STORIES

Simulated systems create stories that prospectively 'unfold' with the reader, unlike traditional stories which are delivered retrospectively with all the story elements and materials available for the listener's consideration. Simulated stories are generated to reflect the perspective that the reader chooses to take at each point within the narrative. In a simulation, a unique story is created 'on-the-fly' (Ryan, 2001 p. 64). Looking at modern interactive technologies, there are still some issues with regard to head-mounted systems having a disruptive lag time or latency in their response to the user's physical movement. Low latency is desired to promote the creation of a totally immersive world. A latency of 20 milliseconds or less is considered acceptable. A high degree of latency can even result in the user experiencing motion sickness.

Shutter release times in electronic cameras has long been an issue for professional photographers. The short delay reduces the sensorial connection achievable in purely manual systems. The camera captures the image some time after the photographer's finger releases, resulting in a temporal distance between image and intention. Some try to shoot early, pressing the button a split-second before the intended shot to compensate, but this is wholly unsatisfactory. Likewise, in the virtual world, the computational power required to generate graphics that instantly correspond to user head movements is significant. A lack of power can result in a visual response delay. This delay reminds the user that the world is computer-generated and not real life. Instant responses that correctly interpret user movements in a predictable and reliable manner provide a totally immersive world. This world is then an alternative to reality, as the 'reality' it creates offers all the sensorial information necessary to 'immerse' the user. Like good plots, good virtual reality systems should offer the element of surprise.

Genre films attract audiences partly because the audience knows what they are going to get for their money. The genre 'rules' may be bent a little to entertain (surprise), but there will be many of the same elements embedded in the film. This reduces the workload of the audience to interpret and deconstruct the narrative. The story is simply another version of a tale they have already heard. Like Propp's analysis of traditional folk tales, genre films consist of a variety of plot elements and character structures that are recognisable and allow complex narratives to be developed in a short space of time. The audience 'understands' how elements within the narrative fit together because of their knowledge of previous films within the genre.

INTERACTIVE STORYTELLING

In VR, the interface itself is often packaged to be part of the entertainment. Again, this technocentric approach ignores the audience's innate desire for a good story. The complexity of narrative development is evidenced by the relatively small number of trusted scriptwriters within the film-making community. These writers can be relied upon to deliver a well-structured, well-developed and entertaining script on time. The lack of such talent in the film industry is only exacerbated in the VR sector. Here, storytelling 'skills' must be fused with a solid knowledge of the technology, the limits of VR and interactivity. Yet VR systems are often marketed on the basis of their technological advances. Each system supersedes the last by being technically more impressive. A larger database, a more intelligent AI, faster graphics etc. feature on the pages of popular digital entertainment sites. The music industry has created a compression technology that is so successful that the music is again primary, not the technology. Advances in cloud-based storage technologies have gradually reduced the impact of the traditional issues of memory capacity, file management and backups. Digital photography cameras have largely (but not completely) superseded traditional film stocks. The aesthetic of digital film no longer replicates film, it has its own aesthetic which is high quality and flexible, but different to film. The Lytro camera captures pixel depth information with unlimited control over depth of field. It offers the ability to adjust focus in post-production and eliminates the need for rotoscoping as depth-based content can be removed based on distance from the camera. Foundry's Elara is a cloud-based platform that offers unlimited storage and significantly enhances the visual effects pipeline. Eventually, computational power will reach speeds that meet all our processing needs to return our focus to the 'story'. In other words, the technology will recede and we will return to conceptual innovation that is not fixated on regular technological advances, but is built on previous conceptual development.

The success of VR rests upon its ability to 'immerse' the user and keep them immersed. Technological glitches return the viewer to the real world, their 'first world'. This is similar to watching a film on television. Immersive narratives are broken by commercial breaks. These breaks make it impossible for the viewer to stay within the text. Less engaging films are not so affected by this stop/start presentation, but others suffer to the point of being unwatchable. The first televisual transmission of Steven Spielberg's *Schindler's List* (1993) in the US was broadcast without ad breaks. The story was considered to be too serious to allow commercials to interrupt the narrative/message of the film.

IMMERSION IN THE TEXTUAL WORLD

Aristotle recommended simulation to ensure consistency of plot (Ryan, 2001 p. 113); it is the reader's method of acting out the script. Visualising the plot allows the writer to know what is appropriate. In his book *Spiritual Exercises,* St. Ignatius of Loyola produced a meticulous description of the mental operations that lead to immersion in a textual world. All the senses are used to engage the reader. Hell is described in terms of the senses. Spatial immersion is often achieved through connective 'words' that mean something to the reader. 'The reader's private landscapes blend with the textual geography' (Ryan, 2001 p. 121). This is reminiscent of Eisenstein's work with visual montage. The broad subjective response to individual images is used as building blocks to create complex responses to a montage of images. Immersion is achieved because the images generate some sort of response in the viewer. The image is recognisable and quantifiable, it means something and can be placed in the sequence of meaning. Some texts lay out the geography of a scene to create a 'memory palace' (Ryan, 2001 p. 125). Action takes place in various places in this geography throughout the text. The images become so clear and yet complex that afterwards the reader may not remember what is from the text and what is from their own mind, like subtitled films where scenes are remembered as being spoken in English. Narrative connections blend so that the primary narrative and embedded narratives become confused/merged; 'Long after readers have forgotten the details of the plot of *Wuthering Heights* they retain the landscape in their minds' (Ryan, 2001 p. 125).

VISUAL WRITING

George P. Landow quotes Terence Harpold: 'most writers on hypertext concentrate on the link, but all links simultaneously both bridge and maintain separation. This double effect of linking appears in the way it inevitably produces juxtaposition, concatenation, and assemblage' (Harpold quoted in Lunenfeld, 2000 p. 159). Noting the differences between authoring for traditional and new media Landow says, 'perhaps it would be more accurate to say that in hypertext (where the author controls more of the layout), writing requires visual as well as alphanumeric writing' (Landow quoted in Lunenfeld, 2000 p. 163).

TEMPORAL IMMERSION

Temporal immersion takes the audience inside the story; it 'is the reader's desire for the knowledge that awaits her at the end of narrative time' (Ryan,

2001 p. 140). 'Human time ... is a quasi-musical experience in which the present is not a moving point but a moving window that encompasses memories of the past and premonitions of the future' (Ryan, 2001 p. 141). Suspense sports such as football and rugby offer total immersion. Suspense films can be watched again and again. In texts, the language must be invisible for immersion to work. This is also true in film where the edit has become invisible in order to immerse the viewer in the narrative. An obvious or clumsily placed edit reminds the viewer that they are watching a film and prevents their immersion within the story's reality.

The story audience is only given a *perspective*, where 'realism is a matter not of resemblance but of ease of decoding, and this ease is explained by the reader's or spectator's familiarity with a certain set of representation techniques' (Ryan, 2001 p. 160). A non-linear story necessitates an attentive audience which can identify, follow and interpret each chronological shift. *Pulp Fiction* (1994) fragments the narrative by representing the chronological sequence of story events out of order. *Dunkirk* (2017) intercuts three narrative timelines, each in turn representing one week, one day and one hour of story, then draws them together towards a single temporal end. *Westworld* (2016) cryptically weaves multiple narrative threads which span decades, made all the more difficult to decipher as we see ageless android hosts repeatedly interact year after year with aging guests. Streaming service distributors – for example, Netflix – are increasingly taking advantage of the long-format model (series and box sets) to present complex out-of-sequence narrative chronologies such as *Ozark* (2017).

While many interactive games are played in real time, some titles offer the player the option of slowing down and even reversing time. The physics of this reality blend seamlessly into the narrative and so are accepted by the audience. This is called the exploitation of temporality. Less dramatically, most films must present the fabula in 'clips' as it would be impossible to follow a narrative in real time. Films that have been presented in real time include *High Noon* (1952), *Nick of Time* (1995) and *Russian Ark* (2002).

'We can no more observe the stages of our own immersion than we can watch ourselves falling asleep' (Ryan, 2001 p. 170). Later, we realise that the virtual was experienced as our primary reality. This is the key objective of the narrative, the immersion of the reader/viewer into the text/film so that they believe they exist within the reality created by the fabula. 'If every text creates its own rules, the reader learns the code in the process of playing'

(Ryan, 2001 p. 182); therefore interpretation of the text is endless, it can be revisited time and time again to find new meaning and significance. Films can also be reinterpreted through subsequent viewings. An interactive film will be no different in this regard. A suitably developed script will exist at several levels of complexity. A cursory glance will provide a different experience than a more thoughtful, engaged viewing.

BACKSTORY

In order to create an immersive environment, the first pages of a story are more difficult to write than the last pages because the fictional world is being set in place. In film, the 'backstory' is the part of the fabula that is not being presented in the narrative but which influences the story. In feature films the first ten minutes usually set the backstory for the viewer to understand the frame of reference of the film's narrative. The backstory is not a story itself but provides a wealth of information that the viewer requires to become properly immersed. Without a backstory the viewer will misinterpret scenes and character development, a continual reminder that they are watching a film. In television the backstory is significantly extended to become a 'story bible', a complete character and plot history of the narrative, which can cover several decades of story development. Scripts for new episodes must conform to the story bible to avoid contradictions and continuity mistakes between events which take place many years apart.

ERGODIC TEXTS

Cybertexts, according to Espen Aarseth, are another example of 'ergodic literature ... a class of works in which "non-trivial" effort is required to allow the reader to traverse the text' (Aarseth quoted in Ryan, 2001 p. 206). Raymond Queneau's *Cent Mille Milliards de Poèmes* is 'a collection of sonnets of fourteen lines each printed on pages cut into so many strips, so that by flipping the strips and combining the lines the reader can obtain 10 to the power of 14 different texts' (Ryan, 2001 p. 185). In *Composition No. 1* by Marc Saporta, cards are laid out at random and the text on the cards creates a story. Roland Barthes states that 'reading is a cubist exercise in which the meanings are cubes, piled up, altered, juxtaposed, yet feeding on each other' (Barthes quoted in Ryan, 2001 p. 191). In *If on a Winter's Night a Traveller* by Italo Calvino, all the chapters of the book are the beginning chapters of ten incomplete novels. Phillippe Bootz, the French media theorist, created definitions of *texte écrit* (the text as written), *textes-à-voir* (the text as seen by the reader) and *texte lu* (the text as mentally constructed by the reader). Interactive text is a machine fuelled by the input of the user. There are many possibilities why the reader would want to submit input. They include: to determine plot; to shift perspective on the textual world; to explore the field of the possible – *The Garden of Forking Paths*; to keep the textual machine going; to retrieve documents, play games and solve problems; or to evaluate the text.

Brenda Laurel considered the psychology of computing and the use of interface metaphors which simplify data access yet create a barrier to exploiting the full functionality of a computer (Laurel, 1991 p. 129). Gunnar Liestol notes that 'in reading hypertext fiction the reader not only recreates narratives but creates and invents new ones not even conceived of by the primary author' (Liestol quoted in Ryan, 2001 p. 220). With electronic literature, the kaleidoscope metaphor allows the same elements to be arranged into multiple patterns – film montage, newspaper and magazine layout (Ryan, 2001 p. 221). The reader cannot freely pick and choose. For each reading to be new, the reader must erase knowledge of previous sessions.

> The kaleidoscope model works better with poetic texts in which the meaning of the sequence is not narrative but lyrical – that is, not logical, causal and temporal but associative, thematic, and quite tolerant of incongruous juxtapositions.
>
> (Ryan, 2001 p. 220)

CONSTANT RECONTEXTUALISATION

In narratology theory the 'fabula' is what happened in the textual world. Discourse or 'syuzhet' is the verbal realisation and dynamic disclosure of the fabula. When time moves back and forward in the narrative (from chapter to chapter) it is the syuzhet that is changing from reading to reading, not the fabula. Therefore reading hypertext affects the reader's experience more than it affects the world created by the text. If the hypertext projects a single fabula, not a new story each session, the reading is cumulative, and the construction of the fabula can span many sessions. Liestol states that 'hypertext promotes a constant recontextualisation' (Liestol quoted in Ryan, 2001 p. 221) where revisiting the lexia puts it in a different context in the linear sequence. Story can also be viewed as jigsaw pieces. But here the connection is thematic, causal rather than temporal. The reader looks at the pieces for the image to be unscrambled, 'rather than a collection of recombinant fragments' (Ryan, 2001 p. 221). Reading hypertext is a solitary experience that cannot really be shared. Reading the hypertext novel involves finding new navigation pathways with every reading, and often, new story outcomes depending on user interaction. How can reader communities establish a generic reading of the text that promotes consensus of opinion on the narrative? Can these reading groups be similar to those who read classic print literature works? The cultural importance of works is established by group exchange of ideas.

DEPTH-FIRST EXPLORATION

Michael Joyce's story *Twelve Blue: Story in Eight Bars* is read for plot or a 'depth-first' exploration. The reader follows links to their conclusion to establish a mental picture of the map, a 'breadth-first' approach that involves backtracking to try all paths that lead out of a given node. As a postmodern text, *Twelve Blue* challenges classical ontology; 'The purpose of traveling around the text is no longer to reconstitute an objective plot but to join a stream of imaginative activity that flows through a network of interconnected subjectivities' (Ryan, 2001 p. 238). 'Hypertext has been credited as offering an alternative to Aristotelian curve of dramatic tension – slow rise, climax and sudden fall – but the pleasure of problem-solving activity follows its own rhythm of mounting and decreasing intensity' (Ryan, 2001 p. 239). Initially there is too much information as the reader tries to identify patterns. The pleasure peaks when the pattern is realised. The reading ends when the reader tires of repeating screen cycles.

Ryan offers two views on narrative. They are: 1) 'Narrative is a form of representation that varies with period and culture'; 2) 'Narrative is a timeless and universal cognitive model by which we make sense of temporal existence and human action' (Ryan, 2001 p. 242). In the first, postmodern literature has radically altered the conditions of narrativity. In the second, the postmodern subversion of plot, character and coherence has merely loosened the ties of the novel with narrative structure. Ryan offers the view that complex narratives are simply more elaborate constructions of simple elements. Therefore postmodern novels are just an incomplete realisation of the narrative or a deliberate undermining of narrative structure. Commercial-sector developers of interactive texts take a narrower, Aristotelian view of narrativity than academic writers and theorists. The popularity of their texts depends on their creating an immersive experience. Time-tested classic narrative structures are best for keeping the user immersed. Compared with literary experimentalists, these writers and designers are more sceptical of the narrative potential of interactive media. It is highly problematic for interactive designers to promote navigation along a line that allows the story to unfold simply, without frustrating and ring-fencing the reader. The reader must feel they can navigate freely and are not simply being coerced into pathways dictated by the author.

STRUCTURES OF INTERACTIVITY

Ryan has considered various structures of interactivity. One is called 'The Vector with Side Branches'. This is used in electronic texts for children because of its:

> cognitive simplicity ... The user moves page by page through an illustrated story, but every page offers hidden surprises ... This structure is the most useful with didactic materials that require an accumulation of knowledge, since it can ask the student to complete separate modules in a determinate sequence.
>
> (Ryan, 2001 p. 249)

The early online interactive fiction title *The Spot* offered a network of diary entries each day but the text as a whole had to be visited daily. *The Spot* eventually failed due to insufficient advertising revenues.

'The Braided Plot' is a classic narrative consisting of a sequence of physical events objectively experienced by a group, where every character in the cast views these events from a different perspective and has a different story to tell. The interactive media can switch windows. An example of this would be moving from room to room where various actions were unfolding. The spectator could move from room to room, but they could still only view one strand of action at a time. Events that have already happened in another room cannot be repeated.

The greater the complexity of the interactive plot, the less control the author has over the viewer's 'navigation': 'the potential of a network to generate well-formed stories for every traversal is inversely proportional to its degree of connectivity' (Ryan, 2001 p. 257). Without control, the viewer follows a navigational path that has not been predicted by the author, and in some ways was never written by the author. The pathway might be random, but without control it will probably fail to entertain.

Emergent meaning is the meaning that is dynamically produced through the interaction of the text and reader. Temporal immersion requires an accumulation of narrative information. Conflict and incompatibility create the best narratives. Complex interactive narratives do not motivate the reader due to the exertion required to navigate the path. The brain is powerful, but the mind can only concentrate on so much at once. Walter Murch states that we can only concentrate on two-and-a-half sound elements (Koppelman, 2004 p. 289). Any more and the complexity of their interaction makes it difficult for the viewer to hear detail. An example of this is the footsteps of many people walking. Once there are more than two people, the footsteps do not need to be in sync with the visuals. The viewer would not be able to keep up with the processing required to compare visuals with audio and instead accepts the general audio array as identifying a number of people walking.

SPATIAL AND EMOTIONAL IMMERSION

In terms of spatial immersion, the hypertext can prevent immersion as the link or jump takes the reader abruptly out of one narrative flow into another. With emotional immersion, the plurality of the worlds created within the hypertext offers a multidimensionality that can only be viewed from a point outside the narrative.

> This conception of hypertext as the super postmodern novel was detrimental to the nascent medium for two reasons. First, the traditional length of the genre motivated hypertext authors to start right away with large compositions that made unreasonable demands on the reader's concentration ... Second, the model of the novel created a pattern of expectations that subordinated local meaning to a global narrative structure, and even though this structure hardly ever materialised, its pursuit distracted readers from the poetic qualities of the individual lexias.
>
> (Ryan, 2001 p. 265)

Writers were focused on the potentials of the technologies and expected the audience to 'keep up' despite the fact that the products were not on a par with traditional media offerings.

The producers of the interactive movie *I'm Your Man* (1992) indicate that the interactive narrative user needs to navigate various pathways, following different characters, to get a sense of the goals and plans that are designed to motivate the action. The functionality of the interactivity acts as a barrier to the narrative. The story must be examined in its segmented form before the user can begin to navigate. The user will therefore start 'reading' with significant plot information already acquired. With the kaleidoscopic model of interactivity the process of interaction produces a distinctive plot. The interruptions do not let the user become immersed in the story. Some plot sections become illogical if they are found through the 'wrong' navigation. This could be solved by adding a memory function to the system.

THE GREEK CHORUS

G.F. Schlegel identified the Greek chorus as the 'ideal spectator' while Nietzsche rejected this on the grounds that the spectator views the play as a work of art (a fiction) while the chorus interacts with the characters as real human beings (Ryan, 2001 p. 297). 'The chorus fulfilled several narrative functions: narrating the past ... commenting on the action, weighing possible developments, or lamenting the fate of characters; but for all its vocal presence it has no influence in the development of the plot' (Ryan, 2001 p. 297). *Peter Pan* broke the illusion by asking the audience to help. Circular theatre architectures allow the audience to see each other. This breaks the immersion in the narrative. Greek style semi-circular seating offers a compromise. The audience has a role in the performance but this role does not permit interference, particularly important in this platform for public discourse 'Greek drama was the way that Greek culture publicly thought and felt about issues of humanity, including ethics, morality, government, and religion' (Laurel, 1991 p. 40). Baroque Italian stage design featured a bright stage and an orchestra pit to separate the players from the audience. Baroque Italian stage design featured a bright stage and an orchestra pit to separate the players from the audience. Spectators could not reach the stage but they were fictionally part of the onstage world, 'a transparent fourth wall ... enables the spectator to spy on characters who live their lives unaware of this observing presence' (Ryan, 2001 p. 300).

AUDIENCE PARTICIPATION: *LIVING THEATRE*

The Living Theatre of Julian Beck and Judith Malina 'approached the theatre as a way of life, adopted a communal lifestyle, developed their spectacles collectively, and regarded them as a means of self-discovery' (Ryan, 2001 p. 305). They would perform even without an audience, as 'when performing becomes synonymous with living, the theatrical experience inherits the immersive and interactive qualities that define our experience of being-in-the-world' (Ryan, 2001 p. 305). In the French theatre of Guignol, spectators yell advice at the characters. They cross the boundary into the fictional world and become characters in the play while remaining part of the audience. But their advice does not influence the script. Other examples of audience participation in theatre includes:

> *Tina and Tony's Wedding*, a contemporary 'interactive' play, the audience is invited to follow the actors around from room to room (kinesthetic), to touch props and sit on furniture (tactile and kinesthetic), and to share in a wedding banquet (taste and smell).
>
> (Laurel, 1991 p. 52)

Antenna Theatre, founded by Chris Hardman, has created experiential performance works using audio technologies, 'where audience members move around a set prompted by taped dialogue and narration heard through personal headphones' (Laurel, 1991 p. 52). Alan Ayckbourn's play *The Norman Conquests* (1973) was performed over three successive nights. Each night the performance of the play covered the same time period but in a different room. Therefore the audience saw the same play over multiple pathways. Each pathway created its own narrative within the same story and was immersive and engaging. The immersion increased each evening as the audience pieced together the intersecting pathways and were allowed to ponder the reactions to events that have happened in another room which they were privileged to view previously (Murray, 1998 p. 158). Radúz Činčera's black comedy *Kinoautomat* was promoted as the world's first interactive film. It was shown at the Czechoslovak Pavilion at Expo '67 in Montreal. At certain points in the film the audience were asked to use red and green buttons to 'vote' on which decision the protagonist should take, and the film progressed along that chosen path.

Ryan suggests ways of creating interactive drama while creating immersion. The aesthetic criteria will be more game-orientated with goals to be achieved. 'I envision the future of interactive drama as investing in Alice in Wonderland type of narrativity, made out of episodic "little stories", rather than being supported by an overarching Aristotelian plot' (Ryan, 2001 p. 330).

Nineteenth-century and early twenieth-century novelists were so successful at developing immersive techniques that later generations fell under intense pressure to search for other types of intellectual satisfaction. Books such as

Wuthering Heights by Emily Brontë and *Madame Bovary* by Gustave Flaubert worked on spatial, emotional and temporal immersion. A major branch of postmodern literature focuses on the process of construction rather than the creation of a fictional world. Readers occupy a position outside of the reality constructed by the text, forced to observe without becoming immersed. However, multiple readings of texts produce multiple interpretations, therefore immersion in the text still creates diverse literary experiences.

THE PERSPECTIVIST APPROACH

Mark Stephen Meadows suggests that all stories are told from a perspective chosen by the author to present the text in a particular light (Meadows, 2002 p. 5). Our awareness of perspective allows us to interpret the text, according to our knowledge of the source. If we know more about the person's background, we have a better understanding of their 'angle' on the story and the reasons why they would adopt this particular stance. Rather than the text being a stand-alone entity, incapable of bias, it is our position in relation to the text that changes our response to it. Just as in a gallery, where we all have a different perspective on a painting, when we hear a story we are all bringing different backstories to the table and we interpret the text differently.

This leads us to 'The Perspectivist Approach' which considers multiple views from both an emotional and dimensional perspective. Multiple perspectives were not mutually incompatible; they all exist, and our relationship to them depends on our position when we approach the text. 'If you have foreground, background, context and decision, you have the bricks of which the plot structures of interactive narrative are built' (Meadows, 2002 p. 17). There needs to be enough information in the virtual world to allow audiences to fully engage in an immersive environment.

THE FREYTAG TRIANGLE

Gustav Freytag created the Freytag Triangle which:

> sliced the classic plot into three primary servings. His rework of Aristotle's definition pointed to the increase, culmination, and decrease of the plot. Plot is expressed as a function of time along a horizontal axis. The density of the plot ... is expressed along a vertical axis.
>
> (Meadows, 2002 p. 22)

The triangle can be subdivided to represent sub-plots and complex narrative arcs. The readers of interactive narratives must be in an investigative mood, for they are required to process information and make decisions in order to progress through the text. Brenda Laurel points out that 'the most engaging interactive narrative relies upon flow; that is, uninterrupted participation in the unfolding action. Poor interaction design can interrupt flow and degrade the experience' (Laurel quoted in Meadows, 2002 p. 37). The interruption in the flow results in a less immersive environment that does not engage the user. Navigation becomes pre-eminent and the text is subjugated. The story becomes all about the process and less about the narrative. Timely response to user interaction is critical if the interactive interface is to succeed:

> in the early days of the web, Stanford, Microsoft and Xerox-PARC all spent many hours showing that a person won't wait more than 20 seconds for a page to download ... This was because there was a need to know that some change was being affected to the system – within 20 seconds.
>
> (Meadows, 2002 p. 39)

Users would believe that the system was not responding to their input, and that their interaction had been lost. The depth of viewer immersion decreases with a less active relationship between stimulus and response. When the user is responding naturally to the text and their interaction is allowing them to navigate without concentrating on the process, the interface is successful.

NARRATIVE CONSTRAINTS

Brenda Laurel identified the need for 'constraints' to guide the user towards a specific intent with regard to their interaction with the system; 'for an interface to work, the person has to have some idea about what the computer expects and can handle, and the computer has to incorporate some information about what the person's goals and behaviors are likely to be' (Laurel, 1991 p. 12). The story should have clearly identifiable borders of the space within which the user can navigate freely; 'Constraints should be applied without shrinking our perceived range of freedom of action: Constraints should limit, not what we can do, but what we are likely to think of doing' (Laurel, 1991 p. 106). In theatre, such constraints on the 'choices and actions of actors improvising characters are probably most explicit in the tradition of *commedia dell'arte*' (Meadows, 2002 p. 63).

JOYCE'S EPIPHANY

Interactivity can be broken down into four steps of observation, exploration, modification and reciprocal change. Observing differences provides information about the text, repetition of text leads to redundancy in the narrative, redundant information ('repetition with variation') provides context, context allows prediction, prediction allows participation, and participation is the cornerstone of interactivity. Interaction with the text encourages the user to better understand the meta-narrative, these are epiphany moments. Epiphany is:

> a term that James Joyce coined to express the moment when the reader understands the entire arc of the story as a single thought ... This is a foreshortening of the story and a compression of information ... [it] is an act of authorship.
>
> (Meadows, 2002 p. 49)

One reason Joyce was able to pioneer narrative structures was due to his extensive literary palette. Like the music band The Beatles, who could play a wide repertoire of musical forms, Joyce was extensively well read and was aware of a great many literary forms in several languages. When writing, Joyce could draw on these forms to find new ways to present his ideas, new ways of constructing the text.

THE LANGUAGE OF TELEVISION

Existing technologies have paved the way to create the audience for new text formats. Television has created a collective space for people to watch the same sound and vision at the same time. Traditional TV viewers are well-versed in the language of television. This language was built around the need to hold viewers' interest and to stop them from changing channels:

> Camera cuts, character introduction, music pacing, colour contrast, volume, and even story structures themselves were built to grapple with the viewer's need to flip over to something faster and more hypnotic.
>
> (Meadows, 2002 p. 56)

Interactive texts require non-passive readers, unlike television; input is required to make the story progress. The input does not have to result in an open-ended storyline with varying outcomes. The objective of reading the text is not traditional, chapters are not read in linear fashion to acquire knowledge of the narrative, nodes are navigated to become immersed in the world created by the author/director: 'in developing an interactive narrative, the plot has to accommodate a more flexible structure that allows for multiple perspectives into multiple viewpoints, each of which work together to assemble an overall and cohesive worldview, or opinion' (Meadows, 2002 p. 62).

IMPOSITIONAL AND EXPRESSIVE NARRATIVES

The lead designer of *Ultima Online*, Ralph Koster, identifies two kinds of interactive narrative: impositional and expressive (Meadows, 2002 p. 63). Impositional narrative involves strict rules and narrow margin of decisions. Expressive narrative is more like architecture as the visitor can roam freely and the specifics of the plot are less defined.

> The interactivity of a modulated structure is more plot-based than in a nodal structure. Modulated plots will, ideally, provide a reader with the option to bore straight through and avoid interaction, or take a more leisurely route and increase the interactivity and participation.
>
> (Meadows, 2002 p. 65)

The foreshortening of time in a narrative is the result of perspectival manipulation. Narratives do not play out in real time, this would be impossible. When time is extended, it is called temporal anamorphosis, the opposite of foreshortening. This relates to the art technique of stretching visuals so that they can only be viewed from a specific angle. 'Foreshortening, anamorphosis, epiphany and foreshadowing all give protracted perspectives. Foreshadowing jumps ahead temporally just as foreshortening does spatially ... both are narrative elements that enable us to understand things from more than one perspective' (Meadows, 2002 p. 91).

Janet H. Murray writes, 'when the writer expands the story to include multiple possibilities, the reader assumes a more active role' (Murray, 1998 p. 38). Murray explains that in the IMAX 3D short film *Wings of Courage* (1995) the traditional cuts from interior to exterior shots are disrupting as the three-dimensional nature of the film already places the viewer in the space. The immersion brought about by the three dimensions is disrupted by the edits. Alternatively, the game *Myst* (1993) achieves much of its immersive power through its sophisticated sound design. Each of the different areas of the game is characterized by distinctive ambient sounds' (Murray, 1998 p. 53). There is a difference between the space that is created in our imagination and the space that can be explored (tangibly) via interactivity; 'Linear media such as books and films can portray space, either by verbal description or image, but only digital environments can present space that we can move through' (Murray, 1998 p. 79). Large-scale hypertext fictions are available on the World Wide Web.

> However, the encyclopedic nature of the medium can also be a handicap. It encourages long-windedness and formlessness in storytellers, and it leaves the reader/interactor wondering which of the several endpoints is the end and how they can know if they have seen everything there is to see.
> (Murray, 1998 p. 87)

The interactive nature of the narrative often ends with the viewer clicking out of the story altogether and moving on to another text.

THE OBJECTIVE CORRELATIVE

Formalist interpretation of the text says that it must contain facts that result in the character's emotion – the emotion cannot simply exist itself without what is known as an objective correlative. 'T.S. Eliot used the term objective correlative to describe the way in which clusters of events in literary works can capture emotional experience' (Murray, 1998 p. 93). Eliot argued that without the external events there was a mismatch between the explicit and the implicit elements in the story.

> Participatory narrative, then, raises several related problems: How can we enter the fictional world without disrupting it? How can we be sure that imaginary actions will not have real results? How can we act on our fantasies without becoming paralyzed by anxiety? The answer to all of these questions lies in the discovery of the digital equivalent of the theatre's fourth wall. We need to define the boundary conventions that allow us to surrender to the enticements of the virtual environment.
> (Murray, 1998 p. 103)

VIRTUAL IDENTITIES

Digital participatory narrative is often played out using an avatar, or virtual representation of the human self that only exists in the digital world. The world itself has its own physics, history, and social infrastructure. The level of participation depends on how the world has been developed in the first place. The world may have been designed to serve some common purpose (for example networking), or may be simply entertainment-orientated. Designers of virtual worlds often describe their audience's avatars as fully autonomous and independent of their control. However, recent developments in online worlds such as *Second Life* have resulted in threats of regulation from the real world. The online article *No Escape from the Bullies* details the findings of an online focus group into cyberbullying (University of Nottingham, 2007). Various traditional proposals have been put forward to curb 'griefing' of online residents. However, they have also identified the unique opportunity of viewing the act of bullying from the bully's perspective. Many virtual world complaints by avatar controllers fall on cynical ears in the real world, with many press stories calling for the users to 're-engage' with reality before they lose all contact with it forever.

> The postmodern hypertext tradition celebrates the indeterminate text as a liberation from the tyranny of the author and an affirmation of the reader's freedom of interpretation. But the navigational software designed specifically for this purpose and celebrated by many proponents of literary hypertext is anything but empowering to the reader.
>
> (Murray, 1998 p. 113)

Even in successful virtual worlds like *Second Life*, audiences are constantly reminded that the world is being controlled by messages from the company that designed the product. These messages often warn of the system going offline to make updates to the software or changes to the capabilities of avatars. This draws into question the success of the system in creating a world where users are empowered to create their own character's destiny within the virtual environment. Therefore the virtual is not progressing the narrative, simply allowing characters to meander around between chapters and plot points, incapable of exerting real influence over the narrative. The capacity for virtual worlds to create memories for avatar-controlling participants is being used by NASA to combat predicted psychological responses to extended isolation and loneliness of future astronauts.

FLAT AND ROUND CHARACTERS

'E. M. Forster thought there were two kinds of characters in fiction: "flat" ones, who perform their shtick in the same way throughout the narrative, and "round" ones, who can learn and grow' (Murray, 1998 p. 242). The latter sound more like the type of characters that work successfully in interactive texts. Conflicting emotions in relation to a single event are much closer to reality. These emotions are closely related to perspective on the story.

> The interactor is not the author of the digital narrative, although the interactor can experience one of the most exciting aspects of artistic creation – the thrill of exerting power over enticing and plastic materials. This is not authorship but agency.
>
> (Murray, 1998 p. 153)

This distinction adequately describes the relationship between interactive narrative author and the interactor/audience. The world created by the designer must create the initial interest in the narrative, just as traditional texts must do. Some audiences are more attracted to science fiction narratives than war history. They will be more likely to engage in the immersive environment of other planets/worlds than simple Earth-based history.

Technical competence is a barrier to producing work that exploits the potential of new technologies and media: there are still few writers who have the technical knowledge and literary skills combined to create an interactive story. Productivity tools such as Shotgun (production tracking and scheduling software) allow international teams to work together despite their geographical distance. Future electronic narratives will probably be the product of teamwork, as are movies and digital art installations. This may change the way interactive books are written but the film industry has been using the teamwork structure for years. Advances in audiovisual technologies has made it possible to use a 'skeleton crew' to shoot a film, and even then the results are mixed. The occupational areas within a film production department are well defined and allow the creative vision of many talented individuals to be realised under the authority of a director. The director exploits the talents and skills of people who have competencies in areas that he/she has lesser knowledge/lower skills. As Michael Caine says in his instructional video *Acting in Film* (1987), when viewing the 'dailies' (the previous day's shots that have just been processed) each crew member is only interested in the success of their department in each shot screened. Only the director and editor are focusing on how each department's work is coming together as a whole. Yet there are small teams and individual story creators working today.

VR STORYTELLING TECHNIQUES

The ability to 'meander' around the story world during a VR interaction and possibly miss important plot events is clearly an issue for story designers. Yet 'missing something' may just be part of a unique and personalised story experience. DEEP Inc's VR documentary *Edge of Space* (2015) employed a technique its team called 'forced perspective' to control where the viewer looks. These carefully placed edits function as a dynamic narrative device, an ellipsis, that will 'naturally direct the gaze towards the focal point of the next shot', abruptly shifting your view to the 'correct' perspective (Cullen, 2016). This brings its own problems, as some viewers find the sudden and repetitious changes in perspective 'nauseating'. So DEEP Inc used another device to encourage viewers to look at a specific part of the visual field. They darkened the less relevant parts of the screen at specific story points, so that the viewer would 'naturally turn towards the light, and hence, the action' (Cullen, 2016). Adding constraints to choice within an interactive story supports the illusion of narrative freedom while ensuring a sufficient rate of narrative progression: 'a key element in its solution is the deployment of dramatic probability and causality to indirectly guide what people think of doing' (Laurel, 1991 p. 73).

Nonny de la Peña's VR 'experience' *Project Syria* (2014) recreates 'a moment on a busy street corner in the Aleppo district of Syria' (de la Peña, 2014). This piece of immersive journalism placed the 'audience *on scene* and evoke[ed] the feeling of *being there*'. Running on Unity game engine with high resolution graphics, *Project Syria* created a 'sense of presence', simulating a rocket attack and its consequences on the local population, seemingly viewed in-situ.

Elia Petridis of Filmatics Creative Services directed the 12-minute VR experience *Eye for an Eye: A Seance in Virtual Reality* (2016). Petridis points out that VR offers an 'element known as inclusion' to create a theatrical experience where the audience is on the stage with the actors (Petridis quoted in Cheong, 2016). The film's scenes were shot with a stationary camera to produce 'stagnant masters'. Actors prepared for their roles through multiple table readings, stage blocking and rehearsals, then performed each scene in a single continuous take. Positional audio allows sound to be heard relative to one's position within the 3D space. *Eye for an Eye* also includes Focus Gaze, where staring at particular 'pre-loaded' visual element causes it to glow. After several seconds, this 'gaze' activates an additional audiovisual experience before returning the viewer to the main narrative. The seance film is a part of a larger transmedia piece, the other materials expand and develop the world and characters within it. Future projects will involve fully interactive 3D spaces that one can 'move around', created using CGI and photogrammetry.

For immersive VR experiences, sound must be consistent with the perceived geometry of the visual space. Spatialised audio recreates sound within a 3D environment, using 'a rendering engine that's capable of attaching sound to objects as they move through the setting' (Lalwani, 2016). Headphones are used to produce personalised binaural audio that precisely locates sounds in a 3D space for the listener; this 'personalized sound feels far enough outside your head for you to forget that you have a headset on' (Lalwani, 2016).

PERFORMATIVE GESTURES

Performative gestures can be used individually or in tandem to communicate the narrative, 'to reinforce, disambiguate, or replace spoken or written language' (Laurel, 1991 p. 155). Gestures can 'also enhance the experience of agency through kinesthetic involvement and the feeling of directness' (Laurel, 1991 p. 158). However, it is worth noting that in storytelling no gesture at all can have a profound impact. This is seen in *Wolf Hall* (2015), a dark tale of political intrigue set in the Tudor court of King Henry VIII. Mark Rylance's rendition of Thomas Cromwell is notable for its stillness. A muted representation of the art of dissimulation. The actor internalised his performance on screen, making Cromwell silent while navigating one dangerous encounter after another, carefully considering his options and formulating strategies. Rylance avoids explicit facial gestures which would have betrayed Cromwell's views in front of potential enemies. His thoughts are communicated only through his eyes while he 'thinks' in character. We, the audience, scrutinise his responses carefully, trying to read his mind.

GESTURE-CONTROLLED INTERFACES

Gesture-controlled interfaces allow physical interaction with the database. Creative approaches include the music artist Imogen Heap's Mi.Mu Gloves which can be used to control and play musical equipment using hand gestures. Heap sets pre-specified gestures to trigger Ableton music sequencing software functionality. This technology is aimed at the maker movement (a subculture of tech creatives that work without supporting infrastructure) and the gloves can be customised through its open source software code. Leap Motion creates a 3D interaction space in front of your screen that enables intricate VR hand-tracking. Magic Leap and Oculus Rift's head-mounted VR displays generate 'an intense and convincing sense of what is generally called presence. Virtual landscapes, virtual objects, and virtual characters seem to be there – a perception that is not so much a visual illusion as a gut feeling' (Kelly, 2016). These wearable displays will soon replace monitors in the office and become the interface for social media platforms. Mixed reality (MR) storytelling places photorealistic and animated content over our real-world vision, providing an augmented experience of entertainment and infotainment. The emotional impact of this enhanced sense of presence produces what Kelly calls 'the "you-person" view, because it's the position of feeling rather than the position of observing' (Kelly, 2016). As a narrative format VR and MR will require new storytelling techniques to be developed, the equivalent of the traditional language of cinema.

TECHNOLOGY AND ART

Ollie Rankin is a VR storyteller and visual effects supervisor. He has previously worked with artificial intelligence to create crowd and battle scenes. This work has helped him to think in terms of 'story graphs and branching narratives' (Rankin, interview 2016). Rankin believes that interactive forms blur the lines between continually evolving software technologies and creative art practices. He encourages experimentation with all aspects of the medium due to the lack of established rules constraining developers; 'there are certain conventions loosely enforced by the underlying platforms (e.g. user input) but the platforms are also in an ongoing arms race, albeit with slower iterations' (Rankin, interview 2016). Rankin suspects that there will be multiple interactive forms, just as there were multiple cinematic forms and VR has the unique ability to turn a passive observer into an engaged, empathetic participant. On interactive story development, he states that 'there's an inverse relationship between interactivity and story crafting, since generally, the more control the participant has on the way the story unfolds, the less control the storyteller has.' The storytelling objective is to allow freedom of interactivity, 'total agency in the virtual world' (Rankin, 2016), while at the same time limiting the user's ability to affect the narrative. Rankin recommends the VR technology demo *Aperture Robot Repair* (2015) created by Seattle-based company Valve. It includes subliminal cues that reinforce the sense of agency:

> the narrative timeline essentially pauses for as long as it takes for you to perform the action that triggers the next progression. But it doesn't feel like a pause, because you are actively trying to do something during that time.
>
> (Rankin, interview 2016)

Rankin's experimental VR film *Framed* used highly crafted 'natural language-based branching narratives' (Rankin, interview 2016) to hide a limited domain of interaction. By understanding the intention behind the participant protagonist's answers to story characters' questions, the responding (pre-recorded) dialogue does not refer to anything that has been said, yet is appropriate within the context of the story. Rankin predicts an interactive narrative platform with a sophisticated level of AI that will respond to any user's input, yet he believes that there will still be room for a storyteller to 'define the parameters of the simulation, to embed complex narrative elements and to curate the overall experience' (Rankin, interview 2016).

HOEY'S *THE WEIGHT OF WATER:* MANUFACTURING PRESENCE IN VR

Irish artist Elaine Hoey won the prestigious RDS Taylor Art Award (Dublin, Ireland) for her VR installation *The Weight of Water* (2016). The work allowed the headset wearer to experience crisis migration 'first hand' in a virtual environment. While researching technological platforms Hoey noted that VR enabled her to 'feel like I was somewhere else' (Hoey, interview 2017). She concluded that VR was the perfect medium to explore the impact of the unfolding European migrant crisis, a story that she believed was becoming less resonant due to waning public opinion. As with Don McCullin's war photography in the 1960s, media saturation and repetition of content resulted in a growing complacency towards economic migrant suffering; stories lost the ability to shock. In developing the piece, the artist was particularly interested in the concept of 'presence'. Hoey intended that her work would build towards an 'empathy-enhancing' sense of presence. She asked herself 'how do I *experience* this rather than simply *viewing* it on-screen?' The screen, which has over the years moved ever-closer to the body (cinema, television, headsets) is now being replaced by an immersive experience within a virtual space.

Hoey's latest digital artwork concentrates on the development of narrative within VR. To achieve this, she has chosen to employ minimalistic or 'less photographic' imagery, so that there is 'less to look at'. The work seeks to disrupt the 'echo chamber' effect of contemporary political and technological discourse. Hoey is considering the notion of digital islands of thought, intending to destabilise the viewer within certain VR spaces.

MIXED STORYTELLING: *FRAN BOW*

Creative developers Natalia Figueroa and Isak Martinsson of Killmonday Games produced the popular interactive title *Fran Bow* (2015). As artists, they had been looking to free themselves from the constraints of traditional narrative structures. Figueroa says she does not have an intended audience, nor does she consider demographics. Instead, she seeks to engage with those who prefer her 'mixed storytelling' approach. Figueroa says her work does not 'follow a prescribed rhythm or formula' but deals with 'life itself as a primary concept' (Figueroa, interview 2016). She diligently records her observations of everyday people and places, noting 'how different people react to different problems'. She then writes these 'problems' into her stories, creating natural interaction points within the narrative. For Figueroa, 'every detail counts', particularly music, which she describes as being 'like the beating of your heart and the rhythm of blood circulating through your body!' She uses music as an emotional guide to the spectator during their immersion within the narrative, to make it 'become real at that moment'.

INTERACTIVE POETRY: *DEAR ESTHER*

Brighton-based interactive story developers Jessica Curry and Dan Pinchbeck of The Chinese Room have created the indie titles *Dear Esther* (2012) and *Everybody's Gone to the Rapture* (2016). *Dear Esther* is a moving and emotional tale, set on a Scottish island. It is 'driven by story and immersion rather than traditional mechanics' (Curry & Pinchbeck, 2016). Sound designer Claire Fitch calls this work 'interactive poetry', where 'the story is pieced together by reading letters that have been written to Esther, who has died' (Fitch, interview 2016). The follow-up title *Everybody's Gone to the Rapture* takes place in an eerily empty village in Shropshire, 'where something has gone wrong'. Audio logs are gathered during the interactive experience to piece together the narrative. Fitch describes it as 'really unnerving ... simply because of the lack of other characters'. In her own work, Fitch creates audio for interactive titles that serves as both a 'feedback mechanism' and 'mood enhancer'.

LOCATION-BASED AR

Mads Haahr of Haunted Planet Studios in Dublin created an early location-based augmented reality product. The designer made (virtual) evidence gathering a key story activity, creating a series of interactive points that advanced both story development and character detail; 'I think it's important to have the narrative and interactive elements resonate in as many ways as possible' (Haahr, interview 2016). Naturalistic audio elements were used to add uncertainty as to which sounds were story-based and which were from the physical environment. Safety is an issue as the story is asking the audience to go to a 'particular physical location'; the developer should have knowledge and provide warnings of any potential hazards/dangers. Haahr recommends *Our Own Storm* (2016) as a compassion-themed story 'that isn't as much told as experienced'. The player takes the role of a refugee who is killed, then takes control of the killer 'only to discover this character too is caught in a system of violence and oppression'.

Brian Vaughan of the Dublin Institute of Technology combines elements of computer science and user interaction design. He sees narrative as method of structuring data, a data model. He recommends Lucas Pope's empathy game *Papers Please: A Dystopian Document Thriller* (2013). The player takes the role of an immigration officer, checking citizens' passports and making decisions on their eligibility to pass through customs. The story creates a moral dilemma in that a pedantic, uncaring approach to narrative decisions will in fact earn more points and secure success.

THE NARRATIVE ARCHITECT

Hartmut Koenitz of the HKU University of the Arts, Utrecht, prefers the word 'narrative' to 'story' as 'there is no *telling* in interactive digital narratives in the traditional sense, instead there is someone who creates a dynamic system, a *narrative architect*' (Rettberg quoted in Koenitz, interview 2017). The interactive narrative author has less control over the audience experience than that of a literary author or film-maker; they create 'opportunities for interaction' rather than a fixed narrative. Interactive games, and more recently, interactive documentaries and features are gradually introducing an interactive narrative paradigm to audiences and will eventually create an 'interactive digital narrative literary'. *Save the Date* (2013) by Paper Dino is a visual novel that exploits 'cross-session memory and meta narrative'. Over multiple playthroughs, the reader attempts to repeatedly navigate an (apparently doomed) dinner date with Felicia to a successful conclusion. ELIZA (1964) is a program (originally developed at MIT) which Koenitz says 'scripted the interactor' in order to superficially emulate a Rogerian psychotherapist. When a user talked about themselves and their life, ELIZA's answers fooled many people into believing that the program was a real person. The atmospheric trial and death story *Limbo* (2010) by independent studio Playdead is a highly creative convergence of visual and sound. German Expressionist-styled aesthetics and richly textured ambient sounds offer clues as to how one should navigate a lost child in a forest to safety. The originality of these titles supports Koenitz's belief that success lies in creating 'new kinds of narrative expressions' and not in the repurposing of traditional story concepts into interactive titles.

EXPERIMENTAL NARRATIVE RIFFS: *GRAMMATRON*

Scott Rettberg states that Mark Amerika's *Grammatron* (1997) 'was pushing toward a *Gesamtkunstwerk* mode of hypertext writing and was as much a philosophical exploration of network consciousness as it was a novel' (Koenitz et al, 2015 p. 31). *Grammatron* contains more than 1000 new media elements – text, visuals, animation, voice and soundtrack to create 'experimental narrative riffs' that remix multiple discourses including 'cyberpunk, dialectical materialism' and the works of James Joyce and Jean-Luc Godard (Amerika, 2011). It satirises the once-liberating potential of our online spaces that have become increasingly invasive, convoluted and tangled.

REMEDIATING STORIES

Film-maker Hank Blumenthal, who produced *In the Soup* (1992), is now working in interactive story development. He states that 'stories remediate easily' and believes that audiences learn new interactions quickly if the interface is non-intrusive and 'the activities are natural' (Blumenthal, interview 2017). His work is aimed at a mass audience. While traditional storytelling models still apply, the interactive 'story, experience, and paratexts point to knowing stories in different senses'. Interactive stories are building new character relationships with more complex levels of conflict and different types of story endings. Blumenthal makes use of 'the best narrative viewpoints' to create works that are 'semi-linear with dynamic action and agency'. He recommends *Façade* (2005), created by Michael Mateas and Andrew Stern, as 'a first-class example of natural language and a first person experience'. This work of interactive theatre allows the audience to actively engage in a text-based discussion with its two characters, a couple living in a New York apartment who are having a domestic argument when *you* arrive for cocktails. As you converse with them, your responses influence the direction of both their relationship with each other and the tone of their interaction with your character. Blumenthal favours a multi-franchise (media products that exist in multiple forms across multiple platforms)/ multi-platform approach to storytelling which features spin-offs and add-on story-building content.

INTERACTIVE DESIGN: TWINE

Interactive story author Christian Divine (*Life is Strange*, 2015) prioritises reader experience in storytelling (Divine, masterclass 2016). He states that 'language is indigenous, part of your toolkit' and this allows the author to layer-in cultural references, to help the audience 'connect' with the narrative. This emphasis on emotion as a device to capture and hold the audience's attention makes the accuracy of language, colloquialisms and phrasing less important. Divine uses the open-source interactive storytelling software Twine to design and build interactive stories, to write from different points of view.

Charlene Putney is a Dublin-based writer who also uses Twine to quickly produce multiple choice-based narratives. She recommends Twine-based interactive fiction works include Anna Anthropy's ten-second-long hypertext fiction, the 'infinitely-replayable love poem' *Queers in Love at the End of the World* (2013). Also, the Thomas Ligotti-inspired *My Father's Long Long Legs* (2014) by the writer Michael Lutz, with its 'palpable creepiness, and some nifty tricks with music and cursor movement used to great effect' (Putney, interview 2017). Putney suggests using Twine to quickly produce stories, assess what works and what doesn't, then release multiple story products in order to develop and populate one's story portfolio. With regard to the future of mobile-based interactive stories, she suggests that *Steve Jackson's Sorcery* (2013) is a good example of the potential of narratives 'to be enjoyed in short bursts of time'. Based on the 1983 *Fighting Fantasy* series of interactive books, these stories will compete with multiple browser tabs eager to steal a reader's attention. They needed to be aesthetically beautiful and designed for this specific mode of delivery (Putney, interview 2017). Sabina Bonnici seeks to accommodate different tiers of audience engagement when developing a narrative; 'some prefer to jump right in into a story, others lurk and observe' (Bonnici, interview 2017). To achieve this, she puts the audience at the centre of the 'creative and technological development phases'.

* * *

This chapter dealt with immersion and perspective in narrative texts. Interactive texts are dependent on the ability of the interface to allow access to their content. This does not make them a barrier to communication; rather, it creates a new access methodology for the reader to comprehend. Interaction creates a non-linear form of storytelling that, as we have seen, is reminiscent of other art forms. The line between textual immersion and reality is blurred. There is no single moment of immersion where we are suddenly absorbed in the text. Interactivity that allows the reader to change their perspective gives a level of freedom to navigate that is reminiscent of the real world. The action of adjusting perspective is part of the immersion process. When we use an interface to change our viewpoint, we are actively thinking about what we are likely to see based on previous experiences. As we continue this active thought process the immersion into the reality of the text becomes complete and we follow a dynamic route through the text, changing perspective, until the immersion is lost at the story end or due to some significant break in the navigation pathway.

The various interactive structures identified by Ryan indicate that the greater the complexity of the interactive interface, the less control the author has over users' pathways through the narrative. This lack of control over emergent meaning threatens the ability of the text to entertain. Ryan gives examples of theatre- and text-based non-linear works, highly creative and non-traditional. Yet interactive developers have not achieved a consensus that could be used to define a 'traditional' interactive film interface. They are all new and all different. It is these differences that make interactivity, from text to text, such a barrier to access. As we learn the interface infrastructure, we are already navigating the story. The authors of interactive texts, including myself, spend so much time designing the interface, the primary component of the text, that the interface becomes a distinct element in itself, fundamentally different from all others and requiring a strict learning curve to understand it.

8

The Business of Transmedia Storytelling

Innovative storytelling concepts are tried and tested across local and international markets in both the public and private sectors. Public service broadcasters distribute content both online and through their traditional media channels. In Ireland, this output is guided by a public service broadcasting charter, a statement of principles and accountability. RTE's chief digital officer Múirne Laffan says that 'people are looking for thematic discoverability, not randomly browsing'. The ability to track users helps to build a relationship and offers a 'tailored discovery'. Data is gathered on individual users to create an incomplete personalisation, to offer 'a more tailored consumer experience. Stories you may or may not like ... we think you should hear them' (Laffan, interview 2016). Commercialisation is not always the primary objective as key players seek to develop content that is recognised as being ground-breaking and new. Technological considerations and complexities may act as a barrier to entry, even for experienced professionals who may not have the specialised knowledge or expertise to exploit new storytelling platforms. Somehow, technological know-how must be combined with storytelling skills to create new products that build audiences to achieve a commercial return. Internet TV providers increase audience share by regularly revising and updating their programmes. New product gives the audience a reason to come back. Some early online broadcast sites had limited success offering scheduled episodic content. In the late 1990s, *The Spot* lacked the necessary funds to purchase bandwidth for their daily online broadcast. Without access to an adequate audience reach, the webcast was unable to generate sufficient advertising revenue. Without the advertising income, the money was not available to purchase greater bandwidth. Many niche online broadcast sites offer quirky or off-centre content. This content may initially attract a limited audience but it is possible for them to gradually secure a significant proportion of the mass market. Providers offering repurposed content have been particularly successful in building large audiences over the short term. In 2014 British Pathé released its newly digitised archive of content. 85,000 historical and cultural films dating from 1895 to 1976. This represents a fundamental shift in online broadcasting: historical content offered online at a time when traditional broadcasters are being accused of reducing production budgets to the detriment of programme quality. British Pathé has recycled quality material in order to build a market share and achieve revenue without production costs. The rapidly changing media sphere creates new opportunities while promoting career obsolescence. This chapter considers several transmedia campaigns, the rise of in-house content creation departments in multinational corporations, transmedia news content, and the development of VR products that are seeking to build a new film language. With this in mind and to promote the development of VR products, the Palo Alto company Jaunt has launched a filming guide titled *The Cinematic VR Field Guide: Best Practices for Shooting in 360°*. The company describes this guide as a 'living document' which they intend to update as VR film-making trends change. Jaunt are asking the VR community to send them their tips and tricks which they can share through this publication.

#FINDTHEGIRL

BBC Three's #FindTheGirl campaign was a transmedia project to promote the five-episode online drama *Thirteen* (2016), the story of 'a young woman who escapes after thirteen years of being held captive by a kidnapper' (Puschmann, 2016). By following the fictional journalist Sarah Hays on Twitter and YouTube, viewers could participate in an interactive detective story, carrying out online research (websites and social media accounts) on behalf of Sarah, to help to track down another missing child and the man who might be responsible for her abduction. Over several weeks, Sarah communicated with users via Twitter, responding to their theories and hunches. The transmedia campaign ran concurrently with the series, to promote audience engagement and retention. There were #FindTheGirl clues included in the *Thirteen* series, picked up by online users, who encouraged Sarah to follow up on their leads and investigate further.

BLAST THEORY: *IVY4EVR*

The Brighton-based artist group 'Blast Theory' creates performance-based interactive art that explores social and political themes. Channel 4 Education commissioned the company to design an interactive SMS drama called *Ivy4EVR* (2010). Delivered directly to individual users via their mobile phone, the project was intended to create a personalised and private space for young people, to allow them to explore issues that affect their day-to-day lives. These issues included drug use, alcohol and sexual behaviour. Written by Tony White, *Ivy4EVR* featured a character called Ivy, a 17-year-old girl who takes drugs, might be pregnant and whose story arc depended on individual audience responses to her text messages. While the themes under discussion were delicate and sensitive, not all her texts were controversial. Conversations with Ivy could even be relatively straightforward. The story world of *Ivy4EVR* used a simple language parser to look for 'tags' that it could respond to. This enabled Ivy to give appropriate replies to texts sent to her. The naturalistic responses that were created resulted in audiences building a strong connection with the fictional character. Developer Nick Tandavanitj notes that *Ivy4EVR* exploited the fact that its audience had mobile connectivity all the time, providing a staccato yet long-term engagement (Tandavanitj, interview 2016).

KAREN

Blast Theory's mobile app *Karen* (2015) was created with the National Theatre of Wales (a theatre with no venues) to develop a performance art piece that would work for an online audience. 'Karen' (played by actress Claire Cage) is a life-coach who communicates with you via smartphone, contacting you at all times of the day (and night). You become a character in Karen's world through a series of context-based conversations where 'night is night'. Her character asks you questions about yourself and your relationships, modulating your responses to her questions, rather than driving major plot changes. *Karen* can be viewed as a parable on oversharing, or the tale of a life-coach with serious 'issues'. The story went through 44 iterations of tone and structure, the team initially shot 19 scenes, then reshot 12. The app was developed in collaboration with Dr. Kelly Page who provided medical advice on psychometric profiling and helped to create a data plan to organise and make use of 30–40 psychometric scales. *Karen* is in fact profiling you. Data collected and collated during your time interacting with her is packaged into a downloadable report which you can access on completion of the story. This project considers the ethical issues around data gathering, the seamless interfaces used by corporations to track your responses and create a profile of your online activities and social media presence. Tandavanitj describes *Karen* as 'the most out-of-the-box project, drawn from theatre, unfolding now, in real-time' (Tandavanitj, interview 2016).

CONTENT CREATION DEPARTMENTS: GOING VIRAL

Companies are increasingly producing branded content in-house and online; video content dominates. 'M-Live' is the global content studio of Marriott, the multinational hospitality company based in Bethesda, Maryland. M-Live looks for experiential marketing opportunities for Marriott's 19 hotel brands. The studio creates content for distribution across multiple social media platforms to engage customers, build trust and promote lifetime loyalty to the Marriott name. The team 'tracks pop culture events across various verticals' to look for marketing opportunities globally (Lazauskas, 2015). In 2015, a $1million reward was offered by an anonymous donor following the theft (10 years previously) of a pair of the famous ruby slippers from the Judy Garland Museum in Grand Rapids, Minnesota. M-Live added 1million Marriott Reward points to the purse, then quickly developed associated creative content and ran a very successful campaign of targeted social media posts and Times Square ads to promote their offer. The company has partnered with content creators to produce story-driven short films, one shot in a Marriott hotel, with no product placement. Marriott has created a media company, where the emphasis is on telling stories to promote audience engagement and build brand loyalty, not direct selling. It does not use many established social media marketing methods such as the brand-damaging 'pseudo-notifications' or 'dark patterns', which effectively trick visitors into meaningless and unrewarding engagement with a site (Wilshere, 2017).

Global strategic consulting firm Accenture have opened a 10,000 sq ft content studio in New York. Accenture Interactive and Deloitte Digital offer 'vertical experts, global consumer insight, the manpower to produce thousands of pieces of content, and – because of their existing consulting relationships – a better understanding of how digital marketing can fit into an overall business strategy' (Wegert, 2016). The LastMinute.com group network of travel brands reaches over 40 countries. In 2016 they created a content development lab in Europe to 'enhance curated, editorial content for its rich and young audiences on its sites and social media pages' (Mortimer, 2016). In 2013, MTV Networks and Sony created their 'next-generation studio' Astronauts Wanted. Their transmedia title *Midsømmer* is 'a gender-bending take on Shakespeare's *A Midsummer Night's Dream*, fed to consumers in non-linear bits and pieces across multiple media platforms like Instagram, Facebook, YouTube, Snapchat and Vine' (Lev-Ram, 2016). Astronauts Wanted have taken an experimental approach to transmedia development, bringing together a group of talented youth, some of whom already have a significant following on social media. The collective, called Flight Club, are encouraged to innovate and create, exploring new possibilities for online story development and distribution and with the eventual aim of monetising their work.

The film-makers behind the independent sci-fi film *The Phoenix Incident* (2016) 'have been cultivating a viral campaign over the past two years on hidden websites, Twitter feeds and Facebook' (Snider, 2016). Part of the film's budget was used to build visual partnerships with online outlets including Shazam. Story elements were scattered throughout the internet on various platforms and distribution channels to create an 'event-based film with an immersive interactive viral campaign', turning a traditional cinematic product into an 'experience' (Snider, 2016).

Companies such as ViralHog seek exclusive deals to license video content from around the world. These clips are then sold on to news organisations and the revenue is shared with the content creators (Judah, 2016). Jukin Media 'represents' potentially viral content which it has found in social media outlets and licenses these 'clips to TV, advertising and digital publishing' (Judah, 2016). While much of the content is 'benign', the company has also sourced controversial footage including scenes from the Shoreham air crash in England. The BBC says it will only pay for footage 'if there is a strong editorial justification for doing so' (Judah, 2016). The monetisation of video clips raises important questions with regard to journalistic ethics. Footage finds its way onto multiple online outlets (both legally and pirated) so quickly that it is unlikely to have been subjected to journalistic rigour. When stories are found to be false or fabricated, they are simply deleted, something traditional print news sources were unable to do.

THE DIGITAL NEWSROOM: TRANSMEDIA AND VR

Forbes publishing platform Brand Voice has around 2000 global contributors. The business magazine has moved from a fixed-rate model to a contributor model (paying for traffic) for its journalists (Goodfellow, 2016). This has resulted in a significant rise in traffic for Forbes. Yet the model has been criticised for allowing advertisers direct access to Forbes CMS, which could compromise the company's journalistic integrity. Forbes' director Paul Mikhailoff counters this by saying that in the digital world, journalists no longer have the sole right 'to inform'. He describes the 'purpose of branded content as value exchange' (Mikhailoff quoted in Goodfellow, 2016) which is not just focused on securing a purchase. Brands are increasingly setting up newsrooms to offer a user experience made up of both advertising and branded content.

Unilever's new in-house content studios are a response to the increasing use of ad-blocking software (which prevent brands reaching their intended market) and audiences' move towards curated content and their desire to seek out brand experiences (Joseph, 2016). U-Studio will create 'how-to videos, infographics, articles, product information', while U-Entertainment will drive the development of 'TV series, web series, games, music integration' (Joseph, 2016). The *Financial Times* has a digital subscriber base and does not fully depend on advertising revenues. It is now creating high-quality long-form video pieces through its film studio in London. The newspaper's competitive advantage is its 'exceptional insights into its audience's interests and reading patterns' (Burrell, 2016). It is distributing news through social media platforms, offering 'one-click-free' high-value content to new customers, with a view to converting them to paid subscribers. The Lantern Dashboard system in the *FT* newsroom gives 'every FT journalist access to detailed analytics on who is reading their stories' (Burrell, 2016).

The *New York Times* has ambitious plans for the newsroom including major investments in visual journalism. With less than half its readers living in New York, the paper must produce content that is both relevant and coherent to an international audience, while still abiding by its original mission statement of accuracy and integrity. Scene-setting video plays automatically when you load a page. Interactive story pages include parallax scrolling, 'a computer graphic effect that makes the background of a webpage load at a different time than the foreground, creating an immersive experience' (Koc, 2015). Rollovers and data visualisations allow readers to access further information and to interact with the data, avoiding clutter and confusing graphical layouts. All video, animation and photographic content are high quality. The paper is restructuring its newsroom to make possible 'smaller, more focused coverage clusters that operate apart from big desks' (Mullin, 2016). In a memo to staff outlining the steps toward digital audiovisual content, Dean Baquet stated that editors 'will not worry about filling space. They will worry over coverage, and the best ways to tell stories' (Baquet quoted in Mullin, 2016). In 2015 the paper debuted its immersive virtual-reality experience *The Displaced* and delivered Google Cardboard sets to its subscribers. The ten-minute film follows three children in Ukraine, South Sudan and Lebanon; 'you hear their stories while walking alongside them in fields, sitting with them in rubble, and witnessing the frantic scramble to receive food dropped from aid planes' (Welsh, 2015). Describing the impact of VR, video journalist Ben Solomon states that it is experientially closer to theatre than film. As in theatre, his VR film uses light and sound to target your attention at a particular subject, to make you 'look' (Welsh, 2015).

STORYTELLING ON SOCIAL MEDIA PLATFORMS

Story Time Twitter is a series of extended narratives created out of a succession of tweets. These live 'performances' can last an hour or so, and the 'likes' and 'retweets' from a 'rapt' and often 'raucous' crowd only enhances the shared in-the-moment experience. The audience can read the story as an archive in the writer's account, or participate 'live', to be entertained as 'the author painstakingly tries to contort a long story into some indeterminate number of 140-character chunks' (Pierce, 2016).

Rob Wittig and Mark Marino have produced several 'netprov' projects that incorporate 'integrated elements of contributory collaboration, social media discourse and online hoax in developing performance fictions'. In their year-long netprov *Occupy MLA* (2012), a story was presented through the Twitter accounts of several members of a fictional academic faculty (Koenitz et al, 2015 p. 31).

Instagram Stories allows users to produce a 'daily story that strings together photos and video' (McAlone, 2016). YouTube stars, whose primary income was previously from Google Ads, are now achieving significant revenue through sponsored, branded content on Instagram.

While user engagement is greatest on these platforms, Facebook still offers an extraordinary potential reach. The platforms are 'major distribution points for these stars' (McAlone, 2016). Creative ideas are developed as 'short-form, half-hour, and feature-length' (McAlone, 2016) packages to be pitched to multiple social media outlets. In this way, they hope to increase their fan-base and ultimately 'branch out' to more far-reaching distributors such as YouTube Red, Netflix and MTV.

Many television shows have successfully exploited their social media following to maintain currency and to increase their audience base. BBC America took to Tumblr, Twitter and Vine to promote *Doctor Who* (Nededog, 2015). *Empire* (2015) has a significant Twitter user-base who actively post tweets during the show (Moylan, 2015). These social media sites are the 'word of mouth' platforms for live audiences to dynamically engage with other viewers and the creators of the show.

DATA ANALYTICS

Data analytics tools like the 'Contently Analytics dashboard' allow stories to be tagged with attributes such as 'topic' and 'format'. A story's performance can be assessed by comparing its audience engagement metrics with similar data about other geostories (Lazauskas, 2016). Content research tool Buzzsumo identifies the most shared content and the key topic 'influencers' on social media platforms. Content producers use this data to guide their selection of subject choices when they are considering content to be developed for online distribution. It informs them about what a particular subset of the online community are actively engaged in reading, viewing and searching for. Skyhook tracks device signals over time to accurately predict consumer intent and to enable location-targeted advertising. The gathered data 'provides both personalization and context' (Rogers, 2016).

Soraia Ferreira is a transmedia producer who develops 'purpose stories' for the business community (Ferreira, interview 2016). The objective of her work is to convey pertinent information to the business audience, short sound bites of detail rather than entertainment. The story elements within each platform are self-contained and readers are encouraged to progress onto other media if they want to read more. Krishna Stott of Bellyfeel has produced a wide range of transmedia titles and interactive experiences for the music sector. By using prototypes of his stories during development, he positions the interaction points of a narrative at the moments where the audience is 'naturally inclined' to engage (Stott, interview 2016). Stott avoids using 'large chunks of linear media' followed by a sudden and disruptive interaction. Instead, he prefers to make viewer interaction an 'expected' part of the experience and so keeps the audience connecting regularly with the story. Stott recommends *The Stanley Parable* (2013) as an example of a highly creative, experimental interactive narrative. A story narrator provides dramatic exposition, but the audience (as the protagonist) can choose whether or not to follow his 'instructions'. If not, the narrator delivers admonishments and encourages a return to the 'proper path'. *The Stanley Parable* considers the very nature of rules and constraints within interactive narratives. The interactive promos *Neon Bible* (2007) and *Reflektor* (2013) are creative music videos by the band Arcade Fire. The latter is an experiential piece that allows the viewer to insert themselves into the work. Stott believes transmedia storytelling has the potential to create new business models which are 'naturally immune to piracy due to the granular form of content' (Stott, interview 2016).

STORY-DEVELOPMENT TOOLS AND TECHNOLOGIES

Story-development tools such as Atavist (media-rich content creation) and VoiceMap (location-aware audio experiences) facilitate the creation of interactive narratives. FrameTrail allows you to produce interactive video content directly in your browser. Online app builders such as Thunkable enables the creation of fully native apps by non-coders. Conductrr is a cloud-based content management system for storytelling. A timeline calendar of 'triggers' is used to schedule content publishing across multiple platforms including email, blogs, social media, websites and mobile. Scripted social interactions allow characters to respond to particular phrases with pre-scripted replies (Conductrr, 2016). iBeacon technologies can trigger push messages and prompts to smartphone apps, enabling story elements to be delivered at specific geographical locations. Emotiv calculates metrics related to brain activity and facial expressions to produce a hands-free brain-controlled interface. Metagram (2016) is a glasses-free holographic film system that uses 'AR to build narrative experiences in the real world' (Lindquist, interview 2016). 'Holograms' can be 'seen from multiple angles by multiple people'. Their first film *End of the Line* (2016), was a Hitchcock-inspired murder mystery where the audience's interpretation and knowledge of the plot depended on their observational position. Viewers later conferred to share their discoveries, to learn what really happened in the story. This perspectival approach to storytelling is also used in Eko's

Broken Night (2017), a short VR film (lasting 8–9½ minutes) starring Emily Mortimer in which you decide which character to follow during four critical moments of a particularly tense drama. The aim was to test individual engagement within a visceral immersive experience. There is no interface and the interaction is driven by emotion. The viewer follows the character that they find to be most interesting at any particular point in the narrative. The result is a varying perspective on the characters and plot depending on where you were and what you saw.

AUGMENTED REALITY

vStream Digital Media has developed an AR solution for the Mercedes AMG Petronas Formula One Team using Epson Moverio glasses. This unique VIP virtual tour of a Mercedes Formula One garage utilises a holographic display to dynamically create an AR experience (Williams, interview 2017). An actor accompanies the participant to guide their progress and to deliver a customised narrative arc. This system places the latest Epson technologies in the hands of 'decision makers and budget holders of leading corporations' (Williams, interview 2016), potential investors in the technology itself. vStream project developer Jermain Williams pays particular attention to how people think when developing these experiential products. He uses gamification techniques, psychological rewards, directional sound and other narrative devices to focus the participant's attention on the most important story elements at each particular point in the narrative. The subtle manipulation of the audience's attention is similar to a magician's sleight-of-hand, diverting their gaze to control awareness and to influence decisions. The audience is given the illusion of navigational freedom when in fact their story choices are predictable and expected.

RECREATING THE THEATRE EXPERIENCE

Camille Donegan seeks to bring the 'liveness' and interactive role play of Forum theatre to her VR projects (Donegan, interview 2017). With Forum theatre the audience can interact directly with actors on stage, add dialogue to scenes and give directions. Donegan recommends Punchdrunk's *Sleep No More* (2011) where the player participates in a 'living performance', an adaptation of *Macbeth*. The setting is the fictional McKittrick Hotel which contains a number of story vignettes that a player can explore. As they navigate the physical space, they are guided by a 'remote actor', who could be located anywhere in the world and whose text-based instructions are interpreted by MIT-built software to 'control' various on-set props. The remote actor receives random visual updates on the player's location. They are encouraged to cause mischief and to make the player jump. The player interacts with both stage actors and this series of VR elements. RFID (radio-frequency identification) and Bluetooth technologies allow the remote actor to geo-locate narrative surprises at the most opportune times within the story experience. The Danish creative media agency Makropol created *The Doghouse* (2015), an interactive 18-minute dinner scene viewed by five people at a time via Oculus Rift headsets. Producer Mads Damsbo calls the individual experience of each viewer a 'subjective reality' (Mufson, 2015). The film was shot as 40 complete run-throughs, with actors wearing fisheye-lensed GoPro cameras on bicycle helmets. This allows each viewer to see a particular perspective of the dinner, each slightly different depending on their character's viewpoint and interpretation of events.

Donegan is exploring the commercial advantages of using VR in eLearning. The 'face-to-face' quality of immersive VR has the potential to provide a more successful training experience and is also scalable. However, she notes that measurements of user engagement will need to be developed and quantified. Metrics of analysis may include biofeedback (sweat and pulse), facial expressions, voice and gestures. An example of this is the Psious VR platform which monitors a patient's physiology to measure their anxiety response to certain virtual stimuli. This behavioural health technology company uses cognitive therapy techniques within a virtual experience to treat phobias and anxieties. Donegan wants to measure engagement while the learner role-plays within a virtual theatrical environment.

Mat Collishaw recreated Henry Fox Talbot's 'seminal' photography exhibition which was originally staged at King Edward's School, Birmingham in 1839. *Thresholds* (2017) is a VR experience where users can navigate a CGI recreation of the original room where Fox Talbot's images were displayed. This is particularly resonant as the original images have significantly deteriorated and are now stored in darkened vaults. *Thresholds* incorporates a physical dimension into the exhibition where visitors can 'touch real objects and feel real sensations that correspond with what they see in the virtual world – whether it's the warmth of a fire or the mouldings on the wall' (Ellis-Peterson, 2017).

Transmedia storytelling offers a unique audience experience. The participating reader/viewer is drawn into the story space and their engagement is accurately measured using data metrics and tracking technologies. Their profile is used to guide the selection of customised content. Martin Reiser suggests we are witnessing the birth of a new art form that 'that lives in the hybrid world of the new "Hertzian" spaces and in the creative mind of its new audiences; simultaneously addressing both the *heimlich* of place and the *unheimlich* of digital space' (Koenitz et al, 2015 p. 255): the familiar and the unfamiliar that exists in the physical interactivity between an electronic device and a person.

9 Conclusion

In writing this book I sought to identify accessible storytelling theories and concepts most relevant to the development of interactive narratives. The future of this storytelling space is difficult to predict. Technology is evolving quickly, so we must keep an open mind, research historical works and experiment with what is available. Interactive narratives and transmedia story developers have a wide range of technical skills and abilities, but it is the ability to tell a good story that is fundamental to their success. Each year I set my students an assignment where they have to return the following week and tell a joke to the whole class. They need to consider the story set-up, the narrative hook, pacing and timing. To be honest, most find telling a joke to be an incredibly difficult piece of business. To begin with, they need to choose a decent joke that has the potential to make people laugh. They must rehearse its delivery and make sure they place the correct emphasis on particular words and phrases. While onstage they need to read their classmates' reactions and deliver the punchline with appropriate intonation and timing. An audience made up of one's peers can be brutal, but it certainly focuses the mind as to the function of a story. A story is always aimed at a specified audience and we must consider how this audience will receive and interpret the story when we construct a narrative.

Hank Blumenthal says that 'a producer must have aesthetic vision. He literally has to be able to see the finished film in his mind's eye. He has to grapple with the way it will situate meaningfulness in the culture a year in the future' (Hope, 2011). Blumenthal's 'storyscapes' describe 'the coordinated transmedia franchise model of games, characters, music, paratexts, and fan participation'. He states that the storyscape is 'spawning an anti-poetics that are revolutionary in the paradigm of how stories help us explain the world' (Blumenthal, interview 2017). They make stories into 'cognitive and emotional landmarks' to increase the level of 'complexity and uncertainty' in the way that drama is used to describe the world.

Several years ago I delivered a lecture on interactive narratives at a UK university. I noted to the audience that in my opinion Tarkovsky's films were almost perfect and that their ponderous style and thought-provoking content was highly suited to interactive storytelling. During the Q&A session at the end of the evening a hand went up and one person spoke frankly: 'If, by your own admission, Tarkovsky's films are in fact a perfect form of storytelling, then what's the point of making any story interactive?' My curt response made reference to nineteenth-century Luddites! The proper answer, of course, necessitates both commercial and creative considerations. Financial success will ensure interactive stories become mainstream, yet non-commercial research and experimentation often produce rich, varied and satisfying results. Storytelling forms, like languages, are plastic, they ebb and flow. Their gradual evolution produces new genres, styles, methodologies and platforms for distribution. This keeps things fresh and maintains interest. In the late nineteenth century the London theatre world needed something new. Looking at historical techniques from abroad, 'directors and designers saw in the elaborate symbolism and apparent simplicity of the Far Eastern stage a way out of the dead end in which they found themselves' (Hartnoll, 2012 p. 229). Japanese Noh theatre involves music, dance and drama and is rooted in religious ritual. It 'takes its subjects from myth and legend ... a drama of soliloquy and reminiscence ... Not as in the West, of conflict' (Hartnoll, 2012 p. 230). Comical interludes called *kyogen* are presented within a main Noh performance. Noh actors play the same role throughout their careers, perfecting each movement and utterance on stage and this prompted a reappraisal of the training of young Western actors. Noh theatre, with its masks, incidental music and evocative costumes was highly influential on the work of Irish playwright W.B. Yeats. Drawing on mythology and foreign theatrical forms, the London theatre revitalised its content and drew in new audiences.

So what does the future hold for interactive narratives and transmedia storytelling? HP chief technology officer Shane Wall describes current

VR as 'the punch cards of our generation', yet he is confident that AR 'display and field of view' limitations will soon be resolved (Bonasio, 2017). SVP immersive media at Technicolour Marcie Jastrow says that for VR to become a mass-market entertainment experience it must have both a strong story and 'stickiness' to create 'a user experience that is both intuitive and comfortable'. Jastrow has emphasised that collaboration is key, as no single company can develop 'VR to its full potential' (Jastrow quoted in Bonasio, 2017).

Achieving widespread adoption of headsets has proved difficult. Various reasons cited for this include fashion change and consumer acceptance, insufficient processing power, privacy concerns and some reported nausea-inducing effects. However, many of these issues are gradually being addressed. The advanced processing power of graphics cards offer an increased frame rate of 90 frames per second which apparently avoids 'simulation sickness' in wearers. Apple has purchased the German eye-tracking technology company SensoMotoric Instruments. Their headsets feature a rendering technique called 'Foveated rendering' which only shows the headset wearer a high resolution image of what they are actually looking at. Peripheral images are delivered at a lower resolution to reduce the computational load. SensoMotoric technology may be 'bigger than making augmented and virtual reality look and feel realistic – it might be the key to making the technology mainstream' (Ghosh, 2017).

Disney is creating a direct-to-consumer streaming service and Facebook will offer factual entertainment to compete with services such as YouTube, Netflix and traditional TV networks (Kelion, 2017). Facebook is particularly interested in the quantifiable social media engagement of smartphone-based viewers. This includes data-mining their likes, shares and comments in order to personalise content and deliver targeted ads. Commercially driven, product-oriented VR storytelling includes brand exploitation of the 'experiential' which aims to produce a 'deeper engagement' with customers and create 'a lasting memory' of a brand (Stewart, 2017).

Future narrative paradigms may realise Anthony Burgess's vision of a complex blend of sound design, text, musical notation and visuals. Increasingly, much of the dynamic content on offer today is registering with us at a subconscious level. The subjective responses of audiences is influenced by their cultural background and knowledge. An audience that can read music, interpret visual composition, framing, timing, tone, colour, contrast and translate languages and consider nuance will successfully deconstruct a complex text. However, this may be a unique repertoire for a limited audience. The interactive story world is a theatrical space, rich in diversity and embracive of change. Whatever future story formats and delivery platforms arise, whether your story is a saga or a vignette, all an audience wants is a 'ripping good yarn'.

Appendix 1

Making *The Little Extras*

The Little Extras story idea was originally developed as a traditional linear narrative. A young woman called Sarah lives with her husband and young child. She is unhappy in her marriage yet cannot afford to leave. In desperation, she takes a second job as a cleaner for an elderly couple. The woman gives her strict instructions for cleaning the house and explains that her husband is permanently bedridden. Each day, Sarah cleans his bedroom and they often chat. Over time, the old man becomes infatuated with Sarah and eventually propositions her with an unusual financial arrangement. He offers her extra money to do the housework in the nude (the original title was *The Last Hurrah). Sarah is thus faced with an interesting moral dilemma and the story has established its dramatic conflict. Should she compromise her virtue and integrity, or are these flexible principles when one is in dire straits. She discusses the offer with her spirited friend, argues with her husband and mulls over her situation. After some deliberation she decides to accept the offer and take the money, planning to use it to create a new life for herself and her son. Later, her friend tries to create a similar arrangement with her own employer, suggesting that he may like some 'little extras' taken care of. Thus *The Little Extras* poses the question, who is exploiting whom?

As the project evolved, in the form of theatrical improvisations and multiple script drafts, it seemed more appropriate to make the story unfold gradually with interactivity becoming a function of narrative exploration.

TOWARDS A NEW FILM PARADIGM

Experimental narratives and digital storytelling offer exciting alternatives to traditional story formats. The aim of the *The Little Extras* was to create an interactive film paradigm that would exploit the potential of fast-evolving digital production and distribution technologies. I wanted to explore user engagement and immersion in a story format which offers the viewer a degree of narrative agency. The audience would be able to choose alternative narrative perspectives as the story progressed. Initially, I intended to distribute the film via an online delivery platform. However, the prohibitive processing power requirements of this interactive, multiple video stream content challenged even the highest specification computers available.

In constructing a method of navigating a metanarrative, which would offer multiple story perspectives, I decided to use the narratological terms 'primary narrative' and 'embedded narrative'. In the film, a primary narrative runs continuously for 30 minutes as a linear sequence, the embedded narratives only play out fully when interacted with. These short duration clips (sub screens) only play if the viewer clicks on them soon after they appear. If left unselected, the embedded narrative fades out again and is not shown. Their spatial and temporal placement on the screen and their concurrent play settings (how

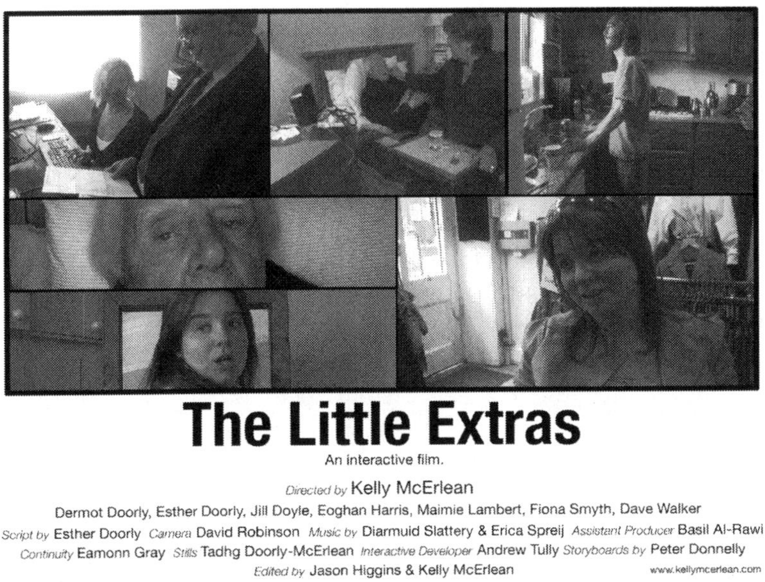

Figure 1 Poster for *The Little Extras*

audio and transitions in overlapping narratives mix) is still dictated by the author. The embedded narratives offer another time frame for the viewer. This may be slower or faster than that presented in the primary narrative. Norman Mailer compared the sense of time experienced by boxers during a title fight to the sense of time experienced by the audience watching them (Mailer, 1991 p. 188). The fighters' appreciation of time passing is utterly heightened; they are living in an experiential moment that is heavily congested with significant incidents; they absorb information at such an intense rate that time appears to be slower for them than for the audience. The narrative 'extras' allow the film's story to be expanded upon to introduce more character details and plot development. They offer the viewer story agency, allowing them to explore the broader metanarrative that traditional films do not show.

By using ambient music and long duration shots inspired by Tarkovsky's work, we are creating the right atmosphere for an interactive film to work. The intensity of scenes can 'speed up' and 'slow down' the perception of time passing. If time is perceived by the audience to be passing slowly they are more likely to interact; 'from this derives Baudelaire's classic claim: "All good and true draftsmen draw according to the image written in their minds and not according to nature"' (Agacinski, 2003 p. 74).

STORYTELLING USING SPATIAL MONTAGE

The Little Extras was shot digitally and the visual aesthetic is characteristic of the low-budget nature of the work. Digital cameras were used by the Dogme 95 film-makers, in part due to their gritty feel and flexibility. Artifice is created when attempting to use this format to produce high-end visuals. Budget constraints impacted heavily on the project, particularly in post-production and the development of the interactive platform and user interface. I experimented with spatial montage by re-editing a sequence from an earlier short film *At Debt's Door* (2005). In a particular scene, a mother and daughter (Brigid and Margaret) argue over money. By reorganising the edited clips onscreen as a spatial montage, the audience are introduced to the story world much more quickly than in the traditionally edited version. The 'comic book' layout of the sequence obliges the viewer to 'navigate' the montage elements, waiting for the next clip which will contain new narrative information and drive the story forward. The scene opens slowly with the elderly Brigid arriving in a taxi outside Margaret's dilapidated old house. Despite her age, she must open the car door herself and carry her heavy bags up the steep steps to the house. She presses the buzzer for Margaret's apartment. The street is noisy and Brigid seems anxious and uneasy, uncomfortable in her surroundings. When inside, a quarter-screen sized shot positioned on the left of the screen, tracks into the kitchen, showing the mother and daughter laying out some crockery on a table. On the right side of the screen we see a series of close-up shots of the various items on the table and tea being poured. This was intended to establish the layout of the kitchen location while also focusing on the minutiae of their lives. It also serves to slow the pacing down and focus the audience's attention on the subsequent conversation. Two clips (Brigid and Margaret in mid-shot) fade-in centre-screen and side-by-side, gradually increasing in size. The fractious conversation plays out like a fencing bout. Both women deliver barbed comments to each other and the atmosphere becomes increasingly frosty. Margaret asks Brigid about some 'love letters' she has been receiving while staying with Margaret's younger sister Jessie. It has been established earlier in the story that these letters are actually unpaid bills that Brigid has been unsuccessfully trying to hide from her daughters. Brigid delivers a swift and calculated retort to her daughter, asking about the employment status of Margaret's husband. She knows that this always puts Margaret on edge and will stop any further questions about the letters. With one final caustic blow directed at Margaret's brittle ego, Brigid's image drifts into the centre of the frame and gradually replaces the fading image of Margaret, a sign that Brigid has once again won the argument.

By positioning the clips side by side onscreen the audience can see the conversation from two perspectives simultaneously. This works extremely well for this scene, as the characters' reaction shots are just as important as the lines being spoken. I have shown both versions of this scene to students over several years and the spatial montage version is always chosen over the traditional linear edit. The feedback is that by presenting various perspectives of the narrative at once, the audience feels more immersed within the story.

THE SPECTATOR'S GAZE

The issue of nudity or semi-nudity was addressed in the early drafts of the script. In these versions Sarah undressed completely in front of the old man and did the housework in the nude. This would have allowed for some comedic visuals and creative camera work that would follow her naked form without appearing salacious and sensational. I was concerned that a fetishistic approach to camerawork would dominate the visualisation of the story; a visualisation that had already been compromised by the demands of constructing spatially presented interactive content. The script was revised to show Sarah instead 'secretly' trying on the woman's expensive clothes, not realising the old man is watching her. He suggests that she can keep the clothes as long as she first wears them while she is cleaning. Soon after, she sells them to a vintage clothing shop.

Laura Mulvey states that fetishistic obsession reveals the meaning behind popular images of women. Women dressed provocatively in film become a male fantasy and fetishistic images already pervade mass media (Mulvey, 1989 p. 13). Mulvey argues that fetishism concerns the narcissism of man, who views the naked female form as his castrated self. The female organs of sex represent a wound while male-dominated representations of women as objects of display do not represent women's own fantasies. For women, this female object they come to represent is not actually there at all. It is only a representation of the man's unconscious fantasy.

In the interactive film, Sarah is encouraged to fulfil the erotic fantasies of the old man. She becomes the object of his gaze but the film stops short of letting her enter the spectator's gaze. This would interrupt the narrative, dwelling on the sexual object. As media entertainment, this would limit the necessity of interaction. The 'gaze' would work as an 'edit' and fix the narrative in a single pathway. For the purposes of creating an interactive film, the erotic gaze could not at this stage be included. The story does however place the 'virtuous' Sarah in a compromising position. While we know that she needs the money, our interaction with the story tells us that the 'gaze' does not threaten her. She places her physical needs before emotion.

THE PRIMACY OF THE AUTHOR

James Joyce employed a lyrical style that turned the act of reading into more of an experience:

> The effect at times is astounding, but the price paid is the entire dissolution of the very foundation of literary diction, the entire decomposition of literary method itself; for the lay reader the text has been turned into abracadabra.
>
> (Williams, 1980 p. 20)

Readers of Joyce must accept the primacy of the author, to accept the reality he has created and the mechanism for accessing that reality. Interactive film necessitates the same commitment of the viewer; the interactivity is working to tell a more complex story, and cannot be viewed in simplistic terms.

The Italian film director Roberto Rossellini discussed realism in film in an interview with Mario Verdone:

> The realist film has the 'world' as its living object, not telling of a story. What it has to say is not fixed in advance, because it arises of its own accord. It has no love of the superfluous and the spectacular, and rejects these, going instead to the root of things.
>
> (Rossellini quoted in Williams, 1980 p. 32)

The Little Extras experiments with new technologies but rejects both artifice and unnecessary user interaction, fragmenting the storyteller's narrative without good reason. This reinforces the primacy of the author in the text and prevents the reader from altering the author's aims and objectives. The story is not formulaic; instead it allows the viewer to journey through the narrative guided by the author, interpreting the world without changing it. The interaction is not fixed, it offers varying narrative pathways. The viewer will find some pathways more interesting than others and they will make decisions based on plot/character preference. By design, in each individual engagement with the story, some navigational pathways will not be explored. In this way, the story interaction reflects the decisions we make in real life, everyday choices and selections, controlling and influencing what we see and hear. This is addressed by the content of the embedded narratives. Each one enhances our awareness of the meta-narrative. The scenes were specifically written to extend the audience's knowledge of the story's reality while avoiding exposition and redundancy. The embedded narratives are not examples of *mise-en-abîme* (a film within a film). They do not deconstruct the narrative nor signify the textual whole. Instead, they conform to the order of connotation established by the *mise-en-scène* within the primary narrative (Hayward, 2006 p. 252). As a function of film, embedded narratives offer the film-maker the opportunity to create meaningful new scenes employing specific stylistic elements representative of the author's oeuvre. These scenes may be a departure from textual linearity, but interactive stories work effectively when structured as non-linear narratives. They change our interpretation of the story and the characters by taking us somewhere new, somewhere we would not have expected to go based on the story material up to that point.

ABDICATING AUTHORSHIP

Interactive narratives blur the lines between author and reader:

> it should be considered that the goal of an interactive narrative is not to author the narrative, but to provide a context and an environment in which the narrative can be discovered or built by the readers of the story ... designers and authors of interactive narrative are far more like architects than they are like writers.
>
> (Meadows, 2002 p. 54)

In the film-making model exemplified by *The Little Extras,* the author/director can create an interactive film text that allows free navigation within the confines of a set narrative. Marc LeBlanc described this as abdicating authorship, 'creating the rules and procedures of the world is an act of authorship that defines the space' (LeBlanc quoted in Meadows, 2002 p. 54). The author creates the world then leaves it to the audience to discover it.

The Little Extras functions like a Bruegel painting presented temporally at 25 frames per second. The spatial montage elements fit together to alter perspective, but in terms of the fabula, they are not happening concurrently. The primary narrative and embedded narratives are separated both temporally and physically. For some embedded narratives, the narrative exposition will be independent of their position within the fabula. They are simply there to develop our understanding of the story by presenting additional perspectives on both the story and characters.

DECONSTRUCTIVE CINEMA

The individualism of narrative deconstruction must also be rejected: *The Little Extras* is deliberately constructed to allow aesthetic content to dominate over form (Hayward, 2006 p. 301). The mode of interaction focuses on simplicity of use instead of creating a techno-centric interface that would alienate traditional film audiences.

> But in challenging all consensual standards of truth and justice, of ethics, and meaning, and in pursuing the dissolution of all narratives and meta-theories into a diffuse universe of language games, deconstructionism ended up, in spite of the best intentions of its more radical practitioners, by reducing knowledge and meaning into a rubble of signifiers.
>
> (Harvey, 1990 p. 350)

The traditional cinematic experience is a shared 'real' encounter with knowledge. Emotions and responses are communicated 'live' through the group to stimulate and enhance specific reactions. The narrative moves forward at a fixed pace dictated by the director and the editor. Audience members connect and read events within the text to form their own interpretation, their thoughts moving back and forward in time, from past events (scenes) to the present. By collecting narrative information the audience construct their own 'real' understanding of the text and its meaning. This is not a collective agreement, but it is a general response to the narrative. Deconstructive cinema makes visible the filmic devices used by film-makers to immerse the audience and can be described as being 'counter-cinematic' (Hayward, 2006 p. 98). By breaking up the film's aesthetic and deliberately contravening the traditional codes and conventions of narrative film, the deconstructive film fragments the text into blocks to be pieced together again by the audience. Narrative flow is overlooked as the film-maker introduces their aesthetical and political ideas. In Godard's *À Bout de Souffle* (1960) jump cuts[1] are used to deliberately break the narrative rhythm in a rejection of the dominant Hollywood storytelling conventions of the period.

The Little Extras uses spatial and temporal montage yet it does not fragment the text at the expense of the narrative whole. The experience offered to the audience is that of meta-narrative with multiple potential perspectives on the story. A deconstructionist approach would fracture these interweaving texts and create a series of redundant fragments: 'the effect is to break (deconstruct) the power of the author to impose meanings or offer a continuous narrative' (Harvey, 1990 p. 51). Fredric Jameson also notes that a deconstructive 'reading' of a text creates closure that is similar to the 'boundaries' of a traditional work of art. A deconstructive reading of traditional art and a deconstructive reading of the text opens narrative boundaries and 'leaves us elsewhere' (Jameson, 1991 p. 157), primarily outside the text and uninvolved. Christopher Norris states that 'deconstruction can never have the final word because its insights are inevitably couched in a rhetoric which itself lies open to further deconstructive reading' (Norris, 2006 p. 83). The aim of *The Little Extras* is to promote a post-viewing deliberation that draws on perspectival references and leads to triangulation of knowledge through debate. The outcome proposed by Norris would take the audience away from the narrative and make their interaction superfluous.

THE FUNCTION OF EMBEDDED NARRATIVES

How can the embedded narratives of *The Little Extras* that were intended to allow the audience to navigate the text be so integral to the plot if they are not compulsory viewing? The aim was for them to each add something that could both exist naturally within the primary narrative and which develops the plot logically. They are conveying the unseen parts of the meta-narrative, which extend the story and develop character. Aristotle said that:

> plots ought (as in tragedy) to be constructed dramatically; that is, they should be concerned with a unified action, whole and complete, possessing a beginning, middle parts and an end.
>
> (Aristotle quoted in Heath, 1996 p. 38)

This would make the embedded elements of the metanarrative essential viewing for the viewer. This 'determinate structure' of the plot requires all the parts to be present for it to work. So the structure of the various elements must be such that the transposition or removal of any one section dislocates and changes everything. If the presence or absence of something has no discernible effect, it is not a part of the whole (Heath, 1996 p. 15).

LEARNING NEW MODES OF INTERACTION

In *Contemporary Problems in Perception* there is an analysis of experiments carried out on subjects who wore glasses that inverted their vision. The experiments resulted in the subjects learning new relationships between movement patterns and visual directions. They proved that people could learn to work with 'up-down dimension and bilateral right-left symmetry' shifts not just due to 'learning' but due to 'an intrinsic organisation of human motion'.

> When we incorporate the concept of feedback into our thinking, we are using a cybernetic model in which not only does perception lead to behaviour, but behaviour inevitably alters sensory feedback. Perception guides behaviour, behaviour guides perception.
>
> (Welford & Houssiadas, 1970 p. 126)

This research suggests that an interactive interface that provides informative feedback will be successful. Audiences interact with the narrative to influence their perspective; this in turn will impact on their relationship with the various narrative elements. The embedded narratives enhance textual comprehension, expanding the metanarrative. As each embedded narrative adds information to a particular part of the metanarrative, audiences are expected to interact with the ones that take the story (or follow a character) in a direction they are interested in.

Tarkovsky did not agree with contemporary experiments in spatial montage:

> In recent years developments in film technique have given birth to (or degenerated to) a particular aberration: the wide screen is divided into two or more parts, in which two or more actions can be shown happening in parallel at the same time. In my view this innovation is ill-conceived; pseudo-conventions are being fabricated that are not organically part of the cinema, 'polyscreen' cinema should be compared not with a chord, or harmony, or polyphony, but rather with the sound produced by several orchestras playing different pieces of music at the same time.
>
> (Tarkovsky, 1989 p. 71)

Tarkovsky preferred images to be presented spatially, like a poem, one word after another, one line at a time. He believed that it was physiologically impossible to watch several visuals at once. Modern texts would suggest that this is not true; in fact spatial montage of blended shots as used in *Europa* (1991) enhances the experience and interpretation of the scene. Parallel timelines are presented spatially using sub-screens within the full screen. Each sub-screen is 'bracketed' several seconds apart. The audience simultaneously views the 'before', 'after' and 'now' of a single event. The result is a more profound experience for the audience. A multitude of spatial information adds to the intensity of the scene and corresponds with the enhanced perceptual ability brought on by an adrenalin rush. Of course, Tarkovsky may be referring to the use of opposing and unrelated visuals that would not present well together.

NARRATIVE IMMERSION

Immersion within a book does not always reflect high literary value or require dynamic engagement with the text. Toni Morrison's *Beloved* is known for its accessibility through effortless concentration. Often, the most familiar texts are the most immersive. Similarly, *The Little Extras* had to achieve a level of viewer interactivity that was natural, not forced and prescribed. The challenge was to present a simple story that drew on the viewers' previous experience. They needed to have some idea of where the embedded narratives might take them. The embedded narratives required a 'lead-in time', to allow the scene to be presented long enough on the screen for the viewer to recognise it, but then gradually fade out during the scene if it was not selected. Immersion in film is partly due to the inactivity of the viewer. The film progresses without aid or interaction; the audience are non-participant observers. The potential conflict between the audience becoming a participant-observer and the ability of the text to retain the immersive qualities of traditional film needs more analysis. The interface may act as a barrier between the immersive reality of the text and the audience's real world. This is only the physical aspect of the problem, in terms of the thought processes going into the audience becoming immersed, even a bad edit can remind the audience they are watching a film, so in fact any user interaction requirement will most likely lead to a similar outcome. In dealing with this issue, I believe that the introspective style of the cinematography, inspired by the reflective use of camera in *Werckmeister Harmonies* (2000) and *Damnation* (1988) by Béla Tarr and *Stalker* (1979) by Andrei Tarkovsky, allowed the interactive interface to become immersed in the narrative text, thereby helping the audience to ignore its function and concentrate on the narrative.

FOVEAL AND PERIPHERAL VISION

Interaction in *The Little Extras* also depends on the audience being able to take in multiple, spatially presented visuals at the same time. This presentation technique relies on the capability of one's peripheral vision to absorb information that is not viewed using the foveal system. Foveal vision is less than one degree wide and is used to concentrate on specific objects. Peripheral vision allows us to see a greater area and to lead us forward. Peripheral vision will guide the viewer through the narrative, both spatially and temporally.

> The temporal process of seeing, as fast as it is, is one of the things that allows a narrative aspect of imagery. This is a temporal process that is implicitly narrative because it provides for a beginning and an end, and it's this motion of the eye that many authors of narrative are able to manipulate and control for the sake of telling a story.
>
> (Meadows, 2002 p. 94)

When reading and viewing texts we 'map' their image; we do not see them, we 'remember' them. If the experiential nature of an interactive narrative seeks to immerse the audience in the story, the engagement methodology should exploit our existing ability to navigate the world.

When reading (or learning to read), 'Colloquialisms and even whole sentences can be parsed in a glance, almost saccadically, because we know what to expect. The redundancy of the information allows us to move easily through it' (Meadows, 2002 p. 94).

ALTERING PERSPECTIVE

Azar Nafisi tells the story of an Iranian teacher who secretly tutors young women in English literature (Nafisi, 2003). The classes are illegal and highly secretive. Some of the students cannot even tell their family they are studying. Azar's friend Mina tells her about her method of teaching the concept of ambiguity. She asks her students to tell her what they see as she moves a chair into different positions. She tells them that despite their different positions in the classroom and thus different perspectives, they are still seeing the same chair. But they now realise that there is more than one way of seeing the chair. This is particularly relevant to the narrative structure of *The Little Extras*. Audiences might watch the same story, but there is more than one way of reading the narrative. The level of interactivity employed in this film increases the potential plot perspectives and this increases the number of interpretations. Audiences are able to engage with the narrative on a more personal level. Through interactivity, their interpretation will be intertwined with perspective.

THE LITTLE EXTRAS SOUND DESIGN

The use of music in an audiovisual text is the surest way of absorbing the audience into the complete experience, 'To the hallucinating mind, the language of music is equally adept at creating horizontal correspondences between the senses and at revealing vertical correspondences between numbers and things' (Ryan, 2001 p. 79). Music is an important part of the story. It was used to create an ambient, immersive atmosphere where interaction is natural. Interacting with the spatial montage has 'rounded edges' because of the music. This is like the traditional edit where we cut audio before the visual. The audio edit takes us seamlessly into the next shot, followed by the visual. The ambient music used in *The Little Extras* aimed to make the interactivity 'seamless'.

INTERPRETING AND RE-INTERPRETING THE TEXTUAL WORLD

Texts create the sensorial atmosphere that allows the reader to 'build' the textual world in their imagination:

> the function of language in this activity is to pick up objects in the textual world, to link them with properties, to animate characters and setting – in short, to conjure their presence to the imagination.
>
> (Ryan, 2001 p. 91)

Film produces a tangible form of this world (audio and visual clips) but they are still creating a new, imagined reality for the viewer. Films may take characters and put them into difficult situations. The entertainment is derived from watching them either win or lose in their attempts to deal with the situation. Here, the author/director controls the visualisation of the world. They dictate what the viewer sees and hears. The viewer can interpret this audiovisual fugue in their own way, but not so freely as they could with a written text. With *The Little Extras* some of this authorial control is given over to the viewer. The viewer can 'navigate the narrative' in their own way by choosing specific story perspectives. The embedded narratives are scenes that will give greater dramatic exposition, but could also have been incorporated into the primary narrative, or existed as deleted scenes. Deleted scenes that we see in home cinema releases are often edited back into later releases of films. This calls into question the actual act of completing a film. Films are often described as being made three times. Once at the script stage, second when the script is shot onto film and third when the film is edited. Clearly, film-makers can revisit this third stage of the film-making process as often as they wish and reinterpret the script and footage. Ridley Scott re-edited *Blade Runner* several times and reshot a scene some twenty-five years after its initial release. However, this is not the norm and on films where digital effects are not used so extensively it is the third film-making process that is revisited. So *The Little Extras* is giving some potential for 'reinterpretation' to the viewer. Like a re-edited version of a film, the perspective on the story may shift, but the story itself remains fundamentally the same. The beginning and ending do not change although we may learn a bit more or less about characters and their journey through the narrative.

STORYBOARDS AND ANIMATICS

The animatics (storyboards edited to dialogue) of *The Little Extras* were particularly useful in terms of timing. They were used to correct issues

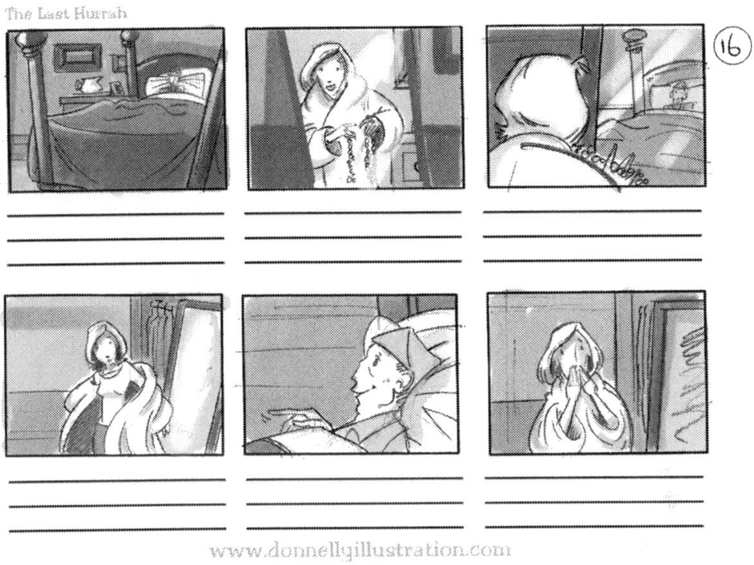

Figure 2 Storyboard from *The Little Extras*

such as overlapping dialogue. Scenes had to be re-timed to ensure that slow motion/speeded up clips are not required in the final film.

Ryan identifies two types of statements made by authors. Counterfactual statements, where we look at different versions of events from our 'native reality' and offer an alternative history, and fictional statements where we are immersed in the text and the text becomes reality. This is called re-centring, which Ryan regards as a basic component of reading fiction. The interactivity of *The Little Extras* re-centres the viewer into the 'reality' of the film text. The immersive nature of the story acts as a function of the embedded interactivity.

Often the enjoyment of a text comes after we have read the whole book and we can contemplate it as a single entity. The aim of *The Little Extras* was that viewers would discuss their navigational pathway to create a shared experience of viewing the same film, but seeing (or focusing on) different perspectives.

NOTE

1 Jump cuts are cuts with no match between shots. They generally interrupt the audience's sense of orientation within the scene.

Appendix 2
Digital Data Compression

Knowledge of digital data compression is very important when working in transmedia, particularly with regard to problem solving and pushing digital audiovisual materials to their limits. Online broadcasters employ compression technologies that reduce file size with minimum quality loss. Smaller files can be sent faster and require less bandwidth for transmission. A codec (compressor/decompressor) is used to 'compress' a file before transmitting it online. The same model codec is used by the receiver to 'decompress' the file when it has arrived at its destination. A great number of codecs are available for music, images and video and some of them are quite similar in performance, but the codec that is used to compress a file must also be used to decompress it correctly.

SPATIAL AND TEMPORAL COMPRESSION: EXPLOITING REDUNDANCY

Compression of images and video work both *spatially* and *temporally* (within each frame and from frame-to-frame). Spatial compression exploits spatial redundancy, repeating pixel values that make up a single 'block' of colour within an image – for example, a clear blue sky. Pixels are positioned at x–y coordinates within the frame. Spatial compression works to eliminate the need to repeatedly transmit the same pixel values when all that is needed is one value plus the number of times it should be re-used. Temporal redundancy occurs where pixel values at specific *x–y* coordinates do not change from frame to frame. This can happen when a camera is in a fixed position and the image background is static. The redundancy here is that the pixels that make up the image background essentially do not change from their first frame values. Therefore, the codec compresses a video file by recording the *x–y* pixel values in the first frame, then indicating how many frames they should be repeated for. Rapidly changing pixels in successive frames require a high *data rate* to store and replay the visuals. Some codecs use two-pass encoding, assessing the data rate needed for each sequence, then raising and reducing the amount of data used for each shot to optimise compression.

QUANTISATION: THRESHOLD LEVELS AND BANDING

A *threshold* value can be used to set the level of compression required. This value is used to *quantise* pixel information according to a fixed scale. For example, a finely detailed image that has millions of colours will result in a large data file if every pixel value is recorded and stored. With quantisation, the codec notes each value, then converts it to the closest value on a preset scale. This is like using a thermometer to record room temperatures to an accuracy of a tenth of a degree (e.g. 32.2°), then 'quantising' the values to the nearest whole number (32°). The threshold indicates how different the compressed value can be to the original. Over-quantising would result in some image quality loss (the new pixel value is an approximation of the original – close but not exact) but would reduce the number of pixel values needed to recreate the image and therefore reduce the data file size. Therefore the codec settings must be adjusted to control the amount of compression applied or *banding* may occur – subtle tonal changes within the original image appear as large bands of colour.

CODING COMPRESSION

Coding compression works at the level of machine code. The codec looks for long, repeating series of bits in the code that make up the file. The codec removes these strings and replaces them with shorter sequences. The transmitted file will contain a *header*, which tells the receiving codec to decompress the file by replacing these short strings with the original longer sequences.

FRAME PREDICTION: KEYFRAMES AND CHECKSUM VALUES

The MPEG (Motion Picture Experts Group) codec is used to encode video. MPEG uses a system of frame prediction to reduce the amount of data that must be sent. The codec encodes and transmits *keyframes* (e.g. frames 1 and 5) then 'predicts' frames 2, 3 and 4. The codec compares the predicted frames to the originals to assess their accuracy, then calculates a *checksum* value by applying an algorithm to the frame data. This checksum is also transmitted to the receiver. On receipt of frames 1 and 5 plus the checksum, the receiver codec uses frames 1 and 5 to predict frames 2, 3 and 4 and uses the algorithm to produce another checksum value. If both the received and locally created checksum values are the same, the frames must have been predicted correctly. MPEG data must be *buffered* in order to allow time for resending corrupted data and dropped files. This means that MPEG broadcasts cannot be fully live; there is a short delay between the live event and the reception, processing and presentation of audiovisual materials on the audience screens.

References

Adorno, Theodor & Eisler, Hanns (2005) *Composing for the Films,* London: Continuum.

Agacinski, Sylviane (2003) *Time Passing: Modernity and Nostalgia,* New York: Columbia University Press.

Aristotle (1996) *Poetics,* London: Penguin.

Arnheim, Rudolf (ed), (1957) *Film As Art,* Berkeley, CA: University of California Press.

Atherton, Kevin (2012) Auto-Interview, Dublin: Flood.

Bal, Mieke (1985) *Narratology,* Toronto: University of Toronto Press.

Barthes, Roland (1978) *Image, Music, Text,* New York: Hill and Wang.

Bazin, André (2005a) *What is Cinema? Volume 1,* London: University of California Press.

Bazin, André (2005b) *What is Cinema? Volume 2,* London: University of California Press.

Bellantoni, Patti (2005) *If It's Purple, Someone's Gonna Die: The Power of Color in Visual Storytelling,* Burlington, MA: Focal Press.

Benjamin, Walter, (1999) *Illuminations: The Work of Art in the Age of Mechanical Reproduction,* London: Pimlico.

Blumenthal, Hank & Xu, Yan (2012) 'The ghost club storyscape: Designing for transmedia storytelling', *IEEE Transactions on Consumer Electronics,* 58(2): 190. http://ieeexplore.ieee.org/document/6227412/ (accessed July 2017).

Branigan, Edward (1992) *Narrative Comprehension and Film,* London: Routledge.

Bruner, Jerome (1991) 'The narrative construction of reality', *Critical Inquiry* 18(1): 1–21. http://www.jstor.org/stable/1343711 (accessed August 2016).

Burgess, Anthony (1975) *Joysprick: An Introduction to the Language of James Joyce,* New York: Harcourt Brace Jovanovich.

Burgess, Anthony (1987) *Homage to Qwert Yuiop: Selected Journalism 1978–1985*, London: Abacus.

Calvino, Italo (1982) *If on a Winter's Night a Traveller*, San Diego, CA: Harvest Books.

Carroll, Noël (2008) *The Philosophy of Motion Pictures*, Singapore: Blackwell Publishing.

Cartier-Bresson, Henri (2004) *The Mind's Eye: Writings on Photography and Photographers*, New York: Aperture.

Chiaramonte, Giovanni & Tarkovsky, Andrei A. (eds.), (2006) *Instant Light: Tarkovsky Polaroids*, London: Thames & Hudson.

Collins, Karen, Kapralos, Bill & Tessler, Holly (eds.) (2014) *The Oxford Handbook of Interactive Audio*, New York: Oxford University Press.

Crary, J. (2001) *Suspensions of Perception: Attention, Spectacle and Modern Culture*, Cambridge, MA: MIT Press.

De Quincey, Thomas (1994) *Confessions of an English Opium-Eater*, Ware: Wordsworth Editions Ltd.

Egoyan, Atom & Balfour, Ian (eds.) (2004) *Subtitles. On the Foreignness of Film*, Cambridge, MA: MIT Press.

Eisenstein, Sergei M. (1986) *The Film Sense*, London: Faber & Faber.

Ellis-Peterson, Hannah (2017) 'Mat Collishaw restages 1839 photography show in virtual reality', *The Guardian*, 14 April https://www.theguardian.com/technology/2017/apr/14/somerset-house-mat-collishaw-restages-1839-photography-show-in-virtual-reality (accessed 26 June 2017).

Else, Liz (2005) 'What was eye and I?' *New Scientist*, 24/31 December.

Fisher, Richard (2005) 'Flogging a dead horse', *New Scientist*, 24/31 December.

Gibson, Ralph (1999) *Deus Ex Machina*, Cologne: Taschen.

Gilbert, Stuart (1934) *James Joyce's Ulysses: A Study by Stuart Gilbert*, New York: Alfred A. Knopf.

Goldman, William (1989) *Adventures in the Screen Trade*, New York: Grand Central Publishing.

Goodall, Howard (2001) *Big Bangs: The Story of Five Discoveries that Changed Musical History*, London: Vintage.

Gorbman, Claudia (1987) *Unheard Melodies: Narrative Film Music*, Bloomington, IN: University of Indiana Press.

Hansen, Mark B.N. (2006) *New Philosophy for New Media*, Cambridge, MA: MIT Press.

Hardy, G.H., (1992) *A Mathematician's Apology*, Cambridge: Cambridge University Press.

Hartnoll, Phyllis (2012) *The Theatre: A Concise History* updated by Brater, Enoch, London: Thames & Hudson.

Harvey, David (1990) *The Condition of Postmodernity*, Oxford: Basil Blackwell.

Hayward, Susan (2006) *Cinema Studies: The Key Concepts*, New York: Routledge.

Heath, Stephen (1981) *Questions of Cinema*, London: Macmillan Press.

Heath, Malcolm (1996) 'Introduction', in Aristotle, *Poetics*, London: Penguin.

Hemming, Sarah (2015) 'Alice in Web-Land: Moira Buffini directs "wonder.land"', *Financial Times*, 20 June.

Hitchings, Henry (2005) *Dr. Johnson's Dictionary: The Extraordinary Story of the Book that Defined the World*, London: John Murray.

Hockney, David (1984) *Cameraworks*, New York: Alfred A. Knopf.

Hockney, David (2002) *That's the Way I See It*, London: Thames & Hudson.

Hodgkin, Beatrice (2015) 'How To Spend It: Katerina Jebb', *Financial Times*, 20 February.

James, Clive (2007) *North Face of Soho: More Unreliable Memoirs*, London: Picador.

Jameson, Fredric (1991) *Postmodernism, or, The Cultural Logic of Late Capitalism*, London: Verso.

Jenkins, Henry & Thorburn, David (eds.) (2003) *Democracy and New Media*, London: MIT Press.

Joyce, James (1993) *Ulysses*, New York: Vintage.

Kandinsky, Wassily (1977) *Concerning The Spiritual in Art*, Boston, MA: MFA Publications.

Koenitz, Hartmut, Ferri, Gabriele, Haahr, Mads, Sezen, Diğdem, & Sezen, İbrahim Tonguç (eds), (2015) *Interactive Digital Narrative: History, Theory and Practice.* New York: Routledge.

Koppelman, Charles (2004) *Behind the Seen: How Walter Murch Edited Cold Mountain using Apple's Final Cut Pro and What This Means for Cinema*, Berkeley, CA: New Riders Press.

Landow, George P. (2006) *Hypertext 3.0: Critical Theory and New Media in an Era of Globalization*, Baltimare, MD: Johns Hopkins University.

Laurel, Brenda (1991) *Computers as Theatre*, Reading, MA: Addison-Wesley Publishing Company, Inc.

Lemaître, Maurice, (1954) *What is Lettrism?* Paris: Editions Fischbacher.

Lister, M., Dovey, J., Giddings, S., Grant, I. & Kelly, K. (2003) *New Media: A Critical Introduction*, London: Routledge.

Livingstone, Marco, (1997) *The Essential Duane Michals*, London: Thames and Hudson.

Lunenfeld, Peter (ed.), (2000) *The Digital Dialectic: New Essays on New Media*, Cambridge, MA: MIT Press.

Mackendrick, Alexander (2004) *On Film-Making. An Introduction to the Craft of the Director*, New York: Faber & Faber.

Mailer, Norman (1991) *The Fight*, London: Penguin Books.

Malkani, Gautam (2014) 'William Burroughs' exhibition at Photographers' Gallery', *Financial Times*, 17 January.

Manovich, Lev (2002) *The Language of New Media*, Cambridge, MA: MIT Press.

Meadows, Mark Stephen (2002) *Pause and Effect: The Art of Interactive Narrative*, Indianapolis, IN: New Riders Press.

Meyer, Pedro, (1996) *Truths & Fictions: A Journey from Documentary to Digital Photography*, Verona, Italy: Aperture.

Michelson, Annette (ed.) (1985) *Kino-Eye: The Writings of Dziga Vertov*, Berkeley, CA: University of California Press.

Mitchell, W.J.T. (1995) *Picture Theory*, Chicago, IL: University of Chicago Press.

Monaco, James (2000) *How to Read a Film*, New York: Oxford University Press.

Mortensen, William (1936) *Monsters and Madonnas: A Book of Methods*, San Francisco, CA: Camera Craft Publishing Company.

Mortensen, William (1948) *The Command to Look: A Formula for Picture Success*, San Francisco, CA: Mercury Press.

Mulvey, Laura (1989) *Visual and Other Pleasures,* London: Macmillan Press.
Murch, Walter (2001) *In the Blink of an Eye,* Beverly Hills, CA: Silman-James Press.
Murray, Janet H. (1998) *Hamlet on the Holodeck: The Future of Narrative in Cyberspace,* New York: The MIT Press.
Nafisi, Azar (2003) *Reading Lolita in Tehran: A Memoir in Books,* New York: Random House.
Nixon, Nicholas (2007) *The Brown Sisters: Thirty-Three Years,* New York: MOMA.
Norris, Christopher (2006) *Deconstruction,* London: Routledge.
Olsen, Mark (2009) 'Steve McQueen's long shot in "Hunger" is paying off', *Los Angeles Times,* March 22, http://articles.latimes.com/2009/mar/22/entertainment/ca-hunger22 (accessed August 2017).
Ondaatje, Michael (2004) *The Conversations: Walter Murch and the Art of Editing Film,* New York: Alfred A. Knopf.
Perec, Georges (2008) *Species of Space and Other Places,* Harmondsworth: Penguin Classics.
Propp, Vladimir (1968) *Morphology of the Folktale,* Austin, TX: University of Texas Press.
Propp, Vladimir (2001) *Morphology of the Folktale,* Austin, TX: University of Texas Press.
Roberts, Russell (2004) *Tony Ray-Jones,* London: Chris Boot.
Reay, Pauline (2004) *Music in Film: Soundtracks and Synergy,* New York: Wallflower Press.
Rieser, Martin & Zapp, Andrea (eds.) (2002) *New Screen Media: Cinema/Art/ Narrative,* London: British Film Institute.
Ryan, Marie-Laure (2001) *Narrative as Virtual Reality: Immersion and Interactivity in Literature and Electronic Media,* Baltimore, MD: Johns Hopkins University Press.
Ryan, Marie-Laure (ed.) (2004) *Narrative Across Media: The Languages of Storytelling,* Lincoln, NE: University of Nebraska Press.
Shklovsky, Viktor (2008) *Literature and Cinematography,* London: Dalkey Archive.
Shore, Stephen (2007) *Uncommon Places: The Complete Works,* London: Thames & Hudson.
Snider, Mike (2016) 'Transmedia film explores "The Phoenix Incident", *USA Today,* 29 February, http://www.usatoday.com/story/tech/news/2016/02/29/transmedia-film-explores-phoenix-incident/80983058/ (accessed August 2016).
Sonnenschein, David (2001) *Sound Design: The Expressive Power of Music, Voice, and Sound Effects in Cinema,* Seattle, WA: Michael Wiese Productions.
Storr, Anthony (1993) *Music and the Mind,* New York: Ballantine Books.
Sutton, Gloria (2011) 'Visualizing the Digital Universe: Interview with Lev Manovich', *Foam Magazine,* No. 27 Summer.
Tarkovsky, Andrei (1989) *Sculpting in Time,* Austin, TX: University of Texas Press.
Van Sijll, Jennifer (2005) *Cinematic Storytelling,* Seattle, WA: Michael Wiese Productions.
Webb, Jonathan (2015) 'Cyber-archaeology salvages lost Iraqi art', BBC News, 19 May, http://www.bbc.com/news/science-environment-32742622 (accessed 19 May 2015).
Welford, A.T. & Houssiadas, L. (1970) *Contemporary Problems in Perception,* NP: International Ideas.

Willett, John (1988) *The Theatre of Bertolt Brecht*, London: Methuen.
Williams, Christopher (ed.) (1980) *Realism and the Cinema*, London: British Film Institute.
Williams, Raymond (1983) *Keywords: A Vocabulary of Culture and Society*, London: Fontana.
Wood, Aylish (2007) *Digital Encounters*, London: Routledge.
Žižek, Slavoj (ed) (1992) *Everything You Always Wanted to Know about Lacan (But Were Afraid to ask Hitchcock)*, London: Verso.

WEBSITES

Amerika, Mark (2011) 'GRAMMATRON', http://markamerika.com/artworks/grammatron-by-mark-amerika (accessed April 2017)
Angelica, Amara. D. (2014), 'Reverse-engineering Hollywood: How to bypass Netflix and create your own custom search genres' Kurzweil. Accelerating Intelligence Blog, 6 January, http:// http://goo.gl/BY67Zd (accessed August 2016)
Ashcraft, Brian (2008) 'Future metal gear involvement, expresses slight cutscene regret', http://kotaku.com/5041131/future-metal-gear-involvement-expresses-slight-cutscene-regret (accessed August 2017)
Baume, Chris (2017) 'The mermaid's tears', http://www.bbc.co.uk/rd/blog/2017-09-mermaids-tears-object-based-audio (accessed September 2017)
Biswas, Sharang (2016) 'The search for emergent storytelling', http://goo.gl/OThcLx (accessed August 2016)
Bonasio, Alice (2017) 'Is VR the future of filmmaking?', https://thenextweb.com/contributors/2017/05/26/vr-future-filmmaking/#.tnw_PD7cQm6q (accessed August 2017)
Burrell, Ian (2016) 'The FT's warning to its media rivals: "If you're trying to play a game of scale, you're going to lose"', http://goo.gl/fbV3mg (accessed 30 September 2016)
Canfield, David (2017) 'Steven Soderbergh says there are two versions of his interactive HBO Project Mosaic, one of which is app-only', http://www.vulture.com/2017/08/steven-soderbergh-describes-sharon-stone-hbo-series-mosaic.html (accessed September 2017)
Cheong, Ian Miles (2016) 'An interview with Elia Petridis and the future of virtual reality', http://gameranx.com/features/id/63655/article/an-interview-with-elia-petridis-and-the-future-of-virtual-reality/ (accessed 30 September 2016)
Conductrr (2016) 'Conductrr', http://www.conducttr.com/ (accessed 15 August 2016)
Cullen, Charlotte (2016) 'Virtual reality can – and will – be used for storytelling', http://goo.gl/BH4jDj (accessed August 2016)
Curry, Jessica & Pinchbeck, Dan (2016) 'The Chinese room – Dear Esther', http://www.thechineseroom.co.uk/games/dear-esther/ (accessed September 2016)
Davies, Char (2008) 'Char Davies Immersence', http://www.immersence.com/ (accessed August 2016)
De la Peña, Nonny (2014) 'Project Syria', http://www.immersivejournalism.com/category/immersive-journalism/, (accessed 6 December 2016)

Ghosh, Shona (2017) 'Apple's latest acquisition could be a major step towards making virtual reality mainstream', http://uk.businessinsider.com/apple-buying-sensomotoric-instruments-might-take-virtual-reality-mainstream-2017-6?r=US&IR=T (accessed August 2017)

Goodfellow, Jessica (2016) 'Forbes on "breaking the back of the economics of traditional journalism" by paying brand journalists based on scale', http://goo.gl/f7KvJm (accessed September 2016)

Guerrasio, Jason (2017) 'Christopher Nolan explains the "audio illusion" that created the unique music in "Dunkirk"', http://uk.businessinsider.com/dunkirk-music-christopher-nolan-hans-zimmer-2017-7 (accessed July 2017)

Hope, Ted (2011) 'Guest post: Hank Blumenthal "Towards an aesthetics of producing indie movies"', http://www.indiewire.com/2011/05/guest-post-hank-blumenthal-towards-an-aesthetics-of-producing-indie-movies-177949/ (accessed July 2017)

Jobey, Liz (2012) 'Paul Graham: "The Present"', http://www.ft.com/cms/s/2/f97e3a3a-5206-11e1-a30c-00144feabdc0.html#axzz2xuYeuvj0 (accessed September 2016)

Joseph, Seb (2016) 'Unilever is building in-house content studios', http://goo.gl/Pyx5Pj (accessed 30 September 2016)

Judah, Sam (2016) 'Cash for catastrophes?', http://www.bbc.com/news/blogs-trending-37222375 (accessed 1 September 2016)

Kelion, Leo (2017) 'Facebook introduces new video service', http://www.bbc.com/news/business-40883588 (accessed August 2017)

Kelly, Kevin (2016) 'Hyper Vision: The untold story of Magic Leap, the world's most secretive startup', http://www.wired.com/2016/04/magic-leap-vr/ (accessed August 2016)

Kisner, Jordan (2015) 'Rain is sizzling bacon, cars are lions roaring: the art of sound in movies', https://www.theguardian.com/film/2015/jul/22/rain-is-sizzling-bacon-cars-lions-roaring-art-of-sound-in-movies (accessed August 2015)

Koc, Elif (2015) 'Review of interactive storytelling at the *New York Times*', http://futurenytimes.org/reviews/interactive-storytelling/ (accessed August 2016)

Lalwani, Mona (2016) 'For VR to be truly immersive, it needs convincing sound to match', https://www.engadget.com/2016/01/22/vr-needs-3d-audio/ (accessed October 2016)

Laporte, Nicole (2016) 'How a Toronto-based storytelling app is becoming a Hollywood idea factory', https://www.fastcocreate.com/3059866/creation-stories/how-a-toronto-based-storytelling-app-is-becoming-a-hollywood-idea-factory (accessed 15 September 2016)

Lazauskas, Joe (2015) '"We're a media company now": Inside Marriott's incredible money-making content studio', https://contently.com/strategist/2015/11/05/were-a-media-company-now-inside-marriotts-incredible-money-making-content-studio/ (accessed 15 December 2015)

Lazauskas, Joe (2016) 'Ask a content guy: How do you keep coming up with new story ideas?', https://contently.com/strategist/2016/08/31/ask-content-guy-keep-coming-new-story-ideas/ (accessed 20 September 2016)

Lev-Ram, Michal (2016) 'Why Sony and former MTV chief are recruiting "transmedia" storytellers, http://fortune.com/2016/06/29/astronauts-wanted-transmedia-mcgrath/ (accessed July 2016)

Lobenfeld, Claire (2016) 'Mica Levi on "Jackie" and how to soundtrack grief', http://www.factmag.com/2016/12/05/mica-levi-jackie-film-score-interview/ (accessed March 2017)

Malkani, G. (2014) 'William Burroughs' exhibition at Photographers' Gallery, London', *Financial Times*, https://www.ft.com/content/a9795374-7e0c-11e3-b409-00144feabdc0 (accessed 15 November 2017)

McAlone, Nathan (2016) 'The way YouTube stars are making millions is changing', http://www.businessinsider.com/adam-wescott-talks-youtube-star-revenue-2016-10?utm_content=buffer82502&utm_medium=social&utm_source=facebook.com&utm_campaign=buffer-ti&IR=T (accessed 8 October 2016)

McErlean, Kelly (2014) 'The construction of a graduate identity: Data-mining the student archive', Cahier Louis-Lumière no. 9: Mémoires d'écoles / Audio-visual archives and Memory in Schools, http://www.ens-louis-lumiere.fr/formation/recherche/cahier-louis-lumiere/cahier-9.html (accessed August 2016)

Media Kunst Netz, (1999) '5 year drive-by', http://www.medienkunstnetz.de/works/5-year-drive-by/ (accessed August 2016)

Metagram (2016) 'Metagram', http://metagram.co/#foundersforum (accessed August 2016)

Mortimer, Natalie (2016) 'LastMinute.com creates content lab as it moves into native video', http://goo.gl/y91wJr (accessed August 2016)

Moylan, Brian (2015) 'Building an empire: How Fox's hip-hop drama broke a 23-year-old ratings record', https://www.theguardian.com/tv-and-radio/2015/feb/18/empire-fox-ratings-record (accessed August 2016)

Mufson, Beckett (2015) 'Virtual reality film installation puts a disassociative twist on awkward family dinners', https://creators.vice.com/en_us/article/virtual-reality-film-installation-puts-a-disassociative-twist-on-awkward-family-dinners (accessed April 2017)

Mullin, Benjamin (2016) 'The *New York Times* of the future is beginning to take shape', http://www.poynter.org/2016/the-new-york-times-of-the-future-is-beginning-to-take-shape/413097/ (accessed July 2016)

Murch, Walter (2005) *Dense Clarity – Clear Density*, https://transom.org/2005/walter-murch/ (accessed Nov 2017)

Nededog, Jethro (2015) '13 TV shows that became massive because of social media', http://www.businessinsider.my/tv-shows-on-social-media-2015-11/?utm_content=buffer8315c&utm_medium=social&utm_source=linkedin.com&utm_campaign=buffer#zTsdvxjmw5wT5buG.97 (accessed August 2016)

Pierce, David (2016) 'Gather around, folks, for the brilliance of story time Twitter', https://www.wired.com/2016/01/gather-around-folks-for-the-brilliance-of-story-time-twitter/?utm_content=buffer636fc (accessed January 2016)

Puschmann, Matthias (2016) 'Inside BBC Three's transmedia campaign ahead of the *Thirteen* premiere', http://goo.gl/XY0mPm (accessed March 2016)

Rogers, Stewart (2016) 'Skyhook launches its new Personas to help solve a $100B industry problem', http://venturebeat.com/2016/03/07/skyhook-launches-its-new-personas-to-help-solve-a-100b-industry-problem/ (accessed September 2016)

Spurrell, Haydn (2016) '"The Witch" composer discusses the unsettling sounds behind the groundbreaking horror', http://www.cultjer.com/the-witch-composer-discusses-the-unsettling-sounds-behind-the-groundbreaking-horror (accessed 29th March 2016)

Stewart, Rebecca (2017) 'Inside the San Miguel experience: Why the brand is investing in immersive events,' http://goo.gl/ijSUuC (accessed July 2017)
University of Nottingham (2007) 'No escape from the bullies,' ScienceDaily, https://www.sciencedaily.com/releases/2007/05/070531120821.htm (accessed August 2016)
Wegert, Tessa (2016) 'Can Accenture take over advertising?,' https://contently.com/strategist/2016/07/29/can-accenture-take-over-advertising/ (accessed August 2016)
Welsh, Madeline (2015) '*The New York Times* hopes its first virtual reality film, "The Displaced" kicks off mass adoption of VR,' http://www.niemanlab.org/2015/11/the-new-york-times-hopes-its-first-virtual-reality-film-the-displaced-kicks-off-mass-adoption-of-vr/ (accessed 11 November 2015)
Wilshere, Andrew (2017) 'Are notifications a dark pattern?,' https://blog.prototypr.io/are-notifications-a-dark-pattern-2c1a177b26e0 (accessed July 2017)

INTERVIEWS

Blumenthal, Hank (2017) interview by email, 14 July
Bonnici, Sabina (2017) interview by email, 19 March
Donegan, Camille (2017) interview, Dublin, 20 February
Ferreira, Soraia (2016) interview by email, 8 July
Figueroa, Natalia (2016) interview by email, 23 September
Fitch, Claire (2016) interview by email, 8 August
Haahr, Mads (2016) interview by email, 11 November
Hoey, Elaine (2017) interview, Dublin, 24 February
Hope, Ciaran (2017) interview, Dublin, 8 September
Koenitz, Hartmut (2017) interview by email, 12 February
Laffan, Muirne (2016) interview, Dublin, 31 March
Lindquist, John (2016) interview by email, 12 October
Meadows, Daniel (2016) phone interview, 25 August
O'Connor, Neil (2017) interview, Dublin, 2 September
Putney, Charlene (2017) interview by email, 17 February
Rankin, Ollie (2016) interview by email, 8 May
Ryan, Nick (2017) interview, Dublin, 25 July
Stott, Krishna (2016) interview by email, 2 September
Tandavanitj, Nick (2016) phone interview, 25 August
Williams, Jermain (2017) interview, Dublin, 20 February

MASTERCLASS

Divine, Christian (2016) Dublin, 19 August

Index